ANDREW SUNG PARK

From Hurt to Healing

A Theology

of

the

Wounded

Abingdon Pre
Nashville

FROM HURT TO HEALING
A THEOLOGY OF THE WOUNDED

This book is printed on acid-free paper.

Library of Congress Cataloging-in-Publication Data

Park, Andrew Sung.
  From hurt to healing : a theology of the wounded / Andrew Sung Park.
     p. cm.
  Includes bibliographical references.
  ISBN 0-687-03881-2 (alk. paper)
  1. Interpersonal relations—Religious aspects—Christianity. 2. Forgiveness—Religious aspects—Christianity. 3. Healing—Religious aspects—Christianity. 4. Mental health—Religious aspects—Christianity. I. Title.

BV4597.52.P37 2004
234'.5—dc22

2004017886

04 05 06 07 08 09 10 11 12 13—10 9 8 7 6 5 4 3 2 1

MANUFACTURED IN THE UNITED STATES OF AMERICA

To Jane Myong,

my best friend and spouse,

and Amos and Thomas,

my two delightful sons

ACKNOWLEDGMENTS

I would like to express my deep gratitude to all those students who took my courses, "Sin and Salvation" or "Sin, Salvation, Han, and Liberation." They have tremendously inspired me to complete this work by making passionate class presentations, submitting well-researched papers, and sharing their personal insights.

To Prof. Julian Pleasants, who sent me priceless materials after reading my previous work and encouraged me several times. As a lay Roman Catholic theologian and a biologist, he (along with Prof. Howard Zehr) has greatly contributed to the movement of restorative justice.

To Dr. Robert Ratcliff, who superbly edited my work. In addition to being an excellent editor, he is also an outstanding scholar and encouraged me on my academic journey to the healing ministry.

To Barry Gannon, who read the whole manuscript and helped me modify it. His help has been indispensable in completing this book.

To Dr. John Cobb, who helped me think creatively and select the title of this book.

To my colleagues at United Theological Seminary who provided me valuable resources, particularly Kathy Farmer, Carolyn Bohler, Larry Welborn, Tom Dozeman, and Tyron Inbody.

To Becky Schram, faculty secretary, who organized the bibliography of this book.

Acknowledgments

To my beloved family: Jane Myong, who tirelessly supported me in completing this book; Amos, who read some portions of this work and helped me revise it; and Thomas, who raised several difficult theological questions. Jane, Amos, and Thomas sacrificed their time by doing a lot of housework on my behalf.

CONTENTS

INTRODUCTION

During his crusade in Dallas on October 20, 2002, Billy Graham mentioned that many believers and nonbelievers suffer from pain. I thought that his diagnosis of the world was relevant to our situation and expected that he would provide a clear message of healing for the pain of the human heart. Yet he concluded his message with his customary theological line, "You are sinners. Repent of your sins and be saved." The message itself was authentic; however, I wished that he could have provided something more than this customary pattern of sin-repentance-salvation. By starting with the topic of pain, he showed his desire to provide a message of healing. Sadly, however, there was no theology for the wounded that could back up his message.

I saw my mother suffering from a deep wound. It is called *han* in Korean. Whenever her deep unfathomable pain erupted, she physically collapsed. I remember clearly as a young boy how helpless I was in the face of this rupture of her pain; she suffered from it deeply, lying down in bed many days.[1] As a simple young woman from the countryside, she went through so many things: the confiscations of her land, house, and all her household goods by the North Koreans; a barely successful escape to South Korea; a refugee life during the Korean War; caring for her sick father-in-law and two young members of his family; the difficult life of a local pastor's spouse; going through and emerging from a bankruptcy; a life of sacrificing for five children; and the overwhelming jobs of saleswoman and housewife. As far as I remember, she spent most of her time grappling with the issues of her wounds, not the issue of her sin. Does the gospel of Jesus Christ care for the resolution of such profound wounds as hers? My hope in this book is to address the healing of the wounded.

The following letter was sent to *Psychology Today* from an inmate awaiting sentencing for armed bank robbery. It tells the story of his adoptive mother, Beulah, who was abused as a child herself, and who became a "nightmare of abuse," and made the inmate's childhood a living hell.

Wrapped up in Beulah's abusive behavior was her tragically warped religious faith.

> Her belief in God was a sincere flame, and she taught me that God made all that is beautiful in the world. She also taught me that this same God would destroy me in the fires of hell for one single sin. I would never presume to know the number of eye-rattling, ear-ringing whacks that marked the hours in Beulah's presence, but I've been knocked unconscious by a stainless-steel pot, a birch log, and the metal end of a vacuum hose. . . . Some vengeful demon fired a rage in her that distorted her thoughts and fueled the vicious cycle of violence.[2]

When Beulah died without reconciling with David, he cried in his emptiness. Later, David almost abused his own eight-year-old son. When he lifted him above his head and saw his face frozen in terror, David saw himself twenty-five years earlier. By "God's grace," he stopped himself, beginning the work of breaking the cycle of violence.[3]

Beulah was a victim of child abuse whose victimization led her to abuse her own child. The physical abuse that she inflicted on David was clearly evil. But what is the role of the cycle of violence in Beulah's sin? Is she more of a perpetrator or a victim? She was a sincere Christian who believed in God. What could the gospel do for her life? Did she need forgiveness for the abuse she committed, healing from the abuse she suffered, or both?

David was the victim of an intergenerational cycle of violence. Even though David was able to stop the cycle by not abusing his own child, his deep wound of child abuse still needs to be treated. Even if the victims of child abuse avoid abusing their own children, they may express the effects of their deep wounds in other ways.

Over the past twenty-five years, many researchers have written about the cycle of violence.[4] Kathy Wisdom examined records on more than 1,500 criminals to find out whether the experience of abuse or neglect during childhood fuels the likelihood of arrest as a juvenile or young adult. The research clearly revealed that a victim of child physical abuse is prone to violence in later years and that victims of child neglect are more likely to surrender to later violent criminal behavior as well. Of all types of childhood maltreatment, physical abuse was the most likely to be linked to arrest for a violent crime later in life.[5] The repetition of physical abuse by the abused is hard to understand, but it is an undeniable reality.

At a collective level, we can see the vicious cycle of abuse caused by the deep wounds of victims. An example is the Jewish people who were persecuted, murdered, and massacred during World War II. Now some Israeli leaders have chosen to persecute and oppress Palestinians in politically complicated circumstances. How could they play the role of the persecutors while the tragic memory of the Holocaust is still vivid? They could have used the power of persuasion and negotiation rather than the power of force and violence, but instead they have ruled the Palestinians with iron fists. The Palestinians need liberation from their grip. The Israelis need salvation from their own oppression of the Palestinians. Why is this so difficult to achieve? Because their experience of the Holocaust has created an insecurity, a terror, that freezes their way of seeing, viewing, making decisions, and dealing with others. In short, they are in the vicious cycle of violence.

When people's deep wounds are not healed, the wounds become vortexes of troubled waters, intertwined with their own instinct of survival and fear. Many victims instinctively *synchronize their wavelengths* with their offenders. They internalize their perpetrators' images and values and externalize them in treating their own victims. In short, they see the world through their oppressors' eyes. Seeing again through their own eyes begins the process of healing.

In this world of violence, the church must address the issue of these deep wounds (han) and the issue of sin if the church wants to be relevant to and effective in transforming and healing the world. In this work, I distinguish between the sinner and the sinned against to help people see the lines of their distinctive journeys. The sinner takes the journey from his or her sin to salvation, while the sinned against goes through a journey from his or her oppression to liberation or deliverance.

Liberation theologians such as Gustavo Gutiérrez treat salvation and liberation as inseparable. Gutiérrez believes in three levels of sin and liberation: liberation from economic, social, and political oppression; liberation from historical fatalism; and liberation from the breach of our relationship with God and neighbors.[6] For him, "the historical, political, liberating event *is* the growth of the Kingdom and *is* a salvific event."[7] However, he does not simply equate liberation with salvation. He construes salvation ultimately as communion with God and neighbors in history and beyond, while he understands liberation as communion in love.[8] At each level of the three dimensions of liberation, he distinguishes the processes of salvation and liberation in unity. His "eschatological salvation"

3

is final communion with God and neighbors, anticipated historically in covenantal communities such as base Christian communities. For him, liberation is sought for the sake of community.[9]

In his context, separating salvation from liberation is dangerous and dualistic, putting down liberation as a temporal deliverance from economic and political oppression and elevating salvation as a lofty spiritual and permanent repose. It is fully understandable and acceptable that liberation theologians unify salvation and liberation in their Latin-American contexts where the oppressed need to determine their own destinies by striving for justice.

My premise is different from that of Gutiérrez: Salvation is for sinners and liberation for the sinned against. From this perspective, it is necessary for us to distinguish salvation from liberation because the deep wounds of the sinned against and the sin of the sinner need to be treated separately. Although society as a whole may experience liberation and salvation as one, the groups of the oppressors and the oppressed in a society experience them separately.

The oppressors need salvation from their own sin, while the oppressed seek liberation from the domination of the oppressors. The event of the exodus serves to explain these two routes. The Egyptians exploited and persecuted the Israelites with the bondage of slavery. That is the reason Moses led his people out of Egypt. What the Israelites needed was liberation from the Egyptians, not salvation from their own sin at that time. The Egyptians needed salvation from their sin of slavery, not the liberation from the Israelites. As a matter of fact, both Israelites and Egyptians needed freedom. The Israelites strived for freedom from slavery. The Egyptians needed freedom from their own oppression. In other words, while the Israelites needed the freedom of liberation from the slavery of the Egyptians, the Egyptians needed the freedom of salvation from their own sin of oppression and dehumanization.

The issue becomes murky when many oppressed people play the roles of oppressors in certain occasions and vice versa. Indeed, most of us find that we are both an oppressor and oppressed. As the oppressed/oppressor, we need both salvation and liberation in life. There are times when we need to focus on liberation more urgently than salvation, and vice versa. But it is important to distinguish between these two, particularly at a collective level. Ethnic minority persons and women are almost perpetually disadvantaged in this society. This does not imply that they are all innocent, or without sin. Yet their primary experience of life is han, not sin.

By drawing these two distinctive lines of liberation and salvation, we can see what we need to pursue in accordance with our situations.

In principle, all Christians are saved. So preaching to the saved about the sin-salvation formula repeatedly is superfluous and unnecessary, if not sinfully boring. Since Christians have been saved from their sins, they more likely need to hear a message of how to heal their wounds. In fact, most Christians struggle with the issue of han, their deep wounds. It is not surprising to find out that there are innumerable Christians who are more eager to discuss their pain and healing than their sin and salvation. Even Jesus himself spent more time healing the sick and the wounded in heart than saving oppressors from their sins.

Furthermore, there are numerous non-Christians who are interested in learning how to heal their deep wounds. Traditionally, Christianity has tried to evangelize non-Christians by using the sin-salvation formula alone. But if we map out a good, adequate course for their healing and liberation from their pain and wounds, we may open up a new avenue to spreading the good news of Jesus to the world. The wound-liberation formula may contribute to the redefinition of Christian evangelism and mission in the world.

Christians are called to spread to the world a more holistic gospel based on biblical teachings. These two lines of salvation and liberation are intertwined in the complex intra- and interpersonal relationships of the sinner and the sinned against, engendering the dynamic dance of life in forgiveness and enhancing the *élan vital* for spiritual wholeness. When people see these two roads, the oppressed and oppressors may understand each other better and work together to bring true reconciliation into their communities by promoting mutual respect, encouragement, forgiveness, and cooperation. Thus, they might be able to accompany each other on their courageous journey to healing and forgiveness.

A poignant issue illustrates our discussion. (Let me point out that the following is not solely a problem of the Roman Catholic Church, but one common to all churches and hurts all Christians.) On April 4, 2002, Rev. Don Rooney, a Roman Catholic priest, killed himself rather than face accusations that he had sexually molested schoolgirls in the 1980s. Speaking at his funeral, Cleveland Bishop Anthony Pilla spoke tenderly of the tragedy of Rooney's life and death.

The depth of Pilla's tenderness surprised some, especially those who say they had tried to raise concerns about Rooney. At least four women say they were touched inappropriately by Rooney when they were schoolgirls

in the 1980s. They say they thought Rooney deserved mercy but also won-
der why church leaders never extended equal compassion to them.[10]

We can see here the Roman Catholic Church softening its stance on
suicide because its priests have committed suicide. Between 1986 and
2002, fourteen priests committed suicide in the United States.[11]
Theological doctrines have been developed by the professional theologians of churches according to the need of specific people. Bishops and
theologians have developed doctrines from their own perspectives for the
sake of their churches and sometimes for themselves.

If the victims' voices had been heard in the beginning, the church
might have saved the life of Father Rooney by confronting him and
reforming his wrong behavior. But their voices were ignored. Had the
church created theological guidelines for the victims, they could have followed them, working toward the healing of their wounds and leading
Father Rooney to repent of his sins. Their wounds need to be treated not
at the level of pastoral care and compassion only but also at the level of
theological instructions. The people abused by priests were left alone in
terms of pursuing the healing of their own wounds. The Roman Catholic
Church has been busy settling a number of the sexual abuse cases of priests
out of court, neglecting the well-being of the victims. In fact, the church
has no doctrine to help the theological journey of healing for victims.

This book intends to shed light on the distinctive paths that the
wounded can take toward healing and that perpetrators can take toward
salvation. The purpose of this book is to sketch a course of a healing journey for the wounded. For example, the woman abused by Rooney in 1980
suffered from the deep wound (han) created by his abuse of power. She
developed shame about the abuse, while Rooney suffered from guilt. She
could not have repented of her wound. Instead, she reported the abuse to
appropriate authorities. Her reporting is a method of confrontation or
resistance. If Rooney had not committed suicide, she could have personally forgiven him in due course. Even without his physical presence, she
can still forgive him. The church's traditional path for salvation is not
the path for this victim. Instead of justification by faith, she needs in
faith to pursue justice. Instead of sanctification, she needs to seek the
healing of her spiritual wounds. Her final step can be jubilee or joy rather
than full sanctification. If the church had provided some theological
guidelines for sexual abuse victims, their wounds could have healed without festering.

In other words, this book is an effort to explore the unfamiliar theological territory of working toward the healing of the victims of sin and wrong. To do so I will draw a contrast between major doctrines for the sinner and their counterparts for the sinned against, working with guidelines drawn from multidisciplinary resources—biblical, theological, psychological, sociological, historical, and scientific. The themes of sin and wounds (chapter 1); guilt and shame (chapter 2); guilt anger and shame anger (chapter 3); repentance and resistance (chapter 4); forgiven-ness and forgivingness (chapter 5); justification and justice (chapter 6); sanctification and healing (chapter 7); and full sanctification and jubilee (chapter 8).

On the one hand, for his or her own salvation, the sinner undergoes the line of sin, guilt, guilt-anger, repentance, forgiveness, justification, sanctification, and full sanctification or Christian perfection. On the other, for his or her own liberation, the sinned against takes the track of wounds, shame, shame-anger, resistance, forgivingness, justice, healing, and jubilee/joy. Even though joy or jubilee is treated at the end of their journey, the wounded need to live it out throughout their journey. Joy enables us to actualize our abundant life in the midst of sorrow and grief. Since the major doctrines for the sinner have been amply discussed and systematically constructed, I will focus on the new guidelines for the sinned-against. I will try to draw these guidelines together from multidisciplinary resources—biblical, theological, psychological, sociological, historical, and scientific. If one victim who struggles in her or his lonely journey to healing and liberation finds help here, the effort will have been worth it.

CHAPTER ONE

Wounds (Han) and Sin

Apatient comes to see a doctor. The doctor diagnoses his or her symptoms and prescribes medicine. If the diagnosis is wrong, a medicine prescribed according to that diagnosis will be ineffective and the patient's health can be in jeopardy. We cannot emphasize too much the importance of a correct diagnosis for the healing of a patient.

In the pews, we find all kinds of people. On any given Sunday the preacher could be looking out at oppressors, exploiters, aggressors, invaders, abusers, rapists, murderers, and more. At the same time, however, the preacher is likely to be confronted with the victims of these sins so that those who have been oppressed, exploited, injured, invaded, abused, raped, and bereft—as well as their families and friends—are also there, waiting to hear a word from God.

In Christian theology, *sin* is the only category we have to diagnose the wrong of the world. We have drawn the map of salvation for sinners and have left those who have been sinned against to find the way themselves. The victims of sins or crimes must turn for help to counselors, psychotherapists, or psychiatrists; pastors and theologians have little aid to offer them. When pastors do counsel those who have been oppressed, they draw on psychological, rather than theological, categories and ideas to help such people deal with their pain.

It is time for the church to face this issue and provide a remedy for it. In this book I propose to see whether the Bible is concerned about the sinned-against and their salvation. Naming a problem is the beginning of its solution, and hence the way to begin is by specifying the pain of those who have been sinned against. This chapter will treat their pain. As far as I know, no general term exists to describe the wound of victims in

Western languages. Fortunately, Korean has a term to describe the deep wound of victims: *han*.[1] To begin, let us look further at what han means and how it relates to the more familiar term *sin*.

Han

Boxed-in Hope

A woman is in a room where there is no door or window. She panics and knocks at the four walls frantically. After a couple of days, realizing there is no use in doing this any longer, she gives up all hope and despairs. Surrounded by the four walls, her life loses meaning, and her spirit dies within her. This slow death of the spirit is han. Sadness, resignation, hopelessness, and despair are all parts of what han means.

Many victims of domestic violence experience hopelessness. They feel that there is nowhere to run from the living hell home has become. They are trapped in their own homes.

> Jan Kuenzel, a criminal justice intervention program coordinator . . . handled a case several years ago where a deputy responded to a domestic violence call at a home where he knew the couple.
>
> Although the woman was badly beaten, the officer did little more than separate the couple.
>
> "All the deputy did was tell the man to go out to the barn and wait until he cooled down," she said. "There are still old attitudes out there." It's like, "If the wife did something, she deserved it. She must have done something to deserve it." [2]

In the United States, domestic violence is an epidemic social problem. Experts estimate that two to four million women in this country are battered every year and that between 3.3 and ten million children witness violence in their homes.[3] In 1999, 1,218 women were killed by current or former partners. According to the Department of Justice, nearly half of the violent crimes against women are not reported to the police.[4] When the person to whom you have been closest violates your basic human rights, han is often the result.

The Collapsed Feeling of Anguish

When pain hurts people repeatedly, it collapses into a compressed ache. Victims of ongoing oppression experience this. Here is a story shared by Bernard Evans, an African American in his late 40s.

> I had just dropped my wife off at the bus stop and had entered my home in a predominantly white neighborhood when a police car pulled up and the cops asked me what I was doing there. They said there had been a burglary in the area. They made me accompany them into my house and walk through it with them—from the third floor to the basement—looking [for] my 'accomplice.' I guess it finally dawned on them that I was telling the truth, and they left. They apologized, but I was so angry I couldn't speak. I tried to forget about it, and I never told my wife. It made me feel sick.[5]

Home is our sanctuary where we rest and have privacy. Evans's home was violated by the police because of the color of his skin! Many African Americans, particularly males, have had a similar violation of their privacy and person. They have been humiliated again and again, but they may not talk about it because talking about it hurts and humiliates them further. Thus, many misplace their resentment by smoking it out, drinking it out, or shooting it out, but they won't and can't talk about it because their self-dignity does not allow them to do so. This bottled and collapsed pain of racial injustice is another manifestation of han. Many members of ethnic minorities have experienced the pain of racial discrimination and bigotry.

Han is the collapsed anguish of the heart due to psychosomatic, social, economic, political, and cultural repression and oppression. When internal and external forces cause our suffering to reach a critical point, it collapses to a singularity of agony. The collapsed sadness, bitterness, rage, and hopelessness become the vortex of our agony, overwhelming our conscious and unconscious modes of thinking. In other words, han is a physical, mental, and spiritual response to a terrible wrong done to a person. It elicits a warped depth of pain, a visceral physical response, an intense rending of the soul, and a sense of helplessness.

An Unfathomable Wound

A wound occurs when external forces damage or break a part of our bodies. Han is the rupture of the soul caused by abuse, exploitation, injustice, and violence. When the soul is hurt so much, it bursts symbolically; it aches. When the aching soul is wounded again by external violence, the victim suffers yet a deeper ache. The wound produced by such repeated abuse and injustice is han in the depths of the soul.

Such a deep wound has, for example, lasting effects on abused children. Jerald Kay, chair of the Psychiatry Department at Wright State University's School of Medicine, says that when a child is badly hurt or terrified, that pain not only produces a traumatic memory, it also changes the developing brain.[6] Kay and his associates have shown that abused children are inclined to suffer from depression, drug abuse, and other chronic ailments as adults. Supported by the research of Paul Plotsky of Emory University, Kay says, "People who have been abused have parts of their brains that are different sizes than other people. And those different parts of their brains will function in different ways."[7] With animal studies to lead them, scientists found strong tendencies in those who were abused as children toward a more active amygdala (the "fear center" of the brain) and a smaller connection between the left and right brain hemispheres, which enables the more rational right brain to better control feelings and anger. Abused children see the world as far more threatening than those who were not abused, becoming hypersensitive or withdrawing and growing numb.[8] Childhood traumas cut into the child's sense of control, leading abuse victims to go to incomprehensible lengths to recover control. They often blame themselves rather than their offenders for their abuse.[9]

The change of brain structure and function in those abused as children is han, a profound wound in the soul. The long-lasting effects of abuse, much deeper than previously known, are the symptoms of han.

Emotional Heart Attack

Our society tends to victimize victims. The powerful receive respect, protection, and appreciation, whereas the victim is further violated and denigrated. Once his or her boundary of protection is broken, it is hard for the victim to restore that boundary again.

Me Ra Koh is a Korean-American woman. She met Jack, a Christian, at a barbecue dinner during her college freshman orientation. He showered her with flowers and affection. After several months, he began to change, leading Me Ra to the decision to end the relationship. Jack responded angrily, insisting that God had told him that the two of them were to be married.

A few weeks later Jack invited Me Ra to dinner as "friends." It was a horrible evening, with Jack acting obnoxious toward the waiters and her. When it was over, Me Ra was relieved to be going back to the dorm— until she realized that their destination was a deserted parking lot instead.

> I remember very few things about the actual rape—the car windshield covered with fog, the struggle, and the moment I felt too overpowered to resist any longer. In that instant I realized there was nothing I could do to stop what was happening. He was simply too strong.
>
> When it was over, Jack took me back to my dorm, told me he would give me a call, and simply left. All I remember about those following hours is standing in the shower with all my clothes on, sobbing uncontrollably, desperately wanting the water to wash away the evening's events.[10]

Eight months later she found herself standing in a crowded courtroom. Even after sharing every intimate detail of the rape (an experience that is itself a second rape), she lost the case on the grounds of insufficient evidence. The case was closed. She fell into a deep depression. Worse, the college allowed Jack to register for classes. In the months that followed, Jack stalked and followed her to her classes, to the cafeteria, and to her dorm. The helplessness she had felt during the rape intensified on campus. Her despair reached a breaking point and she started to contemplate suicide.

A counselor described her condition as "an emotional heart attack." Later she checked into a New Life Clinic: "During the first week I sat in the hall and stared at the floor. On the outside I looked emotionless, but on the inside I was screaming with rage. Rage that demanded to know why I was the one in a psychiatric ward instead of the man who'd raped me. Rage that wanted to have my life back. But instead of the rage coming out, it all just brewed inside me. . . ."[11]

As a rape victim before a court, she experienced the multiple rapes of the legal system. The ongoing victimization, particularly the attacker's continual stalking, was the unbearable burden for her. The "emotional heart attack" is han, a prevalent experience of the victims of injustice. The fusion of helplessness, despair, and rage that brewed inside her was the substance of han.

In 2000, an intimate male partner, a relative, a friend, or an acquaintance of the victim committed six out of ten rapes in the United States. In this country a woman is raped every six minutes and physically abused by her husband every nine seconds. Each year, approximately 1.5 million women are raped and otherwise physically assaulted by intimate partners.[12]

The Void of Abysmal Grief

In the article, "A Skyline Is Conspicuous by an Absence" (24 October 2001, *The New York Times*), Peter Marks expresses the unspeakable absence after the September 11 attacks.

"These days, capturing the New York skyline—on canvas, on film, with the naked eye—has become a complicated, even emotionally wrenching act. The towers are such powerful symbols that they overshadow everything—whether they are present or absent. . . ." "It's our phantom limb," Ric Burns, director of a documentary on the history of New York City that was recently broadcast on PBS, said of the World Trade Center. "You feel it, but it's not there; you look to where you feel it should be."

The World Trade Center is clearly absent, and its absence is vividly present.

The story of Michele speaks to the throbbing pain left by the void of the victims of the disaster. She represents the many who disappeared into the smoke.

"Michele, it's 11 o'clock!" Dennis Eulau would shout. "Could you just come to bed?" After all, her day had started at 5 a.m., with the NordicTrack workout, then the frenzy to roust, dress, and feed their three little guys, ages 2, 5, and 7 and get herself to work, two days a week in the city and one at home, as a systems analyst at Marsh & McLennan. . . .

Mrs. Coyle-Eulau, 38, would go home to Garden City, N.Y., dine on cereal, then supervise the boys' homework and bedtime rituals. . . . She was a to-the-max mom. A coach from an opposing soccer team asked her to tone down the cheering. . . . Here is what the boys did for her: last Mother's Day, they cooked pancakes with red and blue food coloring. She even ate them. What took her so long to get to bed? Packing lunches, making grocery lists, arranging play dates. "I never understood," her husband said. "Now I do."[13]

He feels that at any minute Michele will walk through the door just like she always did. But Michele will never come home again; her bed will always remain empty. The ghostly void of her presence is han.

More than three thousand people vanished into the smoke on September 11, 2001. Mothers, fathers, children, the buildings, and the airplanes disappeared into the thick air of tragedy. Families moan for their sudden departures with no proper closure. There is but one word for the abyss of grief into which these families have fallen: han.

Han is the suffering of the innocent who are caught in the vicious cycle of violence. It is the void of grief that cannot be filled with any superficial patch. This void is the abysmal emptiness that remains after the wound has been inflicted.

Internalized Collective Memory of the Oppressed

Han can be described as *internalized collective memory of victims* generated by patriarchal tyranny, racial discrimination, economic exploitation, ethnic cleansing, massacre, foreign occupation, state-sponsored terrorism, and unjust war. It entrenches itself in the souls of the victims of sin and crime, manifesting itself in such diverse ways as those seen in the survivors of the Nazi holocaust, the Palestinians in the occupied territories, the Iraqi people victimized by the attacks of both Saddam Hussein and the coalition forces, the discriminated-against, battered wives, the molested, the abused, and the exploited. As long as it is not healed, han accumulates and transmits to posterity year after year. It has a collective unconscious dimension.

Han exits on two levels: individual and collective. At its individual level, it is the will to revenge, resignation, regret, diffuseness, absence, bitterness, and helplessness, reacting to a private oppression that can also often be connected to collective and structural oppression. At its collective level, han is the corporate will to revolt, collective despair, communal wrath, group discontent, racial resentment, and racial lamentation. The collective dimension of han includes its structural level that involves chronic and systemic exploitation and injustice. Both individual and collective han contain conscious and unconscious elements. Yet all these factors—individual vs. corporate, conscious vs. unconscious—are inextricably bound up in one another. They create in victims the spirit of an ethnoracial inferiority complex, sourness, desolation, an ethos of a cultural inferiority complex, racial lamentation, racial resentment, the sense of physical inadequacy, and communal shame.[14]

Han and Sin

Where sin is committed, han arises as its corollary. The victims of sin develop the deep agonizing pain of han. They bear excruciating agony and humiliation caused by oppression, exploitation, abuse, mistreatment, and violation. If their situations do not change, their han will only deepen.

Sin causes han and han produces sin.[15] Sin is of oppressors; han is of the oppressed. The sin of oppressors may cause a chain reaction via the han of the oppressed. Sometimes han causes han. Furthermore, unattended or unhealed han gives rise to evil. This evil can regenerate han and sin. Also, sin and han collaborate to engender evil. They overlap in many tragic areas of life.

Han can be resolved either negatively or positively. When it explodes negatively, those in its grip seek revenge and destruction. But when it is resolved positively, han can create the energy to change sinful situations and han-inducing conditions, breaking vicious cycles of sin, han, and evil.

Although for convenience I have divided the sin of oppressors and the han of the oppressed, most people experience sin and han. This does not mean we diminish the difference between the two, but points out the complex entanglement of sin and han. Many people who are oppressed in one aspect of life are oppressors in another. The notion of han may help us transcend the doctrine of sin's one-dimensional approach to the problems of the world. The Christian doctrine of sin addresses the oppressors' need of forgiveness but ignores oppressed people's need of justice and healing. We need a more complete account of human wrong and restitution. To find it, let us turn to the Bible to see whether it addresses the content of han.

Biblical Han

The Bible is full of stories of suffering people. Jesus came into the world to set the wronged free from their grief and burden and to forgive the sins of wrongdoers. But between the two—the wronged and the wrongdoers—Jesus was primarily concerned about the former: "Those who are well have no need of a physician, but those who are sick" (Mark 2:17).[16] Accordingly, the main subject of the Bible was to care for the afflicted and the oppressed. In this section I will thus show the prevalence of the notion of han in the Bible.

Han in the Hebrew Bible: Cain and Abel

The story of Cain and Abel (Gen 4:1-16) is the story of han. The two brothers gave offerings to God. Cain's offering was rejected, while Abel's was accepted. The text is silent on the purposes of their offerings and on the reason for the rejection and acceptance. God's response, however, engendered Cain's anger. Out of his deep jealousy and frustration, Cain struck down his own brother. The dying Abel looked at his brother Cain, his eyes no doubt filled with the question, "Why?"

God was silent at the moment Abel was murdered. God did not intervene! That is the core of han. How can the God of justice be absent in the face of such appalling injustice? Rather, God set a mark on Cain to protect him. A murderer walked out free. Here we witness the conflict between God's mercy and God's justice.[17] Anachronistically speaking, God's mercy interrupts criminal justice, social values, and even the biblical prescription of "an eye for an eye" (the so-called *lex talionis*).

Cain created a civilization, but Abel did not. The murderer became the main character of history. This absurd fact of life is the han of the victim's world. The murdered could not speak! Only Abel's blood—the voice of han—cried out to God from the ground (Gen 4:10).

A Human Sacrifice

The deep resentment of han is shown in the horrible story of sacrificing one's own son. In 2 Kings 3, King Mesha of Moab, a sheep breeder, rebelled against the king of Israel. Allying with King Jehoshaphat of Judah and the king of Edom, King Jehoram of Israel marched toward Moab. When Moab heard the three kings had come to fight against them, from the youngest to the oldest were called out and were drawn up at the frontier. But the battle was in the hands of Israel:

> The cities they overturned, and on every good piece of land everyone threw a stone, until it was covered; every spring of water they stopped up, and every good tree they felled. . . . When the king of Moab saw that the battle was going against him, he took with him seven hundred swordsmen to break through, opposite the king of Edom; but they could not. Then he took his firstborn son who was to succeed him, and offered him as a burnt offering on the wall. And great wrath came upon Israel, so they withdrew from him and returned to their own land. (2 Kgs 3:25-27)

17

The defiance and bitterness of the king of Moab led him to sacrifice the destiny of his dynasty in the person of his own son. What other name can we give this tragic act than *han*? The horrifying vigor of this *han* so repulsed Israel that it withdrew from Moab.

That was then. What about now? Is a suicide bomber a burnt offering for the Palestinians in the West Bank and Gaza Strip? Too often, we witness the explosions of human bodies attached to bombs in Palestine and Israel. With what language can we express the deep agony of the self-explosions of Palestinians and of the deaths of Israeli civilians? We witness the vicious cycle of the explosions of *han* in terrible ways. Some reactions of the Israelis cannot be understood without grasping the *han* of their experience of the Holocaust. In the same way, the actions of the Palestinians can only be attributed to the *han* engendered by losing their homes and hope.

Job

The book of Job was written to contradict the retributive (or "Deuteronomistic") theology that regards suffering as God's punishment for sin and as a tool of God's instruction. Job undergoes a series of unbearable human tragedies. All Job had is destroyed, his sons and daughters are killed, and he is physically afflicted by sores.

Worse, his three friends come to visit him and urge him to reveal and repent of his sin. Their theology represents the orthodox theology. Eliphaz accuses Job of culpability. Job rejects the charge and begs for compassion. Bildad indicts him for hypocrisy. Job insists that he has committed no sin and that God is unfair to destroy both the righteous and the wicked (9:21-22). Zophar rebukes Job as a liar and a hypocrite. Job rejects his rebuke as banality. Finally, Elihu appears and pours out his anger at Job for his self-justification. His argues that God is just and uses suffering as a medium to refine humans. Moreover, he says, Job's afflictions result from his iniquity (36:21).[18]

At the end, God speaks to Job out of the whirlwind. God makes two speeches, and Job replies to them.[19] God's first speech (38:1–40:2) is inappropriate to Job's question, "Why do I suffer such awful tragedies?" God answers him by rhetorically questioning whether he comprehends the divine, mysterious power of creation, of which Job's suffering is part. Job replies with silence and never confesses his sin: "See, I am of small account; what shall I answer you? I lay my hand on my mouth. I have spoken once, and I will not answer; twice, but will proceed no further" (40:4-5). He refuses to talk. God's answer was irrelevant to his suffering. His silence is his noncompliance to such a nonsensical God-talk.

It is strange that God does not reveal the fact that Job's suffering was just a test initiated by Satan with God's own consent. Even God's second answer discloses none of this fact. This is the han of many suffering victims. They do not know why God does not make God's hidden purposes known.

God's second speech (40:6–41:34) starts with the questions, "Will you even put me in the wrong? Will you condemn me that you may be justified?" (v. 8). What God is saying in verse 8 is that justice depends on God. William Occam (c. 1280–1349) recapitulates this theology: Justice is not what we think of as right but rather is simply whatever God chooses to do. Gustavo Gutiérrez, says that, at first, Job views God's justice as retribution for sin. Yet in the end Job understands God's justice as God's freedom. Gutiérrez contends that divine justice is divine gratuitousness. To him, the book of Job centers on the theme of divine *justice* and divine *gratuitousness.*[20]

In his second reply, Job acknowledges God's all-powerfulness and confesses his own ignorance. Although Job obtains no satisfactory explanation for his predicament, he is satisfied with seeing God personally, and with irony repents of his sin.

> "Therefore I have uttered what I did not understand, things too wonderful for me, which I did not know. 'Hear, and I will speak; I will question you, and you declare to me.' I had heard of you by the hearing of the ear, but now my eye sees you; therefore I despise myself, and repent in dust and ashes." (42:3b-6)

Although Job says that he repents, we do not know of what sin he should repent. The fact that a victim should repent of his or her own wound is han. Here the term *repentance* is a wrong word for Job. He cannot repent of his pain but can only regret it.

Sin usually causes han. Han in turn can generate yet more han and sin. Job commits no sin, but agonizes with han. The author of Job tells us that God allows Satan to test Job. Here, a new type of han is introduced. Job's suffering derives from Satan's test. The test for Job was not to refine him, nor to punish him, but to confirm Job's voluntary worship of God in the face of adversity.

If God did not allow Satan to test Job, Satan's claim would be supported: "Job praises and worships God because it is beneficial." This saying of Satan's is a great warning to the theology of glory, which underpins the notion that we worship God for our own benefits. Here we see the author of Job strongly challenging Protestant theology: "This is to know Christ, to know his benefits."[21] Protestant theology is apt to mislead people to misinterpret the doctrine of faith. A distorted Protestant theology asserts that we believe in God because God benefits us. The real meaning of the doctrine of justification is whether God benefits us or not, we believe in God: "Though he slays me, yet will I trust in him" (Job 13:15, KJV).[22] Our trust or belief is not a bargaining chip with God. Our faith itself is an end, not a means to an end. By faith we wait for the God who never seems to come.

Furthermore, the book of Job can correct the preoccupation of traditional theologies with the justification or salvation of the sinner (oppressor). Job shifts our focus from a sinner's salvation to the liberation of the han-ridden. Emphasizing the forgiveness of wrongdoers and their justification, traditional theologies have neglected the liberation or healing of suffering Jobs.

Theology Under God's Wrath

At the end of the book, God expressed anger to Job's three friends for the unilateral theology of retribution with which they afflicted Job. God spoke to Eliphaz: "My wrath is kindled against you and against your two friends; for you have not spoken of me what is right, as my servant Job has" (42:7b). As judgment, God demanded of them burnt offerings and their apology to Job. They forced the innocent victim to repent of his sin and be saved. Job needed comfort and healing from the han of great tragedies, but they demanded his immediate confession of sin.

In pulpits we have preached the one-sided theology of a sin-repentance formula for everyone, including the sinned-against and the wounded: "Repent of your sin and be saved." We have wronged victims by applying this theology to them. The God of Job is angry at this simplistic sin-repentance formula that overlooks the han of victims. It is past time for us to provide a sensible theology of caring about the victims of sin and tragedy. Our present one-dimensional theology is under God's wrath. Theologians owe burnt offerings to God and their apology to the Jobs.

Han and Evil

Job's han arises without anyone's sin, and the source of han is ambiguous. Here han independent of sin is presented. It is the han of uncertain causality.

There are two types of han: the han caused by sin and the han caused by evil. Job is not a victim of sin, but a victim of han caused by evil.

Evil is not an absolute concept but a relative one. Evil might be interpreted as the privation of good (Plotinus, Augustine, and Thomas Aquinas) or as the fullness of good (Lao Tzu). For Simone Weil, evil consists of sin and suffering: "Evil is neither suffering nor sin; it is both at the same time, it is something common to them both. For they are linked together; sin makes us suffer and suffering makes us evil, and this indissoluble complex of suffering and sin is the evil in which we are submerged against our will, and to our horror."[23] A definition of evil can be the cosmic element that gives rise to sin and han. Some theologians believe that sin produces evil.[24] No sin, however, involves the evil of Job's suffering. Rather, evil involves the han that Job experiences. Evil in absence of sin is han; han in absence of sin is evil. Sin causes han and evil. Evil can produce han and sin, and han can regenerate evil and sin.

God's Absence and Han

Job develops han because of God's absence during his suffering. His questions, pain, and agony center on the silence of God in the midst of his suffering and his friends' accusations. His han is caused by *Deus Absconditus*, the God of absence. He experiences God as unreachable and inaccessible in the time of his trial and suffering. This is the reason why Elie Wiesel defies God's injustice and Richard Rubenstein declares the death of a traditional God.[25] We see this in Jesus' cry from the cross, "My God, my God, why have you forsaken me?" a strong protest against God's absence in the midst of the suffering and death of the innocent.

The theophany, however, makes Job realize that God never leaves him alone. God appears in the whirlwind and answered his question through discussion. Job's piercing question, however, is more fully answered in the New Testament. The New Testament theophany takes place at the crucifixion. The answer of the cross is that God is not only present in a victim's suffering but also is fully involved in the suffering, crying out as a victim. Thus, in the Hebrew Bible and the New Testament, God's appearance *resolves* the han of victims without necessarily solving it.

But Job's han is not completely resolved. The deaths of his children, the servants, and his own suffering remain painful in his memory. All the potential of his children and the rest were lost forever. These factors mean that, in spite of God's appearance, Job's han will never be fully resolved. Each year, forty million of the desperately poor die of hunger, hunger-related diseases, and contaminated drinking water.[26] Their han can never be resolved. Jesus' outcry on the cross is a way of replying to Job's suffering and the suffering of millions like him. Yet Job's question continues to reverberate in the souls of the suffering.

Han in the New Testament

Jesus, a carpenter's son, was one of the common people in Palestine. He interpreted the Hebrew Bible from a commoner's perspective. To locate han in the New Testament, we must walk with Jesus in Palestine. The main attention of his service was given to the people of han. He was himself a man of han. Though innocent, he was condemned, rejected, despised, and handed over to be crucified by his own people.

In his hometown, Nazareth, Jesus declared the purpose of his mission: to bring good news to the poor, to proclaim release to the captives and recovery of sight to the blind, to let the oppressed go free, and to proclaim the year of God's favor (Luke 4:18-19). He knew the agony of the downtrodden at that time. There were many who sat in darkness and in the region and shadow of death (Matt 4:16). Jesus diagnosed his time and people and came up with the goal of his ministry, which was to release the downtrodden from their bondage.

The Afflicted: The Theme of the New Testament

The primary reason for Jesus' coming into the world was to bring good news to the afflicted and the sinned-against. Jesus said, "Those who are well have no need of a physician, but those who are sick; I have come to call not the righteous but sinners" (Mark 2:17). Here, "sinners" are not all sinners.

There were two types of sinners in Jewish society at that time. One was a publicly recognized criminal who had broken civil laws. The other was a person in a lowly and socially unacceptable occupation.[27] We can divide the latter type of so-called sinners into two categories. One is the sinner of dishonorable occupation. The other is the sinner of low status such as the sick or the poor. Jesus' followers in general were the disreputable, the uneducated, and the ignorant, whose religious ignorance and moral behavior were problematic to their access to salvation, according to the public view of the time.[28] They were publicans and sinners (Mark 2:16), prostitutes (Matt 21:32), or the sick. They were simply called "sinners" (Mark 2:17; Luke 7:37, 39).

The sinners of the first category were involved in despised occupations. Some examples were herders, tax collectors, and publicans.[29] Others were sinners because of the unclean or ill-smelling nature of their jobs (e.g., butchers, tanners, coppersmiths). They were alienated and could not partake in worship.[30]

The sinners of the second category were the sick people who could not fulfill the duties of the law. As we have seen in Job, the theology that treated sickness as the consequence of sin was widespread in Judaism (Ps 73, John 9, Mark 2:5). Thus, the blind, the lepers, the mentally disturbed, and the hemorrhagic were regarded as either unclean or cursed by God.[31] Although the sick were not defined as transgressors, they were condemned by the religious leaders.

The religious leaders called most poor and powerless people "sinners" because poverty prevented them from observing the Sabbath or the law of purification. The *'am hā'āretz* (the "people of the land") were the uneducated and the ignorant, those whose lack of religious knowledge and moral practice stood in the way of their salvation.[32] During the Babylonian exile, the cream of society was taken captive, while the common people (including the Samaritans) were left behind. These people were called the *'am hā'āretz*. From the time of Ezra, the term was used to designate a lower class of people who were ignorant of the law. Rabbinic Judaism used the term to refer to the poor and the powerless who were despised and marginalized.[33]

Jesus came into the world to take their infirmities and bear their grief (cf. Matt 8: 17). He had compassion for the crowds "because they were harassed and helpless" (Matt 9:36). He proclaimed the good news for these heavy-laden. In Jesus' eyes, the "righteous" were the actual sinners who had to repent of their sins of self-righteousness, religious persecution, and ostentation. In contrast to the religious leaders and scribes, Jesus invited the han-ridden—the despised, the sick, and the poor—to his rest: "Come to me, all you that are weary and are carrying heavy burdens, and I will give you rest" (Matt 11:28). Their burden was double: public contempt and the hopelessness of attaining God's salvation.[34] They were not in fact sinners but were the sinned-against and marginalized by the oppressive religious leaders and their legal system.

This implies that these so-called sinners needed solace, healing, and liberation, not repentance. Jesus used all his means, including miracles, to heal the wounded of their suffering, oppression, and affliction. Contrary to the theology that is basically concerned with the guilt and salvation of sinners, Jesus' teaching centered on comforting the sinned-against, healing the wounded, giving voice to the voiceless, and liberating them from their han while confronting the oppressor. Jesus was the friend of the han-ridden.

The Lord's Prayer

Jesus taught this prayer to his followers. Matthew and Luke contain the two versions of the prayer known to us. Since Luke's version is shorter and thus is more likely the original, we will focus on it.[35]

> Father, hallowed be your name. Your kingdom come. Give us each day our daily bread. And forgive us our sins, for we ourselves forgive everyone indebted to us. And do not bring us to the time of trial. (Luke 11:2-5)

In the prayer, petitioners were the han-ridden: the poor, the sinned-against, and the tempted. They were the poor who had to worry about the next day's meals. In regards to whether "daily bread" refers to necessary bread (today's) or bread for the "coming day," the latter is more appropriate because an Aramaic translation of Matthew explicates it that way.[36]

Jesus did not address well-to-do people, but the poor. Sometimes, the crowd that followed him could not afford food for three days (Matt 15:32-39). His audience was largely the hungry, the tired, and the poor. In Luke, the Sermon on the Plain was directed to those for whom Jesus cared: "Blessed are you who are poor, for yours is the kingdom of God. Blessed are you who are hungry now, for you will be filled. Blessed are you who weep now, for you will laugh. But woe to you who are rich, for you have received your consolation. Woe to you who are full now, for you will be hungry" (Luke 6:20-25). Jesus clearly sided with the poor. His understanding of their life situation of poverty, oppression, and misery shines through clearly in the model prayer that he taught to his followers.

In fact, to the rich, reciting the Lord's Prayer can be awkward. While they have stored surplus food for many days, how can they pray for the next day's meal? Their prayer cannot be answered. The Lord's Prayer is superfluous for the wealthy. For them, it can mean only one thing: relinquishing their accumulated wealth to the destitute.

For the affluent, a saving element in the prayer is "Give *us* this day *our* daily bread," thus including themselves along with the poor. By saying "us" and "our" daily bread, the rich can commit themselves to working with the hungry in fighting against hunger and poverty. Until the time when everybody is being fed, they can earnestly press themselves toward it.

It is easy to notice that Jesus taught this prayer to the sinned-against since they were the ones who could forgive their oppressors' sin. The readiness to forgive was the indispensable condition of all prayers in Jesus' teaching.[37] For the oppressed, their own act of forgiving the oppressor preceded even God's forgiveness of those who have oppressed their fellow human beings. Jesus' other teachings on prayer also focused on victims (Matt 5:44, Luke 6:28). Had Jesus been concerned about the oppressors, he would have said in the prayer that you must ask the forgiveness of others (your victims) prior to asking God's forgiveness.[38]

Jesus further taught his followers to ask not to be brought to the time of trial. The term *trial* is from the Greek *peirasmos* (temptation).[39] In the first century, temptations and trials included apostasy caused by the hardship of discipleship. We should note that it was temptation, rather than sin, that Jesus told his followers to avoid. In general, sin is something the tempters experience, while trials come to the tempted. Jesus addresses this ("Lead us not into temptation") to protect the harassed from possible dangers and victimization.

The Lord's Prayer is for the people of han, particularly the poor, the sinned-against, and the tempted. When the rich and offenders recite the Lord's Prayer, it should be reinterpreted from the other end. For the rich and offenders, it might mean the following: "Our God . . . Use us to help the hungry prepare for their daily bread. Forgive our trespasses and persuade our victims to forgive our trespasses. Lead us not into tempting others, but deliver us from evil-doing." By focusing on the well-being of the poor, the rich and offenders can be the answer to their victims' Lord's Prayer.

Healing a Paralytic (Mark 2:1-12)

At Capernaum, four people brought a paralytic man to Jesus by creating a hole in the roof of the house where Jesus was teaching and lowering down the mat on which the man lay. Seeing their faith, Jesus healed the paralytic by saying, "Son, your sins are forgiven" (v. 5). When some scribes questioned in their hearts about his authority to forgive sin, Jesus said to them, "Which is easier, to say to the paralytic, 'Your sins are forgiven,' or to say, 'stand up and take your mat and walk'?" (v. 9). And then, he said to the young man to stand up, take his mat, and go home. The paralytic did as Jesus said.

In this conversation, even though Jesus said that his sins were forgiven, the term *sin* should be recast. As we have seen in Job, the Israelites connected suffering or sickness with sin. To them, any sin provoked divine wrath, which caused sickness. Thus, the Israelites believed that the forgiveness of sin precedes restoration from sickness. Sometimes it may be true that sin can generate sicknesses, but most times, ailments create false sin-consciousness.

The young man must have suffered from sin-consciousness. While sin might have been the cause of his sickness, far more likely is the possibility that his sickness generated his false sin-consciousness. We know this to be the case because sin requires repentance; without repentance, sin cannot be absolved. In the case of this young man, his sins were forgiven without either confession of sin or repentance of sin. This indicates that he committed no sin of which to repent. Subsequently, Jesus asked which is easier: "Your sins are forgiven" or "Stand up and take your mat and walk." To the young man, the pronouncement of the forgiveness of sin is much easier to understand and accept than the command of "stand up and walk." Jesus' declaration of the forgiveness without demanding repentance indicates that he was not concerned about the young man's sin but about his false sin-consciousness. This is the reason that Jesus treated the forgiveness of his sin as equivalent to "standing up and going home" with his own mat. "Standing up and going home" was letting go of his false sin-consciousness.

Unlike the case of the adulteress (John 8:11), Jesus did not command him to sin no more. Knowing this, we realize that this person's problem was not sin, but a false sin-consciousness caused by his sickness.

Releasing him from the false sin-consciousness, Jesus healed this han-ridden paralytic. As does the story of Job, this story defies the theology of retribution. Sin and human suffering are not necessarily interlocked in the cycle of cause and effect.

In our churches, we see many victims with broken spirits, victims of sexual abuse, homophobia, racial discrimination, and economic exploitation. Rather than demand their repentance of their sins, Jesus would pronounce the words of encouragement: "Stand up, take your mat of han, and go home." For Jesus, releasing people from their han is more urgent than dealing with their sin.

The Victimization of God in the Crucifixion (Mark 15:25-39)

Another benefit of understanding the broader context of sin and han is that it can free us from the lingering effects of the sin-penalty model, the idea that human suffering is the result of divine punishment for individual sin. Many Christians still believe that when we suffer, we do so because God is punishing us for sin. As is clearly shown in the incident of the healing of the blind man (John 9:1-41), Jesus disputed this explanation of human suffering. When the disciples saw a man blind from birth, they asked whether his blindness was caused by his own sin or by sin his parents committed. Although this sin-penalty model (also known as the Deuteronomistic theology for its prevalence in certain portions of the Hebrew Bible) received explicit rebuttal in the book of Job, the idea of sickness as God's punishment was nonetheless prevalent in Jesus' time. Jesus rejected the Deuteronomistic theology by saying that the man's blindness was caused neither by his sin nor by his parents', but for the manifestation of God's work. By flatly denying the popular belief in the sin-penalty model, Jesus opened up the possibility of a new interpretation of suffering: the suffering of victims.

Yet such thinking about sin and retribution has not disappeared from the Christian church. Our traditional interpretations of Jesus' crucifixion demonstrate this fact. The church has understood his execution in terms of the sin-suffering theology: "People sinned and he died for their sins." This formula displays the retribution model at work: People have sinned against God, and someone has to pay for it. Jesus' death is the penalty God required that Jesus pay for people's sin (the penal substitutionary atonement theory).

Does God really require people to pay for their iniquities? Does God have to let God's own son be killed as the penalty for peoples' sin? Setting aside the whole the issue of human sacrifice, we see little of the grace and forgiveness of God in this mode of thinking. If God cannot forgive sinners without the violent execution of Jesus, then God is neither gracious nor merciful, but interested only in retributive justice. In reality, however, our God surpasses the sin-penalty model that we have seen above, and is greatly merciful toward suffering humanity.

Taken as *expiation*—fulfillment of God's requirement that someone has to pay for human sin—Jesus' execution is hard to understand, let alone defend. Let us assume, however, that Jesus died to forgive people's sin. Such a death would therefore be only for those who had lived before Jesus' time, because it is absurd to think that God would forgive sins that have not yet been committed. If Jesus died to forgive the sins of all people, including future generations, people after Jesus should not have to worry about sin and guilt because Jesus has already paid for their sins. In addition, there is no need of repentance because our sins were forgiven through Jesus' death. It is inappropriate to think that God smote Jesus for the sins that people will commit in the future and that God forgave them before they had repented of their sin.

In reality, the execution of Jesus defies the sin-suffering theology, expressing God's han caused by human sins. Jesus did not know sin, yet he knew han through and through. Jesus' last cry was a victim's outcry in han: "My God, my God, why have you forsaken me?" (Mark 15:34). The cross represents the many innocent victims who have suffered injustice and oppression. It is the symbol of God's han. Jesus' cross does not reveal a God who causes human suffering, but rather a God who suffers alongside us. It is the sign of God's great advocacy for the victims of abuse, violence, and unjust oppression, opposing abusive power unto death. The cross offers healing to victims who see God's solidarity and woundedness with them. It offers salvation to offenders by calling them to repent of their sins. The crucifixion signifies God as the victim of human injustice and violence. Only when we interpret the crucifixion as the supreme expression of God's woundedness in the world will we see its saving power.

Sin

Sin is a thought, word, deed, attitude, or intention that goes against God and humanity. It is a damaged relationship that sets us apart from God's creation. It makes people isolated and withdrawn. In the Bible, the tragic history of the world starts with the broken relationship of Adam and Eve with God. The fact that the serpent deceived Adam and Eve points to our imperfection. The story of the fall starts with God's creation of us, imperfect and free. These dual attributes were bound to result in human sin (Reinhold Niebuhr). The story tells us that our sin is not a simple human volitional act but is deeply entangled with the structure of han. It shows what we are, not necessarily what we were.

Let us look further into the biblical teaching on sin. R. Knierim has examined in detail the three most important Hebrew roots for sin found in the Hebrew Bible.[40] Of the three, the root *hātā'* (noun *hēt*) is by far the most common, occurring some 595 times. The primitive sense of *hata'* is the missing of a special goal, one's ethical failure to fulfill a duty, the failure of a vassal to pay tribute to his or her lord, and an offense committed against God.

A second Hebrew root for sin, *pāsha'* (noun *pesha'*) occurs about 135 times and signifies informed, volitional violation of a norm or standard. In general, it would not refer to an unintentional blunder, as might be the case with *hēt*. The noun *pesha'* is revolt or rebellious deeds that are probably to be understood to be such. The verb *pāsha'* can be translated "to rebel, revolt, transgress."

A third important Hebrew term for "sin" is the noun *'āvōn* which occurs some 229 times in the Hebrew Bible. Generally, the acceptable translation of the noun is an error or iniquity. Hebrew *'āvōn* is hardly used to express guilt before humans but is almost always being employed to indicate moral guilt or iniquity before God.[41]

Besides these three meanings of missing a specified target, willful transgression, or error and iniquity, a number of additional terms point to the idea of sin. Sin has a wide range of additional terms. Included among these are disobedience, criminal wrongdoing, wickedness, evil, distress, injury, misery, and calamity.[42]

Like the Hebrew Bible, the New Testament employs several terms for sin.[43] *Hamartia* is the most common. In early Greek literature sin referred to a variety of errors: missing the target in throwing a javelin, committing a procedural mistake in sacrificing, or harming or taking no notice of others. In later Greek philosophy from Plato to the Stoics and Cynics, sin was especially connected with ignorance. In the New Testament, *hamartia* is error, a missing of the mark, and the failure to do what one should do.

Parabasis and *paraptōma* mean respectively "transgression" and "trespass" and thus refer to individual acts. *Parabasis* is going beyond one's boundary. This means invading someone else's territory. *Paraptōma* is a trespassing or a slipping across, a sin less intentional than *parabasis*. It is committed out of our lack of self-control.

Parakoē is "disobedience." It is rebellion, covenantal disloyalty, and hubris. This sin hurts God.

Adikia means "unrighteousness," usually against a fellow human. This sin is a form of injustice.

Asebeia means "impiety," usually against God.

Kakia and *ponēros* mean "wickedness" and "evil." *Ponēros* is very common in the gospels.

Opheiletēs is a "debtor," and sometimes it and the related verb are used to refer to "debt" to God or the neighbor incurred by transgression. This word means a failure to pay a due and a failure in duty.

Anomia is the sin of lawlessness. It is the sin of the one who knows the law, yet breaks it.

In summary, these biblical concepts of sin are missing a mark, transgression, disobedience, unrighteousness, impiety, wickedness, debt, error, iniquity, or lawlessness. We should notice that human freedom is engaged in all these biblical sins.

Sin involves one's will. Without it, it is not sin. In this sense, original sin is not a sin. The idea of original sin is not found in Judaism, but was developed by Augustine. The Augustinian idea of the hereditary original sin is neither biblical nor logical. The Bible never mentions a hereditary transmittal of sin from parents to children. There is a remotely related verse speaking on this in Exodus: "punishing children for the iniquity of parents, to the third and the fourth generation of those who reject me, but showing steadfast love to the thousandth generation of those who love me and keep my commandments" (Exod 20:6). This idea is not about the biological transmission of sin, but the environmental influence of parental sins on their children. This idea of punishment on the children of evildoers shows the structure of han rather than that of sin. Without having committed sin themselves, the children of sinners become victims of their parents' transgressions.

Augustine's idea of original sin is also illogical. According to him, baptism washes original sin away. Therefore, the children of a baptized couple must be free from original sin. Augustine answered this question by saying that the pride of original sin is removed by baptism but its concupiscence (lust) of procreation remains as the channel of transmitting original sin.

> But whatsoever is born of the old nature, which still abides with its concupiscence requires to be born again in order to be healed. Seeing that believing parents, who have been both carnally born and spiritually born

again, have themselves begotten children in a carnal manner, how could their children by any possibility, previous to their first birth, have been born again? [44]

There are two problems here. First, if the content of original sin is eliminated, what will be transmitted? Concupiscence is only the channel of original sin. Second, he regards all sexual activity as lust. On the contrary, the Bible sees it as God's blessing. Were Augustine alive today, he would have to answer the question of whether those children who were conceived by in vitro fertilization and other artificial means are free of original sin. Not having been conceived by an act of concupiscence, they would have to be outside the cycle of original sin. This kind of theological arguments is absurd.

To me, original sin rather shows us our proclivity to sin. It points to the fact that everyone has the potential to commit sin. The universal latency of sin within the human mind and soul may be the reality to which the idea of original sin points.

Walter Rauscehnbusch, champion of the social gospel movement, stands out as one who interpreted original sin in a collective sense. He rejects the individualistic understanding of original sin that supports the biological transmission of sin. His understanding of original sin is social, in that Rauschenbusch saw crimes, social corruptions, and social vices as the sort of things that transmit evil to individuals: "One generation corrupts the next. The permanent vices and crimes of adults are not transmitted by heredity, but by being socialized."[45] For him, sin is selfishness, which negates the common good of humanity and refuses to see the social dimension of God's reign.[46]

Against liberal theologians who they believed underestimated the reality of sin, neo-orthodox theologians stressed sin's seriousness. Among those who focused on the existential reality of sin, Reinhold Niebuhr's depiction "man as sinner" stands out. For him, sin is primarily pride and secondly sensuality; both are based on self-love.[47]

Paul Tillich diagnosed original sin as estrangement from God. For him, our estrangement/separation from God displays itself in three ways: unbelief, hubris, and concupiscence.

In contrast to these definitions of sin coming from male theologians (and hence declaring male experiences of sin to be normative of both genders), Valerie Saiving declare that women's sin differs from men's. To her, most women do not suffer from pride, as Niebuhr insisted, but from "distractibility, the lack of self-centeredness, and the negation of the self."[48]

Saiving refused to accept the doctrine of universal sin that was interpreted by male theologians; women and men suffer from different ills.

Although I greatly appreciate and respect Saiving for her innovative and insightful idea, I differ from her interpretation; distractibility, diffuseness, and lack of organizing center are not sin. Out of a lack of expression, she calls them sin. In fact, they are the embodiment of han. Sin involves a volitional act of offense against God or others. Traits like those Saiving enumerated that result from the infringement of outside forces cannot be called sin at all. That is the very gist of han, the seat of the wound of victims.

Against the individualistic views of sin, Latin-American liberation theologians have presented a sociohistorical actuality of sin. Gustavo Gutiérrez, an exponent of this movement, addressed the threefold nature of sin: economic and sociopolitical oppression, historical determinism, and spiritual sin. With deep admiration, I modify his concepts of sin: economic and sociopolitical oppression and historical determinism are sins from the perspective of oppressors, but they are han from the perspective of the oppressed. However, as the term indicates, economic and sociopolitical oppression tend to be a collective or individual sin of the oppressors, while the historic determinism leans toward a collective or individual han of the oppressed. Gutiérrez' ideas of sin can be strengthened when viewed within an understanding of han.

Sin has at least two levels: individual and collective. At the individual level, sin is a personal offense against God and God's creation, appearing as selfishness, a superiority complex, oppression, and exploitation. At the collective level, sin is a communal aggression, such as the ethos of cultural dominance, a racial superiority complex, physical pride, exclusive ethnocentrism, and nationalism. The collective level of sin includes a structural aspect that sustains such sources of sin as laissez-faire capitalism, racism, sexism, hierarchy, and humanocentrism. From the perspective of the oppressed, laissez-faire capitalism, racism, and sexism are the roots of structural han, while from the perspective of the oppressor, these are the roots of structural sin.

Conclusion

To be effective, pastors have to preach on the particular pain and needs of their congregation, just as they have to know their parishioners' current addresses if they are to minister to them adequately. We have seen that sin may be forgiven by the repentance of sinners, whereas han can be resolved by the healing of the sinned-against. This understanding empowers us, in turn, to more effectively make the fullness of Christian salvation and liberation real and concrete in the world of the sinned-against and the sinned.

It is time for us to address the reality of han in the world. Most violence and crime in the world are the results of the vicious cycle of sin and han. Unresolved han or superficial treatments of han continually produce sin, violence, and tragedies, thus perpetuating the eruption of han by generating yet more han.

We have reviewed the Bible and the church's theology from the perspective of the sinned-against in light of han. The Bible is for sinners and the sinned-against. However, the Bible, particularly the New Testament, was primarily written for the community of faith that was persecuted and sinned-against. If we want to have a more holistic interpretation, it is critical to read the Bible from that perspective. The notion of han may contribute to such an effort to see biblical truth from such perspectives, complementing the doctrine of sin. This notion may free people from the unilateral interpretation of the sin-penalty scheme and provide an alternative theological mode of interpretation for victims like Abel, Job, and especially Jesus of the cross. Imposing the sin-penalty formula upon the victims of sin is a grave injustice. By naming the reality of the suffering of victims, we can begin to heal rather than overlook or condemn them. Such a move will inaugurate a new journey to a theology of holistic salvation and liberation.

CHAPTER TWO

Shame and Guilt

Many people are confused about the difference between shame and guilt. Shame and guilt are two overlapping responses to han and sin, respectively. In general, shame emerges when one is helplessly wronged or hurt by others. Guilt arises when one commits sin or does not do right. The victims of guilt (the offenders) are primarily haunted by an uneasy conscience; the victims of shame (the offended) largely suffer from embarrassment because they could not defend their own territory. Their helplessness is a source of shame. People frequently feel shame when humiliated. People mainly feel guilt when trespassing others' boundaries.[1]

Shame involves discomfort in facing others because of one's own vulnerability. Guilt implies internalization of the moral values of society. Thus, a guilty person experiences the emotional consequence of culpability regardless of whether others are present or are aware of his or her transgressions. Although wrongdoers and the wronged both experience guilt and shame, the wrongdoers predominantly undergo feelings of regret and affliction, while the wronged undergo nervous feelings and pain.

A main definition of shame in *Oxford English Dictionary* is "the painful emotion arising from the consciousness of something dishonoring, ridiculous, or indecorous in one's own conduct or circumstances (or in those of others whose honor or disgrace one regards as one's own), or of being in a situation which offends one's sense of modesty or decency." There is another definition that is "the consciousness of this emotion, guilty feeling; also, the right perception of what is improper or disgraceful" or "disgrace, ignominy, loss of esteem or reputation." To J. P. Tangney, shame-prone persons tend to respond with a personal distress reaction, a reaction to pain that is incompatible with their present state of affairs.[2]

Guilt is defined as "the state (meriting condemnation and reproach of conscience) of having willfully committed a crime or heinous moral offence; criminality, great culpability" or "a failure of duty, delinquency; offence, crime, sin" (*Oxford English Dictionary*). To Tangney, guilt hinges on empathic awareness and response to someone's distress, as well as on awareness of being the cause of that distress.[3] Guilt is the self-consciousness that emerges from reflecting on one's own sin or wrong.

In the 1930s, anthropologists made a distinction between shame cultures and guilt cultures. For them, shame sets up a purely external sanction for good conduct, while guilt internalizes a sense of right and wrong. In the 1950s, psychologists Gerhart Piers and Milton Singer debunked this anthropological interpretation and built a new interpretation pulled out from Piers' psychoanalytic theory of the superego.[4]

Piers distinguished shame from guilt by saying that

> 1) Shame arises out of a tension between the ego and ego ideal, not between ego and superego as in guilt. 2) Whereas guilt is generated whenever a boundary (set by the superego) is touched or transgressed, shame occurs when a goal (presented by the ego ideal) is not being reached. It thus indicates a real "shortcoming." Guilt anxiety accompanies transgression; shame, failure. 3) The unconscious, irrational threat implied in shame anxiety is abandonment, and not mutilation (castration) as in guilt. 4) The Law of Talon does not obtain in the development of shame, as it generally does in guilt.[5]

To Piers and Singer, while guilt internalizes the fear of punishment, shame internalizes the fear of rejection (specifically, rejection by the parent). Shame takes its cue from the loving and beloved aspect of the ego ideal, guilt from the castigating aspect of the superego. Shame derives from the failure to live up to the father's internalized example, and guilt from defiance of the father. The terrifying threat of abandonment arouses shame, and the unconscious image of the punishing father afflicts the guilty conscience. In short, Piers and Singer made it quite explicit: Guilt feelings derive from transgression; shame, from failure.[6]

In the late 1950s, Helen Merrell Lynd developed Piers and Singer's concept further by associating guilt not only with "transgression of prohibitions" but with "violation of a specific taboo." She moved guilt away from its old involvement in sin and associated it with crime and any kind of unconventional conduct. Reducing it to the fear of punishment set up by the community standards, she secularized the religious concept of guilt that had referred to a chronic state of rebellion against God.

In contrast to the cultural anthropologists' claim of guilt as the inner voice of conscience, Lynd theorized that guilt feelings result from efforts toward social adjustment. To her, shame goes deeper than guilt, because the shamed see themselves as condemned by society, not just by their own inner sense of right and wrong.

In 1971, Helen Block Lewis added to this idea by devoting her attention to an individual's proneness to shame or guilt. Women's timid self-esteem is more prone to shame; men's aggressiveness is more inclined to guilty fear of retaliation. Others extended the boundary of shame to underprivileged groups later.

In the early 1990s Gloria Steinem delved into the social implication of low self-esteem, particularly in women. In *The Revolution from Within: A Book of Self-esteem* she contended that when individuals such as women, the poor, or ethnic minorities are repeatedly marginalized, suppressed, scorned, and ignored by a culture, they descend into a sense of apathy and indifference.[7] Unless these external roots of poor self-esteem are not eradicated from the internal self, any chance to transform the status quo, whether within the scope of personal life or in the wider scope of political, social, or cultural life, becomes slim. Steinem argues that only when we end oppression in our "inner lives" can we reduce it in the greater world. Although many feminists have criticized Steinem's book as a withdrawal from political involvements, it can be understood as a new approach to the fact that politics and therapy are inseparable.[8]

To better understand the nature of shame and guilt, one must grasp the many different ways in which these two emotions manifest themselves. It is to that task that I would now turn, beginning with the different types of shame and then turning to the various forms of guilt.

Shame

There are several types of shame: discretion, humiliation, failure, disgrace, and collective shame. Humiliation and failure are manifestations of shame that victims experience. The result of actions by the offender, these destructive kinds of shame require intervention, support, and treatment. The shame of disgrace, on the other hand, is the shame of an offender. It is interwoven with guilt. Discretion shame is a healthy type that everyone should experience. A community of the wronged shares a collective shame of humiliation, while a group of offenders develops a collective shame of disgrace derived from its collective guilt.

Humiliating Shame

Humiliating shame arises as the keenly painful consciousness of something dishonorable, inappropriate, and outrageous done to a person by another. A victim suffers from the shame of humiliation. The primary causes of this type of shame are transgression and crime.

In the Bible there is no event that speaks to the shame of humiliation better than the crucifixion of Jesus. In both the Hebraic and Hellenistic cultures in which the world of the New Testament took part, shame and honor figured prominently.[9] Both highly praised the value of honor and disparaged the experience of shame. Honor meant more than wealth, and shame meant no less than death. The shame of the sinned-against and the shame of sinners are distinguished in the Bible. The shame of the sinned-against signifies humiliation, while the shame of the sinner points to disgrace.

Jesus' teaching in the Sermon on the Mount deals with honor and dishonor. He taught his disciples that when an enemy struck them on the right cheek, they were to offer the other cheek as well (Matt 5:39). Three points stand out in this matter. First, it was an insult for the Jews to slap the face (1 Kgs 22:24, Job 16:10, Isa 50:6, and 1 Esdras 4:30) or break the teeth (Pss 3:7 and 58:6):

> Then Zedekiah son of Chenaanah came up to Micaiah, slapped him on the cheek, and said, "Which way did the spirit of the LORD pass from me to speak to you?" (1 Kgs 22:24)

> I gave my back to those who struck me, and my cheeks to those who pulled out the beard; I did not hide my face from insult and spitting. (Isa 50:6)

> Rise up, O LORD! Deliver me, O my God! For you strike all my enemies on the cheek; you break the teeth of the wicked. (Ps 3:7)

Second, slapping on the face is an "extreme humiliation" in Greco-Roman culture, according to Hans Betz.[10] Third, slapping on the right cheek may mean a strike with the back of the hand or with the left hand.[11] In either case it signifies a sharp insult, for the left hand is unclean due to its use for toilet purpose, and the back of the hand is used for insulting someone. A slap by the back of the hand requires a double penalty.[12] The slapping of the face aims at an insult rather than an injury. This is the reason why a policeman struck Jesus on the face during his trials (Mark 14:65, Luke 22:64-65). "When he had said this, one of the police standing nearby struck Jesus on the face, saying, 'Is that how you answer the high priest?'" (John 18:22). Here, slapping on the cheek points to the shame of humiliation, epitomizing the culture of honor and dishonor.

Furthermore, Jesus' cross was a sign of shame particularly for the Messiah-to-be. When Palestine became Roman territory, the Romans frequently employed the cross to uphold civil authority and preserve law and order against noncitizens. Later on, the Romans used it particularly against thieves and malefactors (Josephus, *Ant.*, 20. vi, 2). In Palestine, crucifixion was a public reminder of Jewish subjugation to the Romans. Thus, Paul called the crucified Christ "a stumbling block to Jews and foolishness to Gentiles" (1 Cor 1:23). We find no Hebrew Bible or other Jewish sources reporting that the Messiah could suffer such a humiliating death. Quite the reverse: To die by hanging on a tree demonstrated that one had been cursed by God (Deut 21:22–23). To the nonbelievers it seemed "foolishness" (1 Cor 1:18) to declare the crucified as the Messiah, the King of the Jews, and God's Son. His horrible death on the cross discredits any such claims. Justin Martyr (ca. 100–165) noted how utterly repugnant it was to recognize a crucified man as God: "They say that our madness consists in the fact that we put a crucified man in second place after the unchangeable and eternal God, the Creator of the world" (1 Apol. 13.4).[13] The utter shame of crucifixion turned many people away from believing in Jesus as the Messiah.

The shame of Jesus' crucifixion is the symbol of victims' shame and the pain of humiliation. Victims of violence are often mistrusted, jeered at, scapegoated, distanced, and blamed for their victimization. Jesus' crucifixion represents the inexpressible han of innocent victims, undergoing all these unjust treatments—the shame of double victimization.

Humiliation shame denotes the natural response of victims to an oppressive and unjust transgression. When offended, desecrated, or overwhelmed by others, victims often withdraw into themselves. Such recoiling into silence can be potentially harmful. Many give in to the pressure of humiliating shame, injure their self-dignity, and develop false guilt-consciousness about their shortcomings, blaming themselves for being helpless. It drives them to the sense of worthlessness, defectiveness, dishonor, and repugnance. At the same time, this kind of shame generates anger and resentment toward the offenders.

The victims of physical abuse, sexual abuse, and crime particularly undergo the shame of humiliation. As people are physically abused and violated, they feel powerless, mortified, and full of shame. Rape cases demonstrate this fact particularly.

The story of Tamar illustrates the nature of the shame of han (2 Sam 13). Tamar was a half sister of Amnon, the firstborn of King David. Having fallen in love with Tamar, Amnon pretended to be sick in order to get her to come see him. When Tamar came to attend him, he seduced her to lie with him. At first she refused to do so by saying, "No, my brother, do not force me; for such a thing is not done in Israel; do not do anything so vile! As for me, where could I carry my shame?" (vv. 12-13). But he did not listen to her and he raped her. After the act, Amnon was seized with a great loathing for her and chased her out of his house. Being driven out by his servant, Tamar put ashes on her head and tore the long robe that was the trademark of the virgin daughters of the king. Putting her hand on her head, she went away with loud crying.

The shame she felt as a result of this rape and incest was too great to suppress. Her loud cry, imposition of ashes, and the torn long robe symbolize the double shame of her helplessness and degradation. Her father, knowing what had happened, nonetheless kept silent out of his need to protect his son and successor, Amnon. David's own sense of his self-interest trumped his sense of justice for Tamar, leading his daughter to suffer the triple shame of humiliation: rape, incest, and her father's knowing silence.

Andrea Dworkin's "The Third Rape" discloses the multiple shames and humiliation that victims of rape experience. The first rape is the act itself. The second rape is the trial. Although nine out of ten rape victims do not report the crime they have suffered, a few do so. For these victims, the trial annihilates what is left of their self-respect. Through intimidation, forced repetition of every detail, insult, and public humiliation before family, friends, and co-workers, the trial rapes the victim, deepening the wound. The third rape is the media. Reporting a rape is equivalent to suicide. Laid bare to the scrutiny of voyeurs by the media, the victim is, in effect, forced to splay her legs before the public eye. Having exposed sexual crimes, the media usually proceed to exploit them. In spite of the fact that a rape victim needs privacy, human dignity, and security, the media exposes every aspect of her life so that there is no place to hide. The media capitalizes on the victim's suffering until it—and she—are used up.[14]

On top of this, the anger and anxiety of the victim slowly chew up the lingering health of her exhausted body. Losing health by the sense of indignation is the fourth dimension of rape. Koh's case in the previous chapter shows another dimension of the shame of rape—the loss of the legal case based on insufficient evidence. The fifth aspect of rape for a victim is the inadequate present legal procedures for rape victims. Before the suffocating and humiliating legal system, the victim can only sigh at the unfair system of legal procedures.

The accumulated quintuple suffering of a rape victim is the mortified shame of *han*. A rape victim agonizes over shame, not guilt. If there is any guilt, it is a false one or a mere regret. The shame that the victim experiences devastate her human dignity and inner space, haunting all aspects of her life.

One can be an offender and a victim simultaneously. When we hurt or injure ourselves, shame arises from within, caused by us. For instance, the victim of an attempted suicide is both a victim and offender. She or he will bear shame as a victim and guilt as an offender. Most addicted people show complex feelings of shame and guilt together. They turn out to be injurers as well as the injured. As they harm their own bodies with abuses, they feel guilty. As they are injured by their own addicted behaviors, they develop shame. Shame and guilt are intermingled in them so closely that the two are inseparable.

The Shame of Failure

When our goals and expectations are not fulfilled, we feel shame at our own shortcomings. The shame of failure, a victim's shame, is a response to our failure to live up to our self-expectations or the expectations of people whom we care about and respect. In Gerhart Piers' term, shame is incurred from a tension between the ego and ego ideal, not between ego and superego as in guilt. As our ideal is unrealized, our ego turns that unfulfilled ideal into shame when we believe our failure affects the survival of our ego or our indispensable condition of respect from others. This is the shame of failure. This type of failure shame burdens us with the uncertainty of our ability to achieve a task. We hesitate before we venture out because of our past shameful experience of failure. Such shame eats up our courage to risk.

Judas Iscariot betrayed his teacher. Whatever reason he may have had for doing this, he felt miserable enough to end his life. It is clear that his expectation toward Jesus was not met and that, when Judas sold him for thirty pieces of silver, he wretchedly failed in his mission as Jesus' disciple. Such feelings of self-pity and misery led him to suicide. His case was one of failure shame. Jesus' shame was very different from Judas.' Jesus faced humiliation shame, but Judas suffered failure shame.

The shame of failure often results from such natural adversities as barrenness. When Rachel bore a son, she said "God has taken away my reproach," and she named him Joseph (Gen 30:23). During the New Testament era, barrenness was still a source of shame. When Elizabeth conceived John the Baptist, she declared, "This is what the Lord has done for me when he looked favorably on me and took away the disgrace I have endured among my people" (Luke 1:25). Childlessness was seen as a form of defectiveness at that time, and hence gave rise to shame.

When an ice skater loses her or his balance and falls down on the ice in a skating competition, she or he shows a shame of failure. In competitions, most athletes express this kind of shame when they make blunders. Most of us experience the shame of failure when we fall short in achieving our given tasks.

The Shame of Disgrace

Sin and wrongs primarily cause the shame of disgrace—a sinner's shame. When we commit a sin, we suffer from guilt-consciousness. The guilt-consciousness we suffer may turn into shame when it is caught by our conscience before God or becomes known to others. As in the story of the fall, Adam and Eve came to the consciousness of guilt and then shame about their nakedness after they sinned (Gen 3:10). Their disgrace shame was a concomitant of the divine judgment upon their sin.[15] When sinners or offenders are caught red-handed in public, they lose face. Through the pain of disgraceful shame, they might come to repentance (1 Cor 4:14, 11:22, 15:34; 2 Thess 3:14). When a sin or crime is concealed from others, the sinner may not grieve over it. But, once the sinner's guilt is disclosed in public, disgrace overwhelms him or her.

For example, charged with downloading child pornography, computer technician Robert Bickerstaffe of Liverpool, England, killed himself instead of facing societal shame.[16] Recently, some states in the United States have attempted to use the idea of shame punishment for the treatment of white-collar criminals. The overcrowding of prisons has led the courts to consider this method of publicly humiliating offenders.[17] The shame of disgrace springs from losing one's self-esteem and sense of self-value. Its foundation is the fear of ruining one's own reputation, relationships, status, and positions. The fear of losing the respect of others is connected with the potential promise of life. With a bad or ruined reputation, one cannot play a normal role in the family and community, and accordingly cannot succeed in one's business and career. Thus, the offender develops the fear that their shameful shadow—be it a sin, error, misconduct, or crime—might become evident in the light of day. People tend to hide their shortcomings and trespasses, secretly harboring their guilt. When their secret comes to light, their guilt-consciousness turns into disgrace shame.

The shame of sin is a form of the disgrace that sinners inflict upon themselves. It is the shame of reliance on false power (Isa 30:3); everlasting contempt (Dan 12:2); folly (Prov 18:13); idolatry (Ezk 7:18, Hos 10:6); or pride in power (2 Chr 32:21). It is the portion of idolaters who are faithless to God or unfriendly to God's people. The shame of disgrace also comes upon those who exalt themselves against God and trust in earthly power and wealth (2 Chr 32:21).[18] It can be removed by giving up sins and offences.

The Shame of Discretion

Shame sometimes works for good. We need the consciousness of shame to protect our decency. This positive form of shame can be called discretion shame. This type of shame arises when our conscience guards against indecent and unacceptable activities. When the zipper of our pants is down, we need to zip it up. Discretion shame dictates to us to do that. When the eyes of Adam and Eve were opened, "they knew that they were naked; and they sewed fig leaves together and made loincloths for themselves" (Gen 3:7). When naked, we need the shame of discretion to cover ourselves with fig leaves.

Particularly, during the tender years of our growth, discretion shame plays an important role in the formation of our values and behaviors. For Erik Erikson, shame is the self-consciousness of being exposed or being looked at "with one's pants down."[19] Carl Schneider compares discretion shame to a darkroom, which protects undeveloped film against the premature exposure to light.[20] This type of shame is an indispensable element in our human development and maturation. In Max Scheler's analogy, discretion shame is like the soil that buries the root of a tree in the ground.[21] To grow the tree, the root must be nurtured through the soil. Covering the part that should not be exposed is necessary for our health. With this shame, we grow trained and well rounded. This shame vitalizes our sense of prudence, decency, propriety, and respectability.

Collective Humiliating Shame (Han)

At a collective level, people of a particular race, gender, or class can develop humiliating shame. In the past, Africans were sold as slaves and were denigrated to the level of objects. Their cumulative dehumanization has continued in the form of racial prejudice and discrimination. They have suffered humiliation shame for hundreds of years. Whenever a racial slur is spelled out, it triggers the accumulated shame of humiliation in the heart of victims. The victims usually respond to an offence with shameful blushing, tears, and rancor, re-living some humiliating events of the past. Most ethnic groups in this country, including Native Americans, Asian Americans, Pacific Islanders, and Hispanic Americans, have undergone various experiences of humiliating shame as well.

There is a different type of collective shame among a group of offenders. Doing something wrong and unjust elicits guilt in them and then the collective guilt turns into collective shame when their act of guilt is acknowledged within their group or society. This shame is collective disgrace. Collective guilt and shame may be major components of the Japanese psyche. The Japanese ignominy over their sneak attack on Pearl Harbor runs beneath the Japanese consciousness because a stealthy attack is an act of dishonor in the samurai tradition. Japan has suffered the collective shame of disgrace after the war. Sometimes, some groups may deny their collective guilt after doing wrongs, but collective shame cannot be repressed for long. The culture of those experiencing this shame reflects it one way or another. Collective shame transmits itself to posterity.

Guilt

Guilt is an awareness of having done wrong or having committed sin. It is the primary conscious experience of a sinner. We find in the Bible a close affinity between crime, guilt, and punishment. This is seen in the Hebrew word *'āshām*, translated fifty-five times as "offense" or "crime," 159 times as "guilt," and seven times as "punishment." The whole idea of sin in the Hebrew Bible and New Testament is structured around this word.[22] Some people find it irrational to suffer guilt over what happened in the past. For them, the rational look toward the future, not the guilt of the past. Nietzsche construes guilt as a self-imposed course, an illness that needs to be cured if we are to live.[23]

Some Christian theologians think that Christian theology should treat the issue of guilt rather than that of shame. Donald Capps in his *The Depleted Self: Sin in a Narcissistic Age* argues that while contemporary culture is dominated by shame, Christian moral theology should focus instead on guilt as it emerges from the sin of pride. Capps believed that the focus on shame was the result of living in an age of narcissism.[24] Capps's perspective makes sense when we see that his starting point is the traditional doctrine of the guilt of sinners. For me, shame manifests itself among victims, and because Christian soteriology has traditionally ignored them, it has ignored shame as well.

The term *guilt* has several dimensions. There is *legal, ethical,* and *religious* guilt. Legal guilt involves culpability and responsibility for crimes. Ethical guilt is a matter of moral accountability rather than legal liability. Drinking for alcoholics is legal, yet it may cause moral guilt for them. Religious guilt concerns our obligation before God and neighbor. A sin of omission or lust in our hearts may not be legally or ethically wrong but can be religiously wrong.

For Protestantism, sin is universal and so is guilt. Reinhold Niebuhr felt uncomfortable with the idea that sin and guilt are identical in every person or group, because there is a difference between the sin of oppressors and the sin of the oppressed. To distinguish them, he invented the brilliant phase: *the equality of sin* and the *inequality of guilt*. For Niebuhr, oppressors and the oppressed are all sinners (the equality of sin), but there is a difference in guilt. Oppressors are more guilty than the oppressed (the inequality of guilt). This distinction is better than Protestantism's implicit generalization that the universality of sin produces an equally universal experience of guilt. Guilt emerges from the exercise of freedom. Victims have not exercised their freedom in ways that produce within them the same kind of guilt as their oppressors experience. The universality of sin and guilt needs to be reinterpreted in Protestantism.

At this juncture, we need to distinguish the guilt that wrongdoers feel from the guilt perceived by those who have been wronged. While wrongdoers' guilt is natural, that of the wronged is unnatural. When we commit a sin or wrong another, the guilt we experience over that act is healthy. Unhealthy guilt, on the other hand, arises from a defense mechanism.[25] One of the symptoms of the wronged is self-blame, shame, and guilt. Their feeling of shame is normal, but their feeling of guilt is unjustified, for they have not done anything wrong. Guilt requires repentance, but shame needs remedy.

Appropriate Guilt

Appropriate guilt for the offenders is the awareness of their offence, crime, sin, and failure of duty. The superego, our internal authority, produces the sense of guilt whenever we transgress the highly charged barrier set up by the superego.[26] True guilt is guilt at the remorseful awareness we have for our offence, and the obligation we owe to ourselves to be our best selves.

The Christian idea of guilt engages three components: responsibility, blameworthiness, and obligation.[27] Responsibility means we have the power to use our freedom to make ethical decisions and are hence answerable for our conduct. It also means that the degree of our guilt depends on the degree of our freedom. Blameworthiness means that our actions and attitudes merit reproach, discipline, or penalty. Blameworthiness also depends on the knowledge and intention of the sinner. Obligation is a debt made good through payment or compensation. It is a course of action by which one is bound and that is imposed by conscience, law, or society. Put another way, guilt involves questions of cause, motive, and consequence on the part of the sinner.

Guilt can direct us toward those who have been wronged or damaged, and demand reparation, sanctions, or punishment in the name of what has happened to them. As guilt pressures us to communicate and to confess, it can be forgiven or it can be punished. When guilt is recognized and confessed, it can be alleviated. There are several steps in removing guilt: admit one's culpability, take responsibility for an action or event, and amend wrongs.

To be effective, punishment must connect with a sense of guilt and a desire to be accepted back within the community. A sense of personal shame, however, is more related to the expectations we place on ourselves rather than those placed on us by society or a group. When we have these expectations of ourselves, shame can motivate a change in our behavior as effectively as guilt and punishment can for others.

Inappropriate Guilt

While appropriate guilt leads us out from inauthentic situations, improving our interpersonal and social relationships and increasing our sensitivity to others' needs, inappropriate guilt traps us in a repetitive self-blame and destructive self-denigration, escalating our irrational anxieties. People express their unhealthy guilt in several ways.

Unhealthy guilt tends to distort our authentic self-image, making us believe that we are after all not guilty of anything, when in reality we have obviously hurt others. This, in turn, leads us to compulsiveness, and releases us from our sense of responsibility.

Perpetrators in unhealthy guilt deny their guilt. When confronted, many perpetrators deny their misconduct and guilt in the hope that they may get off the hook.

Some people with unhealthy guilt are super sensitive or compulsive. They feel guilty for things they have not done. They feel guilty for the death of their family members or friends—even their friends' divorces. This is a misplaced guilt. Feeling inadequate and guilty for their inability to help victims, these people apologize incessantly. They assume an unreal sense of responsibilities for others. After the September 11 attacks, Robert Maddalone, a firefighter in Brooklyn, described the misplaced guilt well:

> "I'm thankful I'm alive, but I feel guilty I'm alive," he said. "I'm trying to remember the guys who aren't here. Their wives and children. It's a hollow feeling. You try to laugh sometimes to keep your sanity, but you feel bad about laughing."[28]

His feeling of guilt derives from a sense of solidarity. He, of course, is not responsible for the deaths of his fellow firefighters. His boundary of responsibility is overextended because of his strong sympathy for his fallen friends. The development of misplaced guilt usually drives people to digress from their healthy selves and to suffer from frustration, discontent, and low self-esteem.

Some other people of inappropriate guilt cannot accept forgiveness from victims and from themselves, and thus develop a distorted self-image. They become withdrawn and rigid in their personalities. Their ensuing identifications tend to be with disparaging images, inactivity, passivity, or turning against their own selves. They focus on personality, not on issues, when things go wrong: "I am bad" or "I am a failure," instead of "I made a mistake" or "I failed this time." Guilt-driven activity is at best restitution, which rarely frees, but brings with it resentment and frustration rage that in turn nurtures new guilt into the system.[29]

Collective Guilt

Collective guilt is the communal liability that a group of oppressors shares for the unjust conduct of its members. In spite of the fact that individuals in the group, society, or nation are personally innocent, everyone in the group experiences a collective guilt for the group's unjust behavior. Karl Jaspers sees it as "a co-responsibility for the acts of members of our families."[30] His understanding of collective guilt is, however, not a condition but a mission: "Because in my innermost soul I cannot help feeling collectively, being German is to me—is to everyone—not a condition but a task."[31] Elisabeth Fiorenza echoes Jaspers' sense of mission with being a German: "As a German youth I learned to understand myself as victim and victimizer at the same time. Yet I never accepted the notion of 'collective guilt' or Helmut Kohl's 'grace of the late birth.' Rather, I accepted responsibility and committed myself to do everything in my power to stop dehumanization, vilification, and prejudice so that the reign of terror, injustice, and genocide that marred my childhood would not be possible again."[32]

The guilt that everyone in a group shares can become the guilt for which no single individual takes responsibility. However, a group's collective guilt can lead individuals to commit themselves to rectify past wrongs. In this way two timelines—a horizontal one and a vertical one—come together in a group's collective guilt. The horizontal line relates the group to its contemporaries; the vertical, to its ancestors. Those Germans living under the Nazi regime experienced horizontal collective guilt. Their descendants bear the vertical one. In 1995, America's largest Protestant body, the Southern Baptist Convention, adopted a resolution repenting of the pro-slavery stand that led to the denomination's formation 150 years ago. The delegates, meeting in Atlanta, also made an apology for condoning "individual and systematic racism in our lifetime."[33]

In 1992, Pope John Paul II in Africa offered an apology for the church's complicity in the African slave trade. In early 1995, he was in the Czech Republic to ask forgiveness for Catholic-Protestant wars in Europe during the Counter-Reformation. Several years ago, hundreds of German Christians gathered in the Netherlands to ask pardon for Nazi belligerence during World War II.[34] Although they are indirect and second-hand, these confessions of the collective guilt engendered by their predecessors or ancestors help to alleviate the collective han of the victims.

People of collective guilt should not identify themselves as villains nor perceive self-vilification as a sign of informed sensitivity. Weary of being on what Kenneth Minogue calls a moral treadmill, unable to avoid guilt even by leading blameless lives because guilt arises from membership in a guilty society, people might repudiate the notion of collective guilt altogether.[35] Thus, it is important to emphasize the connection between collective guilt and collective responsibility. Without commitments to the common good of a hurtful society, collective guilt can be nonproductive and destructive in society. In the end, *communal responsibility* might be the better term than *communal guilt* because it can point toward actions in the present that seek to make restitution for guilt incurred in the past.

CHAPTER THREE

Shame Anger and Guilt Anger

A nger is a repulsive, unpleasant, antagonistic, emotional response to a threatening situation. It is a necessary reaction to preserve one's own boundaries or integrity. Prolonged anger, however, can be physically harmful, causing anxiety and depression, compromising the body's immune system. It increases impulsive actions and reduces our problem-solving abilities. But its timely expression can energize our constructive behavior, strengthen our creativity, and work toward solving problems. By communicating our anger moderately and respectfully, we are empowered.[1]

There are many types of anger, but for our discussion, we will treat two major forms: shame anger and guilt anger. Shame anger is the anger of the wounded, and guilt anger is the anger of the offender. Shame anger can be assertive and guilt anger aggressive. Assertive anger is positive and constructive; aggressive anger is usually self-justifying and offensive. Assertive anger comes from the heart of fairness; aggressive anger might emerge from a desire to control and a superiority complex.

Shame Anger: The Assertive Anger of the Offended

As Christians, can we be angry? Will it fulfill or thwart the will of God? We learn that God became angry a few hundred times in the Old Testament. Many prophets were angry at Israel and its neighbors because of their idolatries and injustice. Jesus himself showed his anger toward the scribes, Pharisees, and religious hypocrites.

The Bible in general treats the issue of anger cautiously. It neither encourages nor discourages our expression of anger in general. Sometimes it allows us to be angry, and other times it dissuades us from being angry.

It is, however, clear that we should be angry like the prophets, Jesus, and God when facing injustice, idolatry, evil, and transgressions. Without being angry at wrongs, we are wrong and cannot be the people of God. Honorable anger is part of our Judeo-Christian faith. Even though the Bible allows us to be angry, it bars anger accompanied with hostility and violence. Being unjustly violated or seeing others unjustly treated, we must be angry, but not in such a way that our anger gives rise to violence.

Violent or hostile expressions of anger often result from experiences of shame, rather than guilt.[2] This anger is shame anger, which is the anger of the offended, a spontaneous reaction to the injustice done to them. By expressing anger intemperately, we can suffer the consequence of ruining our relationships; by expressing it repressively, we run the risk of injuring our health. This is the reason why the Bible advises us "Be angry but do not sin; do not let the sun go down on your anger" (Eph 4:26). The Bible recommends that we express our anger in moderation. Anger at injustice, wrongs, and evil is necessary if we are to rectify these ills. However, extreme or prolonged anger will lead the wounded to harming others and themselves. Because of this reality, the Bible prohibits a lengthy or extended anger.

Many victims fall into the trap of holding in their anger for a long time, thereby destroying their health and faith. Anger has long been associated with possible causes of health problems. A study published in the Journal of the American College of Cardiology reveals that anger poses a risk to people who already have heart disease by speeding up atherosclerosis, the hardening of the arteries. Peter Angerer of the Medizinische Klinik der University Munchen-Innenstadt in Munich, Germany and his colleagues used a technique called angiography to examine patients' blood vessels and invited patients to answer questionnaires measuring their levels of social support, anger expression, and hostility. Two years later, they performed a second round of angiography to see whether the atherosclerosis of the patients had worsened.[3]

The results from 150 of the patients were striking. The researchers detected that patients who combined high scores on anger expression and low scores on social support had a highly increased risk of disease advancement, regardless of medication use or other risk determinants. Hostility levels had no impact on disease furtherance.[4]

A study reported in the American Heart Association's journal *Circulation* (1 October 1995) showed that outbursts of anger doubled the risk of suffering from a heart attack. The researchers reported that the average risk of heart attack during the two hours after an incident of anger was 2.3 times higher than among those who were not angry.[5] Another study found the effect of anger and vital exhaustion on recurrent events after percutaneous transluminal coronary angioplasty (PTCA) was studied. The 123 male patients with high anger were significantly more likely to have multivessel disease before PTCA, and they also had a threefold increased risk for recurrent events after PTCA.[6]

By bottling up our anger inside, we suffer from anxiety, depression, despair, and various kinds of psychosomatic illnesses. In 1971, the University of Michigan began to conduct a study with 696 men and women aged thirty to sixty-nine on "Life Change Events, Anger-coping Styles and Psychological Well-being." By 1983, fifty-three persons from the group had died. Those who scored high on suppressing anger had a 2.1 times higher mortality rate than those who said they express anger or protest.[7] Communicating our anger constructively is better for our health than burying it.

The wounded would be better off to take a middle path between explosively venting anger and the repressing it. Jesus declared, "Blessed are the meek, for they will inherit the earth" (Matt 5:5). For Aristotle, meekness (*praotēs*) means to take the middle ground of any extreme positions. The meek are those who abstain from extreme anger or extreme angerlessness.[8] The anger of meekness is that of moderation and discretion. It means that we express our anger gracefully, not explosively. This does not mean that we deny our anger; on the contrary, we honor the passion of anger. Unbridled passion will not resolve any problems, but transforming our passionate anger into a more temperate form will. This anger of meekness concurs with the spirit of Paul's saying in Eph 4:26; we can be angry, but should not be swept away by our anger. The anger of meekness is assertive anger. Assertive anger is a just response to injustice and evil, or a self-protective response to a threat. Its intention is to keep, mend, or improve our relationship with others. This moderated form of anger seeks to communicate with offenders, rather than do away with them. It can be a creative energy that builds up better relationships by bringing forth necessary changes.

Here is an example of assertive anger that demonstrates its constructive intention. Gary Hankins tells the story of Dr. Nash, a psychologist, and Dr. Corkum, a physician, who work on the same patient care team. One day in a team meeting, Dr. Nash found it necessary to take a brief phone call. As soon as his colleague hung up, Dr. Corkum berated him for accepting a call while in team meeting and instructed him to tell the person who called (another colleague, as it turned out) never to interrupt him in team meeting again. Dr. Nash's first inclination was to lash out at his accuser, reminding Dr. Corkum that he took calls anywhere and anytime he wanted to do so.

Instead, Dr. Nash waited for the next day to approach Dr. Corkum with his feelings about the exchange.

> Dr. Nash said, "Dr. Gorkum, I didn't appreciate you telling me I couldn't take any more calls from my colleagues. . . . The more I think about your request, the less comfortable I feel about complying with it. . . . I don't believe we should get into the practice of censoring each others' calls. I respect your right to screen your own calls and I expect you to respect my right to do the same." [9]

Nash's intention was to make the relationship good by removing the hurdle instead of putting the other physician down. He respected Dr. Gorkum, yet was forthright about his position, challenging Gorkum's wrong. This anger combined with a constructive will is assertive anger. Jesus never prohibited the assertive anger of the wounded. Jesus himself was angry at religious hypocrisy.

Anger and Rage

Rage is an emotional anomaly that can be dangerous, leading us to depression and aberrant behaviors. It is called the "nasty cousin" of anger.[10] When anger negatively mixes fear and the unhealed pain of the past, anger changes into rage. Anger is controllable while rage is uncontrollable. Anger can be a strength that protects us, while rage's explosive energy can harm us. When something threatens us, fear is our primary response; after that comes anger, the secondary reaction; and rage is the final response.

Anger and Hatred

People often confuse anger with hatred. When we are angry with children, many times they think that our anger means we hate them.

Similarly, when we are infuriated at adults, they often misinterpret that anger as abhorrence and subsequently sever their relationships with us.

We need, however, to distinguish anger from hatred. In young children, anger is a normal response to reduce frustration, displeasure, and peril. When children's anger is inadequate in alleviating menace or threats, it turns into hostility that over time condenses into hatred.[11] In adults, foiled by disillusionment and threats to inner security, normal anger is transformed into hatred based on primitive defenses. Hatred is a potentially explosive, pathological condition.[12] While anger is normal and healthy, hatred is abnormal and unhealthy. Anger in its assertive form can be benevolent, while hatred is malignant. Assertive anger can be an expression of care while hatred is a sign of spite. Assertive anger can be a constructive force while hatred can become a destructive one.

Feeling hate toward perpetrators is, however, part of the natural recovery process from abuse, but counter-dehumanization can lead victims to the vicious circle of dehumanization.[13] Thus it is important to transform the negative energy of hatred into a positive one.

Assertive Anger Resolution

How can we transform the passion of anger into compassion and use anger to work toward the will of God?

The first step is to wait until our fury cools down. As long as we are excited with the heat of anger, our perception is exaggerated and warped. In this heated state, we might attempt to assail or injure others with our words and deeds, and consequently ruin the opportunity to right the wrong.

To cool off anger is to acknowledge its authenticity. Acknowledging our anger helps us to be angry in a way that is not harmful to ourselves or to others. It gives us a moment to look at anger and transcend it. Acknowledgment is a way to balance the hotness of our emotion with the power of reason.

However, it is important that we not lose the passion of our anger. The passion of anger differs from the rage of anger. The former is controllable energy, and the latter includes uncontrollable energy.

The second step is to accept our anger as it is. This means not to deny or repress the anger, but to be aware of it and own it. Instead of dismissing it, we need to acquaint ourselves with it, listen to it, and understand our anger, thus gaining the power to transmute anger into compassion.

It is important for Christians to accept our anger before God and people when we are violated. Our bodily response to any violation should be recognized for what it is: a reasonable response to the violation. We must accept our feelings in this situation. Anger is not something we can simply deny or repress. Getting angry is a natural response to any injustice, encroachment, or threat. Feeling angry is not necessarily a bad thing or a sin.

The biblical writers reported God's anger with the Israelites when they served idols. Prophets arose with anger when Israelites breached their covenant with God. Jesus was angry when people turned the house of God into a den of robbers and when religious leaders misled and exploited their own people. The instrument of anger aided God and God's people in accomplishing justice.

To be aware of and accept our anger, we need to locate its source. Doing so does not mean that we are trying to rationalize our anger, but rather that we wish to understand its real source. By honestly facing our anger, we can find a handle for resolving an anger-provoking cause. When we find the source of anger, we can decide what our response to the one who has provoked the anger will be.

The third step is to understand our offenders. Central to this effort is transposing our position with theirs. Understanding the bondage our offenders are in can give us compassion for them. When we understand our offenders in their vulnerability, anxiety, fear, false security, and brokenness, the heart of concern emerges from within us. Also, although our offenders may appear to be invulnerable, strong, and arrogant, they are in reality miserable before God. They condemn themselves by their own actions. The offended have the key to the salvation of the offenders. Thus they must have compassion and a merciful mind toward those who have offended them.

A sage was walking with his disciples and met a man who disliked him. The sage greeted him, but the man turned his face and walked away. One of the sage's disciples was so angry that he wanted to harm the man. The teacher calmed the disciple from his burning anger by asking a question: "Do you get upset when you see an ugly person?" "No, Sir," answered the disciple. "Then, why do you get angry when you see a person with an ugly heart?" The disciple was then able to understand his irrational fury and transcend it.

Guilt Anger: The Aggressive Anger of Offenders

Aggressive anger is not a response to a threat, but people's belligerent hostility toward their victims. It is the oppressive or controlling action of offenders toward those whom they have targeted. Some typical aggressive behaviors are to humiliate, denigrate, dominate, exploit, and hurt others. Some bosses vent their anger through shouting, threatening, and blaming when they are frustrated. Such aggressive anger might receive momentary attention but diminishes cooperation, effectiveness, trust, and respect from others. Aggressive anger hurts aggressors and their victims. Giving expression to aggressive anger is destructive and, unlike assertive anger, incapable of bringing about good. While assertive anger helps resolve problems, aggressive anger only aggravates problems.

Jesus himself forbids anger: "You have heard that it was said to those of ancient times, 'You shall not murder'; and 'whoever murders shall be liable to judgment.' But I say to you that if you are angry with a brother or sister, you will be liable to judgment" (Matt 5:21-22a). Some ancient authorities insert "without cause" after a brother or sister.[14] The text indicates that this anger is directed to a victim. This anger is obviously that of an offender. Jesus forbade the anger of offenders, not that of the offended. The purpose of his saying was to prohibit any aggressive anger ("without a cause" in the KJV) against brothers or sisters. In Matt 5:27-28, the sin of intention was reiterated: Jesus regarded lust in the mind as equivalent to adultery. To him, anger at a brother or sister is murdering, just as lusting for someone is adultery. It is clear that whoever looks at another with lust is an aggressor. In the same way, the person who is angry with a brother or sister is an aggressor. Thus, this anger is the aggressive type, that of the offender.

In the classical Christian tradition, anger takes its place alongside pride, envy, sloth, avarice, gluttony, and lust as one of the seven deadly sins. The kind of anger to which the tradition refers is guilt anger. It emerges from sin and is thus prohibited. Guilt anger involves denying one's own sin and wrongdoing. It is part of a self-defense mechanism. When God faced Cain about his murdering, Cain angrily responded: "Am I my brother's keeper?" The guilt of sin turns into anger when the guilt is exposed. Facing one's own wrong is painful, and, when provoked, the pain turns into anger.

Second Samuel 13 tells the story of Amnon's rape of his half sister Tamar. Before the rape, he proclaimed to Tamar his overwhelming love for her. After the act, all he discovered in his heart for her was loathing (13:15). Amnon's response reveals guilt anger welling up from his painful consciousness of the immorality and violence of his actions.

Paul disallows sinners (offenders) any anger and wrath: "These (vices) are the ways you also once followed, when you were living that life. But now you must get rid of all such things—anger, wrath, malice, slander, and abusive language from your mouth" (Col 3:7-9). He addressed this message to those who lived the life of licentiousness and aggression. Likewise, James noted that such aggressive anger does not work the righteousness of God, but disrupts it (Jas 1:20).

Therefore, the Bible proscribes the aggressive anger of the offenders toward their victims. They need to understand the pain of their victims, acknowledge their wrongs, come to repentance, and seek for the forgiveness of God and the offended.

Collective Anger: The Anger of the Oppressed and Oppressors

Although we have distinguished the anger of the oppressed from that of oppressors, it is difficult sometimes to draw a clear line between these two groups. We often become oppressors and the oppressed at the same time.

"Oppressed" and "oppressors" are designations that apply at the individual and collective levels. At the individual level, we can be oppressors in one situation and the oppressed in another. At the collective level, we can delineate a general line for the oppressed and oppressors by considering the collective history of a group.

In the collective sense, we need to understand the anger of an oppressed person from his or her long history of communal repression. Often the categories of race, gender, and class can assist us in distinguishing the oppressed from the oppressors.

According to a new study, race plays a major role in the data of stroke deaths. The study reports that the risk of death from stroke is much higher in African Americans ages forty-five to fifty-five than among Caucasians in the same age range. The probability of a forty-five-year-old African American dying of a stroke is four to five times higher than the average forty-five-year-old Caucasian.[15] Injustice doubly victimizes the groups of the oppressed. Prejudice and discrimination marginalize them in their career and social lives, and anger harms their health and mental well-being. Anger provokes their hearts to beat faster, their arteries and veins to increase blood pressure, and their lungs to breathe heavy. Continual anger generates ceaseless stress. As a corollary, their hearts, arteries, and lungs become weak and stiff. The oppressed collectively undergo double victimization.

Disregarding such aspects of human relations, Protestantism has underscored the sinful nature of all people. Thomas Hanks stresses this universal nature of sinfulness: "All of us are simultaneously oppressed and oppressors (Acts 10:38; Rom 3:23). . . . Thus the first step in genuine Christian discipleship is humbly to recognize my own situation: I am an oppressed oppressor."[16] He generalizes the sinful nature of all human beings, without distinguishing oppressors from the oppressed.

While his diagnosis may be right at an individual level, it is improper at a collective one. Collectively speaking, there is a qualitative difference between a group of German Nazis on the one hand, and a group of the Holocaust victims on the other. In terms of sin and han, guilt and shame, and guilt anger and shame anger, these two groups are not the same. The latter experiences collective han, shame, and shame anger, while the former bears collective sin, guilt, and guilt anger. To the oppressed, anger is sacred and thus should never be dampened or denied by an appeal to the universal human experience of sin. Anger at injustice is necessary for the transformation of social structures. No anger against evil is possible without God's grace. It encourages victims to express their assertive anger; it empowers them to transmute their passion into the strength needed to make the oppressors repent of their sins. One of the tasks of the church is to hearten victims to communicate their collective anger creatively for the eradication of the root-causes that generate structural han.

CHAPTER FOUR

Resistance and Repentance

Resistance

The wounded naturally seek revenge in anger. However, anger can be used destructively or creatively. Here we will focus on the assertive—or creative—use of anger. If an offender takes the initiative to seek forgiveness from his or her victim, that will be an ideal situation. If this does not happen, the victim has no choice but to confront the offender. Doing nothing means doing something. By not challenging the offender, the victim allows that person to live with his or her wrong.

To punish or eliminate the offender is to cause a new cycle of resentment, oppression, and violence. Violence begets violence. Oppression begets oppression. A violent reaction is not a solution to violence at all. Thus, to a victim of injustice and violence, Jesus says, "Turn the other cheek." Is it biblical then to resist evildoers? What does it mean to turn the other cheek to racists or criminals? Do we encourage them to strike their victims again?

Martin Luther King Jr. struggled with this issue of how to resist the evil of racism. He found the answer in the spirit of Jesus' love and in the method of Gandhi's nonviolence. To him, the teaching of turning the other cheek is not clear enough to implement a Christian way of dealing with injustice. But the example of Gandhi's nonviolent resistance reveals the true meaning of Jesus' love in the context of violence and blatant injustice. By advocating the principle of turning the other cheek, does Jesus literally teach us to submit to the power of unjust violence?

In the Sermon on the Mount, Jesus provides a new set of laws in contrast to the law of retaliation (lex talionis) found in the Hebrew Bible

(Exod 21:22-25; Lev 24:19-20; Deut 19:15-21). We should see his teaching on turning the other cheek in the context of this long-standing tradition on how to respond to violence directed against our person.

There are several ways to respond to a slap. The first response is to give vent to our anger and strike back repeatedly and with greater force than the original slap, hurting or even killing our assailant. To prevent this vengeful reaction, the law of retaliation was given: "a tooth for a tooth and an eye for an eye." This is the second level of exact retaliation: one slap for one. The third level of response is to protest at a verbal level in the absence of a physical retribution. The fourth level is to respond with neither words nor physical violence, thus displaying the strength of silence. The fifth level is to respond with love beyond silence. This response is the way Christ taught us. In Christ we are able to return others' insults and assaults with love.

Three Principles of Confrontation

There are three principles in Christian responses to victimization: challenge, care, and respect. The order of these responses is important. Care should come first, then respect, and finally challenge. When we challenge the aggressor with the mind of care, we treat him or her with respect. According to Howard Clinebell's "growth counseling," confrontation without care would not change people's hearts but only lead to further conflict.[1] People listen to others when they detect care for them.

Challenge

"Turning the other cheek" is not an act of subservience but the proactive gesture of confrontation in love. This act is much stronger than the act of silence or resistance alone. It is rooted in fundamental care for the oppressor.

For Walter Wink, Jesus' core sayings in Matt 5:38-42 have been misinterpreted as requiring the suffering of injustice rather than the restoration of sufferers' rights through resistance. This misguided interpretation has created a false requirement to endure violence.

Step by step, Wink recasts the meaning of Matt 5:38-41: "You have heard that it was said, 'An eye for an eye and a tooth for a tooth.' But I say to you, do not resist an evildoer. But if anyone strikes you on the right cheek, turn the other also; and if anyone wants to sue you and take your coat, give your cloak as well; and if anyone forces you to go one mile, go also the second mile."

Jesus commanded not to resist an evildoer (5:39a). The meaning of the term "resistance" (*antistēnai*) is more than simply "resist" or "stand against." It denotes violent resistance, revolt, or rebellion. An early Hebrew text of the Gospel of Matthew reads at 5:39a, "But I say to you, do not repay evil for evil." Wink supports this version and interprets the verse as "do not react violently to evil" or "do not mirror evil."[2]

This term is employed in the Septuagint mainly for armed resistance forty-four out of seventy-one times and Josephus's writing for violent struggle fifteen out of seventeen times.[3] Matthew 5:39 does not signify submission to evil or armed resistance to evil, but rather a low-conflict protest. Thus, Matt 5:39b-41 suggests nonviolent resistance stirring the oppressor to repentance.

It is important to understand what Jesus' original context was. His listeners were subjugated by the Romans and marginalized by the Jewish authorities. Knowledge of their situation is necessary to understanding Jesus' message. What, then, would his message have meant in that context?

First, "turn the other cheek" symbolizes nonviolent resistance. "But if anyone strikes you on the right cheek, turn the other also" (v. 39b). The only way one can typically slap the right cheek with the right hand is with the back of the hand. As we saw in chapter 2, slapping this way is an act of humiliation and dishonor. In Jewish rabbinic law, a backhand slap was twice as insulting as a flat-hand slap. In Jesus' days, a backhand slap signified an insult; it was a way of humiliating inferiors. Masters used the backhand to humiliate slaves; husbands, wives; parents, children; and Romans, Jews.

To the one who is already humiliated, turning the other cheek indicates the action of robbing the oppressor of the power to humiliate: " 'Try again.' Your first blow failed to achieve its intended effect. I deny you the power to humiliate me."[4] Striking someone on the left cheek with the flat of the left hand takes place, not between oppressor and victim, but between equals. Thus, offering the left cheek to the one who has just struck you with the back of the right hand is a way of demanding equality and the end of dehumanization. It is an active form of resistance.

Second, the act of giving the undergarment (*chitōn*) in a court would mean stripping off all the clothing: "If anyone wants to sue you and take your coat, give your cloak as well" (v. 40). It means parading out of court completely naked. Nakedness was taboo in Israel. However, the shame of nakedness in this case would fall not on the person without their clothing, but on the one who caused that person to go naked.

The law of Moses demands to return a cloak every evening at sunset: "If you lend money to my people, to the poor among you, you shall not deal with them as a creditor. . . . If you take your neighbor's cloak in pawn, you shall restore it before the sun goes down; for it may be your neighbor's only clothing to use as cover" (Exod 22:25-27a). Further, Deuteronomy prohibits anyone to pawn a poor person's cloak: "If the person is poor, you shall not sleep in the garment given you as the pledge. You shall give the pledge back by sunset, so that your neighbor may sleep in the cloak and bless you" (24:12-13a).

This act of disrobing will unmask the cruelty of the creditor and the entire system that oppresses the poor debtor. In the Old Testament, God asked Isaiah to walk naked and barefoot as a prophetic sign and omen (20:1-6). As he did for three years, the poor walks out naked and barefoot in a sign of protest against the suer. To Wink, the poor in fact says by the action: "You want my robe? Here, take everything! Now you've got all I have except my body. Is that what you'll take next?"[5]

Challenge demands an explanation, or the doing of justice; it calls the unjust act into question. It is not a Machiavellian act that schemes to put the offender to public shame. Rather, it is an act of courage that faces injustice and evil with truth.

Another form of challenge can be found in 2 Sam 12:1-25 where the prophet Nathan challenged David with the tool of reflection. He used a parable of the poor man's lamb, which mirrored David's own outrageous sin. David was outraged by the rich man who stole the poor neighbor's lamb in order to treat his guest while sparing his own herds. After inducing David to judge and condemn the rich man, Nathan told him that David was himself the man, pronouncing God's judgment upon him. David humbly repented of his sins before such a powerful confrontation. In his confrontation Nathan used a parable of reflection that clearly showed the unjust and sinful situation for what it was. Further, he induced David to see the pain of the victim and guided him to repentance. Finally, he pronounced God's judgment and forgiveness. Grounded in authentic divine authorization, his reflective method of challenge was powerful enough to make King David repent of his sin.

Offenders can be challenged in several ways: nonviolent resistance, noncooperative resistance, reflective resistance, civil disobedience, boycotts, sit-ins, street demonstrations, and picketing. The offended must resist injustice and evil, choosing an effective tool wisely without losing the fundamental principle of care. Challenge is not a choice but is an obligation for Christians in the face of injustice. Its goal is not to punish or destroy the offender but to help him or her be penitent.

Care

The act of going the second mile (Matt 5:41) could be an act of defiance. Roman soldiers had the legal right to impose forced labor (*angareuō*) on subjected peoples, requiring them to carry a burden up to one mile. To use the forced labor, however, the soldiers needed written permits from the prefect. The soldiers abused these rules, stirring up resentment, which in turn led the Roman authorities to punish violators. Wink contends that in this context, Jesus' teaching was neither to aid nor to abet the enemy. Carrying a soldier's package the second mile could be interpreted several ways: "Is this a provocation? Is he insulting the legionnaire's strength? Being kind? Trying to get him disciplined for seeming to violate the rules of impressment? Will this civilian file a complaint? Create trouble?"[6] It could be a humorous scene, in which a Roman infantryman pleaded with the forced laborer to return his baggage.

Wink is convinced that Jesus did not mean his fellow Jews to walk a second mile in order to pile up merit in heaven, or to practice a supererogatory piety, or to smother the soldier with kindness. Rather, he was trying to help the oppressed protest and neutralize the unjust practice of the impressed labor.[7]

Wink believes that Jesus counseled neither flight (submission, passivity, withdrawal, and surrender) nor fight (armed revolt, violent rebellion, direct retaliation, and revenge). Instead, Jesus taught a third way: Find a creative alternative to violence, assert your own humanity and dignity as a person, meet force with ridicule or humor, break the cycle of humiliation, refuse to accept the inferior position, expose the injustice of the system, shame oppressors into repentance, stand your ground, recognize your own power, force the oppressor to see you in a new light, deprive the oppressor of a situation where a show of force is effective, be willing to undergo the penalty of breaking unjust laws, seek the oppressor's transformation, and so on.[8]

Wink sums up Jesus' third way in the following sentence: "Jesus, in short, abhors both passivity and violence. He articulates, out of the history of his own people's struggles, a way by which evil can be opposed without being mirrored, the oppressor resisted without being emulated, and the enemy neutralized without being destroyed."[9]

His critic Richard Horsley agrees with Wink that Jesus' strategy in Matt 5:39-40, 42 was socially revolutionary, but disagrees with him that the focal point of the sayings was not whether the strategy was violent or nonviolent but whether it was focused on renewal of local communities or not. Horsley contends that in the broad social-historical context, Jesus addressed the saying for the improvement of local communities, not for the amelioration of the relations between oppressed Jews and oppressive Romans or Jews.[10]

For Horsley, the backhanded insult was not limited to the relations between the superior and the inferior but could address the issues of local quarrels and conflicts. Since slapping on the cheek was a formal and serious insult, not a spontaneous action of violence nor a "damage to person," the context of this saying is the local village.[11] Also, since Matt 5:40 refers to the case of the seizure of a garment as a pledge, the saying manifests a local interaction between creditor and debtor: "the creditor asking for the cloak would more likely have been a local than a wealthy absentee official or landowner."[12] As to going the second mile, Horsley has doubts about Wink's sociopolitical context of the occupied troops. He holds that since Galilee was ruled by the client king Antipas, it was unlikely for the Galileans to be burdened by the presence of Roman soldiers.

Wink's rebuttal was that we cannot confine the perimeter of the application of Jesus' teaching to local compatriots. Jesus taught to love enemies in reference to Romans and their puppets, too.[13] While Wink stresses that these passages aimed at the relationships between oppressed Jews and oppressive Jews or Romans, Horsley emphasizes that they focused on the relationships of local people.

I believe that Jesus' teaching could be applied to any relationships between villagers, between the Romans and the occupied, or between creditors and debtors. It is, however, clear that Jesus addressed these sayings to the offended, not offenders. He wished to instruct the violated about how to react. Since Jesus' audience largely belonged to a lower class, he had compassion for their situations.

Although I agree with Wink's position on resisting oppressors with nonviolent strategies, I would emphasize resistance with unrelenting love. Our motivation to resist evil forces is not only for our own liberation but also for the change of our opponents with resilient love. Jesus taught us to withstand wrongs in order to lead wrongdoers to their repentance. It is easy for us to receive the slap on the right cheek, say nothing, and avoid our oppressor, all the while regarding him or her with brooding hatred. It is a different matter to confront the oppressor with justice and care. Only the love that humanizes our enemy enables us to deal with him or her again. By turning the other cheek we demand justice and equality from our oppressor and enter into an ongoing relationship with him or her. Only when we care enough for the oppressor can we challenge him or her to change. This care for the oppressor becomes the essential ingredient in resistance. Without it, resistance would turn into hatred and retaliation, dehumanizing us and failing to change the oppressor.

Jesus does not teach us an easy love, but an unrelenting love that will not let wrongdoers continue in their wrongs. If we care for a person, we would rather correct his or her wrongs than disregard them. The Hebrew Bible teaching underpins this point: "You shall reprove your neighbor, or you will incur guilt yourself" (Lev 19:17). If our child intentionally steals someone's jacket, we do not let him or her wear it but make him or her return it to the owner and make sure that such stealing will not recur. Jesus taught us such a responsible love.

Only such responsible love enables us to give the undergarment to the person who pursues the coat and go the second mile to the one who compels us to go one mile. Jesus asks victims to exercise such tenacious love toward their opponents or enemies. Christ's love is the durable and caring love that does not return evil with evil, but evil with good. By avoiding resistance, we return evil with evil. For instance, by not challenging slavery or apartheid systems, we allow evil to continue, thus answering evil with more evil. Resistance may be burdensome to victims, but it is a privilege for them as well. Resisting evil with resilient love is the core message of Jesus.

Respect

Everyone needs respect, including our enemies. Respect is an attitude of regard and admiration. To respect is to provide positive self-esteem.

People do not change while their self-esteem is low, but only when it is high. Jesus gave special regard to the sinner and the sinned against. Such respect elicits transformation in the sinners, as the story of Zaccheaus (Luke 19:1-10) demonstrates.

Publican Zacchaeus was a chief tax collector, having contracted for the right to collect revenues in his district through his subordinates. He was rich. Consequently, his neighbors despised him for working for the Romans and being rich through his unclean occupation.

Jesus gently challenged Zacchaeus by declaring that he would stay in his house that night. By staying with the "sinner," Jesus would become unclean. Zacchaeus was an oppressor to his compatriots. Jesus regarded him as a human being, a child of Abraham, and one of his friends. Jesus' risk-taking presence was good enough to restore Zacchaeus' lost humanity. His low self-esteem and dehumanized self-image were confronted by Jesus' true humaneness. Jesus' staying with him evoked the repentant spirit in Zacchaeus so that he declared he would give half of his possessions to the poor and pay back four times what he defrauded anybody.

Zacchaeus' offer went far beyond the requirement of the law. According to Moses' law, if one confesses a sin voluntarily, he or she "shall make full restitution for the wrong, adding one fifth to it" (Num 5:6). When one steals an ox or a sheep deliberately, "the thief shall pay five oxen for an ox and four sheep for a sheep" (Exod 22:1).

Overwhelmed by Jesus' presence, Zacchaeus truly changed his heart before Jesus and other people. Jesus was elated and said, "Today salvation has come to this house" (Luke 19:9). Jesus' challenge was intertwined with the care and respect for the oppressor. He would not roughly demand his immediate repentance as might have been expected from a prophet.

Jesus consistently treated sinners with respect. Jesus' way of confronting the Samaritan woman (John 4:6) was not one of condemnation. Instead of saying "You, repent of your sins of wantonness," he asked her "Go, call your husband and come back." It was a gentle challenge with respect, which eventually led her to confess the state of her unsatisfactory life, since she had had five previous husbands and a current illegitimate partner (4:16-18). Impressed by Jesus, she turned around and voluntarily became a messenger of his good news. With respect and care, Jesus gently challenged her to be what she could be.

Former President Jimmy Carter shows a case of the challenge of respect.

> Every now and then, one of my Sunday school lessons is about forgiveness, and it is a difficult subject for me to teach. Almost invariably, a feeling of hypocrisy gnaws at me as I remember people against whom I still hold a grudge. In some cases, I have said, "I can't forgive that jerk!" But when I forced myself to consider the original altercations more thoroughly, they usually seem somewhat silly—some I couldn't even remember. Teaching these lessons has induced me to correct some of my mistakes.[14]

When Carter was asked whether he had trouble forgiving political opponents, he candidly said "yes." For a while, he could not have forgiven the "jerk" who ruined his political career.

> One of the most important events in my political life was the debate between then-governor Ronald Reagan and me during the 1980 presidential campaign. Afterward we learned that a copy of my personal briefing book for that debate had been stolen beforehand by a Reagan supporter who worked for me in the White House. A noted columnist and author had used the purloined briefing book to help prepare my opponent for the debate. My positions on all the important issues, my analyses of Reagan's positions, my assessment of his vulnerabilities, my tactical plans for the debate—all of these were known and used against me by a respected journalist who professed fairness and objectivity.[15]

For years after the event, he could not bring himself to forgive the journalist. One day he was preparing a Sunday school lesson on forgiveness. The topic was difficult for him to teach. He determined to think of some concrete step he could take to break down the barrier of anger.

> My family and I have long been avid baseball fans, and I knew that he had written a book on the subject. I bought a copy. After reading it, I wrote the author a note, expressing appreciation for the insights he had given me into some of the intricacies of baseball, and offering reconciliation after our long feud. He responded in good humor.[16]

President Carter is a person of integrity and courage. In a mild form of challenge, he gently induced the journalist to reconcile with him. His initiative to reconciliation is laudable and admirable. I hope the journalist was led to repent for his actions when challenged that gently. With deep respect for President Carter, I would like to point out two things. The first point is that although President Carter had brought the journalist to the table of cease fire, he could have challenged him to repent of his wrong at a personal level. The journalist should have apologized to him more directly. The second is that since that act contained a criminal aspect related to the destiny of the nation, the journalist should have faced the consequence of his act at a legal level. The case was similar to the Watergate scandal. President Carter should have filed a grievance against him, letting the proper authorities take care of the case so that such a preposterous act might never repeat itself. Filing a grievance against a crime is part of Christian care. Its aim in this case would not have been to destroy the journalist but to build up a true relationship with him and to reform the society.

If a case is criminal, we need to forgive the perpetrators, but we should not and cannot acquit them of their crime. Christian forgiveness is not a legal action, but a moral one. It does not overlook the consequences of a wrong act or the issue of justice. A criminal can be forgiven by the victim but must be accountable for his or her act.

In brief, confrontation should be done with care and respect. Unless we confront the wrongs of others, we do not fulfill Christ's commandment of love. The worst thing we can do to them is to excuse their sins and let them away with their wrongdoings. Unless we care about and respect them in our challenge, they will not change their ways. It is not the power of confrontation that changes them, but the strength of care and respect that moves them to repent of their sins. Care and respect can be so strong that even a stubborn opponent may realize the love that is in the heart of the victim.

Steps of Christian Confrontation

So far we have treated relationships in non-Christian setting and between unequal persons. The early church was also concerned about the offensive relationship between fellow members of the church community. When a member of the church committed sin against another, how could the sinned-against respond to it?

The Matthean author offers three concrete steps to resolve a conflict in the case where offenders are peers: "If another member of the church sins against you, go and point out the fault when the two of you are alone. If the member listens to you, you have regained that one. But if you are not listened to, take one or two others along with you, so that every word may be confirmed by the evidence of two or three witnesses. If the member refuses to listen to them, tell it to the church; and if the offender refuses to listen even to the church, let such a one be to you as a Gentile and a tax collector. Truly I tell you, whatever you bind on earth will be bound in heaven, and whatever you loose on earth will be loosed in heaven" (Matt 18:15-18).

For the Christian community, the Matthean author detailed the commandment of rebuke of Luke 17:3b: "If another disciple sins, you must rebuke the offender, and if there is repentance, you must forgive."[17] We find a similar statement in Leviticus: "You shall not hate in your heart anyone of your kin: you shall reprove your neighbor, or you will incur guilt yourself" (19:17). Here, kin refers to those who share religion, and neighbor refers to those who share nationality. The present Matthean context is limited to fellow church members.

It was unusual for a Jew to challenge another at the time of Jesus. It was rare for Jesus' contemporaries to try to regain a lost one, believing instead that self-restraint was the best policy. An erring person was challenged and claimed back only in a strongly knitted community like Qumran.[18] Here Jesus' teaching was rather given to the church community.[19] The early church community had asserted its responsibility for each of its members (1 Thess 5:11, 14-15).

The first step to regain a lost one is a private admonishment. If a fellow disciple commits a sin against you, you must settle the matter with him or her privately. This private encounter without a witness was designed to preserve the full honor of the straying person.

The second step is a conflict resolution with one or two witnesses. The presence of witnesses was to protect the sinned against and the sinner. Either party could be wrong and be corrected. It was noticeable that unlike the Qumran community where an overseer intervened, the witnesses in the church community were fellow disciples, having no hierarchical authority.[20] The encounter was between equals.

The third was the challenge of the church. If the first two steps were unsuccessful, then the community had to be involved in the resolution of a dispute. The entire community had the last word. If the offender did not listen to the church, it treated the person as if he or she were a Gentile and a tax collector. This was not, however, an act of excommunication, but rather of waiting for his or her return. A Gentile or a tax collector was not an enemy of the church but a target of evangelical mission.

Let us think for a moment about what such Christian confrontation should look like in the contemporary world. The first step is to talk to the offender. Rather than complain about the offender, the injured needs to communicate with the person involved directly. If the offender is in a position of authority over the victim (such as a boss or employer), the situation can be difficult. Yet it is necessary to resolve the problem. One should confront the offender with goodwill and positive intentions. Remember that the principles of confrontation consist of care, respect, and honest challenge. The offended party should express his or her points of view with a constructive attitude, making appropriate use of assertive anger.

If the first step does not work, the second step is to talk to the offender through an intermediary. Alternatively, the offended can talk to some person who can exercise influence on the offender. This third party can be a pastor, counselor, or a friend of the offender. The mediation of the third party can release the excessive tension and promote an effective communication between them through objectivity and fairness.

The third is to talk with a group to which both parties belong or which can understand the case. The group can be internally supportive to the victim by listening to his or her story and by praying with him or her, and it can be externally supportive by organizing a collective challenge to the offender.

The fourth is to take a legal action. If criminal acts are engaged in—as with cases involving child abuse, sexual abuse, or domestic violence—then the case should be reported to police and the offender taken to court. This action is not to destroy the offender, but to reclaim him or her. The purpose of the legal action should be the rehabilitation of, rather than retaliation against, the offender.

Collective Resistance

Resistance must be done at two distinct, yet inseparable, levels: individual and collective. Its individual level includes personal protest against sexual abuse, authority abuse, malicious attacks, privacy invasion, unjust lawsuit, and vicious backbiting. Its collective level encompasses gender discrimination, racism, labor exploitation, classism, ageism, handicappism, homophobia, ecological disruptions, militarism, and nationalism.

If a wrong is done to a group, the wrongdoer, whether it be an individual or a group, is supposed to repent. Hard as it is for an individual to repent of his or her sin and wrong voluntarily, it is all the harder if the culprit is a corporate one. Historically, it is rare that the corporate wrongdoer voluntarily recant its wrong unless the wronged group exercises its corporate resistance. Usually when it is cornered, the corporate group changes its wrong involuntarily. A corporate injustice involves a systemic dimension of oppression. So it is necessary for the wronged to use effective methods of resistance that will break through systemic injustice. Some of these methods include boycotts, street demonstrations, sit-ins, picketing, noncooperation, letter writing, civil disobedience, and fasting. Whatever methods the wronged use, they should not forget that if genuine change is to occur it will be a result of love and respect, not their own cleverness in confronting the wrongdoer.

Repentance

Some sinners or offenders, racked by guilt and guilt consciousness, come to repentance. If their repentance is genuine, then their attempts to secure forgiveness from those they have wronged will be more likely to succeed. The ideal situation is true repentance on the part of the offenders and true forgiveness on the part of the offended.

Biblical Repentance

Three different New Testament terms describe repentance: *epistrephō*, *metanoeō*, and *metamelomai*. The first two signify "turning around" and "turn oneself round," indicating one's conversion and faith in God. The third refers to the feeling of regret for error, failure, sin and debt, but does not indicate an active turning toward God, as do the other two.[21]

The term *metanoia* means a turning away from one's own sin and going back to God. It has two levels: divine and human. In Jesus' and his disciples' message, repentance before God includes faith (Mark 6:12). The Great Commission statement in Luke declares, "Repentance and forgiveness of sins is to be proclaimed in his name to all nations, beginning from Jerusalem" (24:47). And at sinners' repentance, heaven rejoices (Luke 15:7). At the human level, repentance requires the forgiveness of neighbors.[22] Most of the times, repentance demands the recompense of the wrong done to a neighbor. This word is commensurate to the Hebrew term *nihām*, to be sorry about something. It lacks, however, the physical aspect of the Hebrew term *teshūvāh*.

The term *metamelomai* means regret, remorse, and the change of one's mind. This term cannot always be neatly distinguished from *metanoeō*. In Jesus' parable in Matt 21:28-32 (the two sons of the vineyard owner), the second son initially refuses to work in the vineyard, yet regrets his decision and winds up working. His attitude is similar to *metanoia*.[23] The remorse (*metamelomai*) of Judas, however, did not elicit his complete change of heart, or his action (Matt 27:3).

The word *epistrephō* connotes a lifestyle transformed on the basis of the change in perspective and intention achieved by *metanoia* (cf. Luke 3:8).[24] Luke uses this term in Acts 26:20b: "Also to the Gentile, that they should repent and turn to God and do deeds consistent with repentance." It is a complete transformation under the inspiration of the Holy Spirit. As in Acts 11:21 and 26:20, this term includes conversion and surrender of the life to God/Christ in faith and a fundamental change of a whole life.[25] Without a converted life (*epistrephō*), *metanoia* (a change of thinking) would not be authentic repentance.

In the Hebrew Bible, two verbs signify the idea of repentance: *shūb* (to return) and *nihām*, (to feel sorrow). Judaism emphasizes the redeeming power of *teshūvāh* (the noun form of *shūb*), which is a prerequisite of all expiation. It is human self-redemption from the serfdom of sin. Sincere repentance is equal to rebuilding the Temple, the restoration of the altar, and offering sacrifice.[26] In the Prophets, repentance goes far beyond mere words. It leads to a new heart (Jeremiah); justice, mercy (Amos); and faithfulness (Hosea). Repentance has also its cultic expressions; it calls for wearing coarse garments, rending raiments, throwing ashes, and fasting.[27]

The second term, *nihām*, connotes acknowledgment, regret, sorrow and contrition over one's own wrong. This repentance consists of a change of mind and decision to do something anew (Ps 110:14; Jer 4:28; Amos 7:3, 6; Jonah 2:9). Its exemplary case is a prayer for healing and moral renewal (Ps 51), which shows the contrition of a sinner (David) in connection with religious sacrifices and observations.[28]

Judaism distinguishes sins against God from sins against humans. If one sins against God, she or he needs to grieve or confess her or his sin. If one sins against humans, *teshūvāh* requires four processes: regret, abandonment, confession, and resolve.

Regret (*harātah*)

Regret, as opposed to guilt, is that state of discontent in which the offender feels a sense of loss. In striving for their growth they must first see that their mistakes in life have resulted in the loss of something they deem to be precious and significant.

Abandonment (*'azīzbāh*)

This stage is to see what it was that enticed the offenders into the snare of their sinful behavior, to understand the basic untruth that is the core of their rationalizations about that behavior, and to decide how to avoid repeating the same mistake. They need to abandon the distorted rationalization and put a halt to the action it sanctioned.

Confession (*vīddūy*)

This is the act of asking for forgiveness from victims. There is no escape. The truth about the actions of the offenders and their hurtful consequences are laid bare for all to see when they utter those simple words: "I'm sorry. Forgive me for what I did, it won't happen again. I promise."

Resolve (*qabbālāh*)

This act is to reconcile with the victim by changing the offender's behavior. When offenders say, "I'm sorry," and, "It won't happen again," they are saying what they mean and mean what they say. With this final act of commitment never to repeat the same mistake, the offenders have come full circle. They have reconciled with the victims.[29]

Repentance in the Church

Sinners are haunted by guilt, anxiety, and fear of death and punishment. Their salvation starts with repentance. In the Roman Catholic Church, reconciliation or penance is one of the seven sacraments. The sacrament of penance involves four parts: contrition, confession, absolution, and satisfaction. Contrition is the state of *metanoia*, a change of the heart. It takes "sins as material to grieve over."[30] Confession is to tell all the sins we can remember to a priest who stands in for Christ. While contrition is in itself the inner repentance of the heart, confession "carries the power of external penance in it, including the resolve to confess and make mends."[31] Satisfaction is an act of reparation allotted by the priest, primarily hymns, prayer, or an action of restitution such as almsgiving. "What is sought here is not just restoration of the balance of justice (as in retributive justice) but reconciliation between friends."[32] Absolution is a declaration of pardon by a priest. The form of absolution derives from Christ's own words to Peter: "Whatever you loose on earth will be loosed in heaven" (Matt 18:18). However, "only God can be the original source of absolution and forgiveness."[33]

These Roman Catholic guidelines are helpful, but they need some modifications for effective healing. It is necessary for sinners to undergo the process of repentance with victims if the victims are available. There can be six steps of repentance: (1) contrition; (2) confession; (3) changing one's behavior; (4) performing acts of recompense; (5) asking forgiveness from the victim; and (6) reconciliation. The first two steps represent a change of heart (*metanoia*); the third and fourth, a change of lifestyle (*epistrephō*).

To elaborate on these steps of repentance:

1. Repentance begins with contrition for one's own sin. The first step of contrition is to listen to others' voices attentively. Attentive listening can enrich the process of contrition. Confronted by the wounded or convicted by one's own guilt, a wrongdoer can listen to the story of the wronged. Earnest listening will lead the wrongdoer to genuine contrition. How sincerely one listens to the wounded determines how truly one will be penitent. While listening to the story of han, people understand the pain of the wounded and experience deep contrition. God often speaks to the offender through the voice of the wounded.

Contrition is an internal transformation; it means having the heart of remorse, regret, and sorrow for what one has done. The act of contrition needs to converge with emptying one's own heart. The work of emptying is an internal deed. In this respect, the soul can be likened to a cup. Into the cup we have poured the fullness of our sin and evil desires. By the grace of God, sinners can empty these sins, evil desires, and guilt from the soul. A sure way to empty the cup is to invite Christ into the soul; Christ pushes our own sin and guilt out of the cup, filling it instead with his presence.

Central to the act of contrition is to decide before God not to repeat the sin. The Roman Catholic Church furthermore distinguishes perfect contrition from imperfect contrition. The latter, also called attrition, arises out of the fear of punishment and hell. The Roman Catholic position is right on the idea of contrition that should come out of loving God, rather than fearing hell. The love of God moves us from ourselves to God. It is the change of the heart, not merely change of the mind, denoting the move from us to God. True metanoia leads us to love God and thus love others.

2. Confession is the next stage in the journey of repentance. The Roman Catholic Church keeps the penitential system of confession, in which individuals confess sins to a priest (auricular confession). It claims that the priest on behalf of Christ, as in John 20:21-23, has the power to offer assurance of forgiveness toward the penitent who confesses serious sins and shows contrition with the intention of correction (absolution). Most Protestants oppose this idea of forgiveness (many of them thinking that it is the priest who does the forgiving) on the ground of the belief that God alone can forgive our sins.

Confession is an important process in being forgiven. If he or she wants to be forgiven, it is essential for him or her to confess his or her sins before God and before his or her victim. Confession is an uncomfortable move but an effective step toward halting the repetition of our sins. In the next four steps, we enter the realm of forgiveness. While I will treat these ideas more fully in the next chapter, a brief discussion of them is in order here.

3. Repentance means changing one's behavior. This is the concrete expression of contrition. If anyone wants to repent of his or her sin, he or she must turn back from sin and walk in the right way.

4. Repentance requires acts of recompense. Any repentance without compensation is not genuine repentance.

5. Repentance involves asking for forgivingness. To ask forgiveness from the wronged is not to ask him or her to forget the events of injustice, but to give the wrongdoer new opportunities. This part of repentance can only happen when humility accompanies it.

6. Repentance seeks reconciliation. A genuine act of asking for forgivingness leads the penitent and the one who forgives him or her to reconciliation.

Above all, repentance is the act of loving God. In fact, such love precedes repentance. This is Luther's point. He tried to repent of his sins but realized that he did it out of a fear of God and a sense of self-interest.[34] We often forget that loving God leads us to repentance, not the other way around. Loving God does not derive from God's irresistible grace over our will, but rather from our free decision to respond to God's love. Repentance is a Copernican revolution from a self-centered life (a geocentric worldview) to a God-centered life (a theocentric worldview). It is a reverting to God, through whom we also turn to our neighbors. Repentance without caring for God and neighbor is not possible. Repentance means we heed God's call and our neighbors' needs.

Collective Repentance

In the Hebrew Bible, we see multiple occasions of collective repentance. From the exodus to the postexilic period, Israel had rebelled against God and had repented of its sin a number of times. The sequential pattern of the salvific cycle of Israel was rebellion, repentance, and the forgiveness of Yahweh. Here we see the collective dimension of sin, repentance, and salvation. Collective repentance is an indispensable element in the life of Israel.

A vivid scene of collective contrition is at Mizpah where Samuel called all Israel who went astray and asked them to return to God and put away the Baals and the Astartes. All Israel fasted that day and confessed, "We have sinned against the LORD (Yahweh)" (1 Sam 7:3-6). It required public fasting, confession, and contrite action.

A contemporary example of corporate contrition is the Dutch Reformed Church in South Africa. In 1991, the Dutch Reformed Church officially apologized to black South Africans for having furnished religious justification for apartheid. Archbishop Desmond Tutu was present and accepted the apology. The Dutch Reformed Church's compunction was regarded as sincere. But the Reformed Afrikaners had shown a true courage in this act of collective repentance. They apologized when their country needed their voice most—in time of a turbulent transition. They made their collective declaration of public repentance when it counted heavily, and it helped. Meeting in Atlanta in 1995— more than thirty years after the height of the civil rights struggle—the messengers (delegates) to the Southern Baptist Convention offered their apology for the past pro-slavery position that led to the birth of the denomination 150 years before. They also apologized for condoning the present forms of racism.[35] It was an important move for the church that was still struggling with the issue of racism. Timely corporate contrition and confession are crucial for any effective social transformation.

Furthermore, collective repentance requires follow-up. Public declaration of repentance is one thing, but the enactment of the repentance is another. Without the latter, the former becomes cheap. Collective repentance is completed when the guilty party puts into practice the compensating action of repentance.

CHAPTER FIVE

Forgivingness and Forgiven-ness

L et me begin this chapter with some definitions. The customary English term "forgiveness," because it can be used in so many different ways, is often susceptible to a lack of precision. Therefore, in this chapter when I refer to the forgiveness that takes place in the heart of victims, and which they offer to their offenders in acts of reconciliation, I will often employ the terms forgiving or forgivingness. Because English does not have a precise term for the forgiveness that offenders receive, I have coined the term forgiven-ness.

Christianity is a movement of forgiveness. Jesus proclaimed God's forgiveness for humanity. Based on his teaching, the church was established and has continued to herald the good news of forgiveness. When asked about the uniqueness of Christianity, Huston Smith, an eminent scholar of world religions, replied that the Christian emphasizes forgiveness as the way of God and that no other faith places forgiving as the focal point of God's attributes and the central requirement of its discipleship.[1]

According to the New Testament scholar William Klassen, forgiveness is a pervasive motif in the Bible. In the Hebrew Bible, forgiveness is chiefly an action of God toward Israel who breaches the covenant relationship. Contrary to the common view, the Hebrew Bible gives more explicit attention to forgiveness than the New Testament. Be that as it may, however, the New Testament depicts Jesus Christ as the one who brings God's grace to forgive sins down to earth and leaves it there in the church, the forgiving community.[2]

The basic Hebrew term for forgiveness is *salakh*. The origin of this abstract verb prior to its appearance in the Hebrew Bible is not known, but it probably derives from the Akkadian *salāhu*, "to sprinkle." In cultic connections, this word is often connected to sacrifice. In a secular con-text, it is used in medicine to describe sprinkling someone with water, oil, or other healing liquids. The Hebrew Bible writers frequently relate for-giveness to cleansing. [3]

The meaning of forgiveness in the Hebrew Bible varies according to the different stages in the history of Israel, but can be summed up in five images: carrying off the sin, the removal of sin, covering sin, sweeping away sin, and washing away sin. "Taking away sin or guilt" is the expression used in the writings considered the "Deuteronomistic history books" (Exod 10:17; Gen 50:17; 1 Sam 15:25; and 1 Sam 25:28). "The removal of sin" can be found in two preexilic passages: 2 Sam 24:10 and 12:13. It is also used in postexilic passages: Job 7:21 and Zech 3:4. "Covering sin" is employed several times: Neh 4:5; Prov 17:9; Ps 32:1 and 85:3. The image of "sweeping sin away" is found in such passages as Isa 44:22, 43:25; Neh 4:5; and Jer 18:23. "Washing away sin" is used in Ps 51:2, 7.[4] The New Testament and early church fathers employed the term *aphiēmi* (to forgive) and *aphesis* (forgiveness, release). These terms were used prior to the New Testament in the Septuagint (e.g., Lev 16:26). In major cases, the term *aphiēmi* signifies to let (Mark 1:34; 5:19, 37; Acts 14:17); to release, dismiss, and divorce (Matt 13:36; 1 Cor 7:11-13); to leave and leave behind (Matt 1:20; 10:28; Mark 1:18); and to abandon (Mark 7:8; Rom 1:27). It is used also for the forgiveness of trespasses (Mark 11:25; Matt 6:14); sin (Mark 2:5, 7; Luke 7:47); and debts (Matt 6:12). In contrast, the term *aphesis* stresses the sense of forgiveness (cf. Mark 1:4; Matt 26:28) and points to release from captivity (Luke 4:18).[5]

In the life of the church, forgiveness is pivotal. The forgiveness of God, the theme of the Bible, has been the matrix of historical church movements including the Reformation. As the earthly agency of Jesus Christ and God, the church has been identified as the forgiving commu-nity—the community to proclaim the forgiveness of God and to foster forgiveness for one another. Thus, it is crucial for the church to announce God's forgiveness of sinners.

Recently the topic of forgiveness has emerged as a major theme of research in the fields of psychology and sociology. These forgiveness stud-ies are from the perspectives of physical health and mental health. Their discoveries are informative and helpful for the Christian understanding of forgiveness.

Most people experience forgiveness often. "Forgiveness is the way to set yourself free" to get on with life, says psychologist Bernie Zilbergeld, author of *The New Male Sexuality:* "People have to understand that holding a grudge is one of the most self-destructive things you can do. If you want to have a happy life, you have to move on and let go."[6]

Forgiveness is close to our daily life. To forgive or to be forgiven is important to everyday life, yet we find it hard to be comfortable with either of them. Forgiveness is the "gift you give yourself," says Bonnie Weil, author of *Adultery: The Forgivable Sin.* "If you don't forgive a grudge, there is a part of you that dies inside. You lose your optimism, your enthusiasm, your zest for life."[7] The purpose of this chapter is to delve into the meaning of forgiving and being forgiven. I will take the victim's perspective to examine forgivingness and then turn to the point of view of the offender to look at forgiven-ness.

Forgivingness

We often treat the issue of whether or not we should forgive, but discuss little about the contents of forgiveness. What is forgiveness? According to Oxford English Dictionary, *forgive* means "give or grant," "to give up, cease to harbor (resentment, wrath)," "to give up one's resolve (to do something)," or "to give up resentment or claim to requital for, to pardon (an offence)."

The New Testament teaches the offended to forgive the offender, based on God's unconditional forgiveness toward him or her (e.g., the parable of the unforgiving servant in Matt 18:23-35.) The noteworthy point is that human forgiveness is closely connected with divine forgiveness. While the Hebrew Bible emphasizes divine forgiveness, the New Testament focuses on human forgiveness built on divine forgiveness— the unlimited forgivingness (the active offer of internal attitude and external reconciliation) that the offended can offer the offender because of God's unconditional forgivingness.[8]

The Content of Forgiveness

In her book *The Fall to Violence*, theologian Marjorie Suchocki interprets forgiveness as willing the well-being of an offender instead of having ill-will toward him or her. It is not a once-for-all event, but a time-spent event. Although forgiveness does not require feelings of love or acceptance, it can make room for warm feelings or acceptance for both the victim and the violator. Forgiveness thus can be the foundation of transformation.[9]

Theologian Gregory Jones describes forgiveness as reconciliation with God. It is not "primarily a word that is spoken or an action that is performed or a feeling that is felt. It is a way of life appropriate to friendship with the Triune God."[10] He contends that forgiveness declares pardon in some situations, corrects wrong in others, and sometimes even makes retribution. He differentiates Christian forgiveness from therapeutic forgiveness, making it clear that popular therapeutic understandings internalize and privatize the significance of forgiveness. In contrast, true forgiveness is integral to Christian belief in the Triune God of self-giving communion.[11]

Pastoral counselor John Patton shifts our concern from the definition of forgiveness to the perspective of forgiveness. He describes forgiveness not as something we do, but something we discover. To forgive the one who injures us, we need to discover ourselves in him or her: "I am like him or her."[12] Some injured persons wield forgiveness as a defensive power. Authentic forgiveness is an act of surrendering one's own power to forgive rather than holding on to the power. Patton warns the injured against any attitude of superiority to the offender. In the humble process of forgiveness, the injured can overcome the pain of rejection.

In *The Spirituality of Imperfection*, Ernest Kurtz and Katherine Ketcham define forgiveness as letting go of the feeling of resentment and of seeing the self as victim. It is the readiness to accept one's own accountability instead of blaming his or her problems on someone else, and starting to clean oneself up. Then forgiveness and healing, not only by God but even of God, can take place. One cannot, however, generate forgiveness by himself or herself since it is a gift (for-give-ness).[13]

The Phases of Forgiving

Both pastoral theologians and psychotherapists have described the phases of forgiveness. While psychotherapists commonly stress the healing of the injured, pastoral theologians generally extend their interest to the reconciliation between the injured and the offender. It is natural that psychotherapists focus on the well-being of their clients, while theologians are more concerned about the biblical principles of reconciliation beyond forgiveness.

Beverly Flanigan, a clinical professor at the School of Social Work, University of Wisconsin, wrote *Forgiving the Unforgivable* for those who want to transcend deep and unforgivable injuries. To her, forgiveness is a journey. It requires a process—picking a place to go, outlining an itinerary, and packing the luggage and setting off. She suggests six steps toward a journey of healing our injury:

1. Naming the injury—to admit our woundedness, to construct the meaning of the wound, and to talk to others to validate our feelings.
2. Claiming the injury—to give up the struggle to fight off the changes that will result from the unforgivable injury.
3. Blaming the one who injures—to identify the offender whom we must forgive.
4. Balancing the scales—to see all the methods of balancing the scales—punishing, loading the scales,[14] mock punishment.
5. Choosing to forgive—to choose to release the offender from debt and move forward to the emergence of a new self—to become more relaxed, less defensive and brittle.[15]

This journey is a rational process, a self-conversion, and a reconceptualization of our belief system.[16] The journey of forgiveness is a profound, and a profoundly personal, one.

Recent research shows that forgiveness boosts people's self-esteem and lowers their blood pressure and heart rate. Forgiveness also helps people sleep better at night and increases a positive change in their attitude. "Forgiveness is an intellectual decision you make to give up your anger and feelings of revenge," said Richard Fitzgibbons, a psychiatrist based in Philadelphia. He offered several tips on how to forgive:

1. Admit your anger.
2. Decide to forgive.
3. Do no harm. Do not act negatively against the person who hurt you.
4. Consider the source. It may help you to forgive if you understand the background of the offender that could explain his or her behavior.
5. Put yourself in the other person's shoes. Empathize. Consider what was going on in the offender's life when he or she hurt you.
6. Give yourself some time.[17]

This forgiveness is a rational decision based on practicality and experience. These processes of forgiveness take weeks, months, and sometimes years to help us get over anger and bitterness.

The Stanford University Forgiveness Project, one of the largest and most noted studies on forgiveness ever conducted, shows that gaining knowledge of how to forgive improves our emotional and physical health. Fred Luskin, the cofounder and director of the project, suggests nine steps to forgiveness in his book *Forgive for Good*.[18]

1. Understand how you feel about what happened, and be able to articulate what about the situation is not okay.
2. Make a commitment to yourself to do something that will make you feel better.
3. Know your goal. Forgiveness does not necessarily signify reconciling with the person who upset you or condoning his or her action.
4. Obtain the right perspective on what is happening.
5. At the moment you feel upset, practice the Positive Emotion Refocusing Technique (PERT)[19] to ease your body's flight-or-fight response.
6. Stop expecting things from other people, or life, that they do not choose to give you.
7. Pour your energy into looking for another way to get your positive goals met than through the experience that has hurt you.
8. Bear in mind that a life well lived is your best revenge.
9. Alter your grievance story to remind yourself of the heroic choice to forgive.[20]

So far we have dealt with psychological approaches to forgiveness. What appears below reflects the position of Lewis Smedes, a theologian who has devoted his energy to advancing the Christian concept of forgiveness. His approach is different from the psychological approaches because he includes the dimension of reconciliation. His six steps for forgiveness are:

1. Forgiveness is a redemptive response to having been wronged and wounded. This is simple but important. Only those who have wronged and wounded us are candidates for forgiveness.
2. Forgiveness requires three basic actions. First, we surrender our right to get even. When we forgive, therefore, we place the out-

come of the matter in God's hands and often choose to live with the scales unbalanced. Second, we rediscover the humanity of our wrongdoer. When we forgive, we rediscover that the person who wronged us is a complex, weak, confused, fragile person, not all that different from us. And third, we wish our wrongdoer well. We not only surrender our right to revenge against him or her, we desire good things to happen to him or her.

3. Forgiving takes time. God can forgive in a single breath. But we need time.

4. Forgiving does not require forgetting. Does God not remember that Peter denied his teacher? But we can refuse to let a harmful incident control our lives. We can detoxify the memory; we can purge its poison from our souls.

5. Ideally, forgiving leads to reconciliation. But we often have to put up with less than the ideal. Sometimes the forgiven person will not want to be reunited with us. Forgiving happens in our hearts. There can be no reunion without forgiving, but there can be forgiving without reunion.

6. Forgiving comes naturally to the forgiven. Nothing enables us to forgive like knowing in our hearts that we have been forgiven.[21]

Notice that Lewis Smedes' steps incorporate reconciliation, while psychotherapists do not mention it. A Christian approach mandates a full cycle of restoring forgiveness. Another point is that Christian forgiveness counts heavily on the inspiration of the Holy Spirit, making forgiveness of the offender possible.

Conscious and Unconscious Forgivingness

Forgiveness allows room for error, sin, or failing. This means that we keep our feelings about the offenders' sins and mistakes separate from our perspective about their persons. If we truly forgive offenders, we do not attack their personalities, but focus on issues. We respect them as persons but deal with the issues of sins, injustice, or mistakes.

Forgiving at a conscious level is one thing, and forgiving at an unconscious level is another. Our rational decision to forgive may provide peace of mind for a while, but it may be overcome by a vortex of unconscious feelings that refuse to forgive. How can we forgive the offender at the unconscious level? To do that, we need to change our images of the offender. The world of the unconscious is governed by images, feelings, or intuitions, while the world of consciousness is ruled by words or reason. Images or feelings touch our unconscious mind while reason deals with the conscious mind. By bringing up redeemed and fresh images of the offender, we can finally forgive him or her at a deeper level. Our unconscious connection to an event is always stronger than our conscious one, as the fact that we forget the details of an occurrence far sooner than we forget how we felt about it proves. Although we say that we have forgiven our offender, we may harbor negative feelings towards him or her. Consequently, we try to find ways to avoid seeing or meeting that person. This is not genuine forgiving. To forgive our offender more fully, we need to exchange our bad or negative images of him or her for good, positive, and redeemed ones. When we change our images of the offender, our unpleasant feelings toward him or her fade away, and we can relate to him or her pleasantly again. Thus, it is necessary to forgive others both at the level of words and of images, if we want to forgive them fully.

Internal and External Forgivingness

One of the most urgent issues is when and how we forgive our offenders. Do we forgive them before or after they ask for forgiveness? Some argue that we should forgive our offenders immediately, while others contend that we should not forgive them unless they change their wrongs and ask us to forgive them. In response to the issue, it is necessary to develop two phases of forgiveness: internal and external.

Internal Forgivingness: An Intrapersonal Dimension

Joram Graf Haber argues that we should not forgive offenders unless they repent.[22] Without the offender's repentance our forgiveness betrays self-respect.

My position differs from his. The offended needs to internally forgive the offender as soon as possible. But the offended does not have to declare his or her forgiving until the offender repents of his or her wrong. The offended has the task to work toward the repentance of the offender.

Internal forgiveness is to forgive our offenders or enemies before they ask for it. This type of forgiveness is agreeable with theological and psychosomatic practices. Theologically, as God has forgiven us, we forgive our offenders unconditionally. Jesus forgave his own killers before they asked his forgiveness: "Father, forgive them, for they do not know what they are doing" (Luke 23:34).

Peter asked Jesus how many times we should forgive the offender: "As many as seven times?" The Jewish tradition stipulated that the offended should forgive the offender three times. Peter was generous in suggesting seven times. Jesus, however, said to him, "Not seven times, but I tell you, seventy-seven times" (Matt 18:21-22). This means forgiveness beyond reckoning. It is Jesus' mandate that the forgiven ought to forgive the offender.

The sinned-against suffer the psychosomatic effect of anger and resentment as long as they brood over them inside. Kathleen Lawler, a psychologist at the University of Tennessee, traced the blood pressure and heart rate of victims as they discussed being betrayed by a friend, lover, or parent. She discovered that while burying the hatchet did seem to ease strain on the heart, nonetheless, once the interviews about their grievances started, all of the participants experienced an initial sharp rise in blood pressure. Those who had forgiven their offenders saw their blood pressure return to normal quickly, while the readings of the unforgiving stayed high. "Carrying around resentment can take a physical toll," says Lawler. [23]

The sooner we forgive, the better. However, we cannot force anybody including ourselves, to forgive offenders prematurely. Before forgiving them, we need to sort out issues and work through our hearts and souls. This form of forgiveness involves an internal process.

There are several steps in forgiving: brokenness with sorrow and grief, a willingness to let go, and the courage to envision a fresh image.

1. Sorrow and Grief

The wounded cannot easily forget their deep pain and grief. Forgiveness involves an angry and sorrowful period. According to the nature of offences, some people undergo this phase for a long time, others for a short time. It is necessary for the wounded to express sorrows or wail over their tragic events of injustice and evil. In the parable of the Lost Son (Luke 15:11-31), the father grieved over the son who went away and longed to see his son return (Luke 15:20). It takes courage to acknowledge our wound and pain. The process of forgiveness starts when we demonstrate the courage to put ourselves in the vulnerable position of acknowledging our wound and weakness and undergoing sorrow and grief over han. This spirit of grieving over han opens the process of healing by transcending its own helplessness.

2. A Willingness to Let Go

Forgivingness means letting go of our woundedness, sorrow, and anger—a difficult thing indeed. Some psychologists suggest that we let go through breathing deeply in and out from the belly to relax and to visualize a time when we felt cared for and loved.[24] This is in truth a helpful way to deal with our hurt. However, a more fundamental way to let go of our woundedness is to be connected to God. When prayer, meditation, and contemplation link us to the God who knows our depths, we can let our woundedness go. God also gives us the strength to envision something positive about our offenders, making it possible to release our feelings of anger and hatred toward them.

Willfulness is different from willingness. Willfulness is an uncontrolled state of the will; willingness is a state in which the will is under control.[25] With the former, people seek to take revenge, while with the latter, they let go of someone's offence. By refusing to hold on to a painful event, we experience the energy that heals our body, mind, and spirit. Forgivingness enables us not to dwell on the pain of shame but to transcend it for good.

Forgiving others is forgiving ourselves. Retaliating against others injures ourselves again. Controlling our will, and exercising forgiveness release us from the dungeon of anger and shame. Forgivingness is our own forgiven-ness. Without forgiving our offenders, we become captives of the destructive force of anger and hatred. We need to forgive others seventy times seven. Otherwise, we never learn how to forgive ourselves. In this sense, forgiving is not a choice, it is a must. Every unforgiving moment causes us damage. This does not mean that our forgiving is cheap and easy. On the contrary, it is costly. The father in the parable of the Lost Son could not hold on to his frustration, bitterness, and anger and at the same time embrace the son who once was lost but became found.

3. A Redeemed Fresh Image

Even after the son left home for a far country, the father did not give up on him. He did not disown him but waited for his son to come home.

He never gave himself up to despair or to a negative image of his lost son, but clung to the good image of his son who would return to him.

We have a tendency to demonize or dehumanize our offenders when we are injured. By separating an individual's personhood from his or her actions, we can condemn that person's sins and errors without rejecting his or her as a person. All sinners deserve human dignity and respect. Forgiving those who injure us means seeing in them the same kind of scared, vulnerable, fragile, confounded, and struggling human beings that we see in ourselves. We need to restore their humanity in our thinking and remember that God redeems them, too.

Most offenders suffer from negative images of themselves. To forgive them is to refuse to accept their own denigration of themselves. A forgiving heart foresees a redeemed, good, and accountable image of the offenders, while not forgetting their past.[26] Forgiveness allows to see our offenders through the lens of hope. In other words, we cease harboring resentment against them, and picture them to ourselves as transformed persons. It is the courage to exchange the hurtful understanding of them that we have so carefully nurtured for a new, positive image of who they might be.

As a parent, I have experienced the power of positive and negative images of my young sons when they do wrong. When I forgive them, I have to engage two sets of negative images: mine and theirs. On the one hand, when I see their wrong behaviors, I can easily conjure up negative images of them: "Here he goes again. What's wrong with him?" To combat this, I try to bring to mind positive images of my children, seeing them as good, kind, gentle young men, even when they have behaved in ways I disapprove. Those good images, in spite of negative acts, are redeemed images. On the other, before I judge them, they judge themselves: "You don't have to tell me. I know I am a bad boy." When I say something about their inappropriate behavior, I need to remind them of the fact that they are good boys. Forgiveness involves maintaining a good image of the wrongdoer's person. As long as my sons perceive this fundamentally positive image I have toward them, they can accept my words of challenge to their behavior without conjuring up a bad self-image. They then are freed to try to live up to my understanding that they are good persons. Forgiving is to keep renewed images of the offender.

Here is another feature of Christian forgivingness. A Christian approach to forgivingness presupposes the forgivingness of God and our debt to God in the distribution of forgiveness. Its essence is to regard the offender as the redeemed.

External Forgivingness: An Interpersonal Dimension

So far, we have discussed forgiving from the perspective of the inner life of the injured. This internal forgiving can take place whether the offender asks for forgiveness or not. Let us turn now to see how the injured needs to be engaged with the injurer in a relational act of forgiveness, which can be called "external forgivingness."

Ideally, the offender will offer to recompense for his or her wrong and ask for forgiveness. If the offender fails to seek forgiveness, the injured person is not obligated to offer it. Only when the injured cares about the offender will he or she challenge the offender to repent. To provide this external forgiveness when the offender has not asked for it and does not want it is to waste one's time.

External forgiveness is to pronounce the offender forgiven when he or she has sought it. This external forgiveness leads to reconciliation.[27] When the offended and the offender come to settle their discord through forgiveness, they begin to reconcile with each other. Ideally, the offender is supposed to seek reconciliation with the offended. If the offender has no intention of seeking forgiveness, the offended needs to initiate the process of external forgiveness with the offender through resistance. There are several steps to take in the course of resistance. First, the offended has to challenge the offender to admit his or her wrong. This is the stage of confrontation.

Second, the offended has to guide the offender to repent of his or her wrong. Repentance brings both parties back to neutral ground and prepares them to enter into a full relationship again.

Third, the offended needs to engage the offender to recompense whatever damage he or she has done. Without repentance and recompense on the part of the offender, apology is cheap and forgiveness is empty. Dietrich Bonhoeffer calls forgiveness without repentance "cheap grace." Forgivingness proper transpires after recompense.

Fourth, external forgiveness restores a mutual relationship. Forgiveness alone cannot bring reconciliation. While forgiveness is entirely within the power of the victim, reconciliation can happen only if both parties agree to restore their relationship. Reconciliation makes the offender a family member, a friend, or a community member again.[28] As time goes by, the offended will resume a good feeling toward the offender. When it has reached maturity, reconciliation may reconstruct a relationship that exceeds the one that existed when the original offense broke the relationship.

In the parable of the Lost Son, when the son returned home, the father had the compassionate heart to embrace and kiss him. A forgiving heart does not condemn returning sinners but accepts them as they are. A forgiving heart restores the dignity of the sinner. The father did not treat the lost son as one of his servants, even though his son asked for just that. Rather, the father restored the son to his previous status. The son in turn truly respected and loved his father. Reconciling means restoring the offender to his or her dignified state and solidifying the relationship again.

If possible, we should aim for reconciliation, but we live in an imperfect world. So we sometimes must settle for something less—external forgiveness. The offended or the offender may pursue their relationship to the point of forgiveness, but no further. That desire should be respected. After forgiveness, they can go their own ways. The Christian way of forgiveness, however, does not stop there, but compels us to reconcile with the opponent on the basis of the love of enemy. Even treating unrepentant sinners as outsiders ("Gentiles" or "tax collectors," as Matt 18:17 says) is not to abandon them or to let them be ruined, but to gain them back to a Christian community by temporarily distancing them from the community. True forgivingness is not to overlook the wrongdoing of offenders, but to challenge them to change their ways and encourage them to rectify and recompense what they have damaged. In this sense, the internal forgivingness is interwoven with the external one. They are inseparable for a Christian.

When we forgive our offenders, we accept them as they are, while expecting them to become more, and aiding them in this gradual self-transformation. It is not easy to help our offenders, for they often don't wish to ask for our help. However, patiently and prayerfully waiting for their change is the best thing we can do for them.

Collective Forgiving

Can a group forgive another group? Does an individual victim have a right to forgive the group that victimized his or her group? Can an individual forgive an institution that injured his or her group? Can a victimized institution forgive another institution that victimizes it? These questions beg us for answers, difficult as they are.

A group can forgive another, if the offending group asks for the forgiveness of the injured group and makes compensation for its wrong.

Donald Shriver in his *An Ethic for Enemies* provides rich insights on this topic.[29] Japanese Americans were unjustly interned during World War II. In response to their demands for redress of the losses and damage they suffered during the war, the U.S. government in 1988 officially apologized for the internments and passed legislation (H.R. 442) offering partial monetary compensation to the approximately 60,000 surviving internees. In October 1990 President George H. W. Bush sent a letter of formal apology with a $20,000 check to each survivor.[30] Japanese Americans have responded to this action with gladness and forgiveness. Grace Uyehara, president of the Japanese American Citizens League, saluted H.R. 442 with the following: "Their votes show that civil rights violations are taken seriously, and that amends go beyond mere apology. . . . H.R. 442 affects all Americans."[31]

Unlike the Japanese American case, the victims of the Holocaust have not accepted the apologies offered by the German government and people. Although the Germans have made a public apology and offered large monetary restitution to individual Jewish survivors, to the nation of Israel, and to other non-Jewish victims of German aggression, the Jewish victims have not yet been able to forgive them, probably because of the magnitude of their han-ridden heartbreak. It takes time to resolve such deep han.

There are, however, many individual Jewish survivors who forgave Germany long ago. Frank H. Boehm shared the conviction of his father, a survivor of the Nazi's brutality: "He spoke of a need not to forgive those Germans who were responsible for the unbelievable crime against nature, but rather for a need to forgive the Germany that had evolved into a civilized nation and now lived within its borders."[32] The new Germany that Boehm's father depicted embodied the essence of the offender seeking forgiveness. Collective forgiveness invokes a fresh image of the offending group, treat its members with dignity, and helps make it possible for them to live up to that image.

An individual victim does not have a right to forgive a group of offenders or an institution in the name of his or her group. He or she does have, however, an individual right to forgive the offenders or the institution. The question of whether one institution can forgive another is answered by Reinhold Niebuhr. For Niebuhr love is between persons, but justice is between institutions. The forgiveness between institutions is possible only when the offending institution restores justice.

Forgiven-ness

Let us turn now from the forgiving that the offended do, to the for-given-ness that offenders receive. In the Hebrew Bible, the first essential condition of God's forgiveness is repentance. The second essential condition is the intent to avoid repetition of the offense. With these conditions, a sinner could reconcile with God.

The animal sacrifices about which one reads in the Hebrew Bible were made for sins committed unintentionally, and for actions committed out of ignorance that resulted in ritual defilement. There is no sacrifice that can atone for volitional offenses (Num 15:30). While repentance is based on a change of heart according to the prophets and Psalms, for-giveness depends on free acts of divine grace and mercy (Mic 7:18, 19; Ps 103:3).[33]

In Judaism, Yom Kippur, the Day of Atonement, brings about the "ten days of repentance." The purpose of Yom Kippur is to achieve individual and collective purification by the practice of forgiveness of the sins of others and by sincere repentance for one's own sins against God. Yom Kippur is marked by abstention from food, drink, and sex.

Jewish people spend the eve of Yom Kippur and the entire day in prayer and meditation. On the eve of Yom Kippur friends confess, ask, and accept forgiveness from one another for past offenses, since obtaining forgiveness from one's fellows signifies God's forgiveness. God forgives the sins of those who sincerely repent and show their repentance by improved behavior and the performance of good deeds.[34]

Maimonides (C.E. 1140–1204), a great rabbi, philosopher, and physician, elaborates on the process of return (Teshuvah) in his Mishneh Torah, integrating the Bible, Mishnah, Talmud, response (rabbinic rulings in specific cases), customs, and the ongoing tradition. Rabbi Elliot Dorff sums up his teaching in eight points.

1. Acknowledgment that one has done something wrong.
2. Public confession of one's wrongdoing to both God and the community.
3. Public expression of remorse.
4. Public announcement of the offender's resolve not to sin in this way again. (These first four may possibly take place amid crying and entreaties for forgiveness and, in the most serious of cases, may even include changing one's name.)

5. Compensation of the victim for the injury inflicted, accompanied by acts of charity to others.
6. Sincere request of forgiveness by the victim—with the help of the victim's friends and up to three times, if necessary (and even more if the victim is one's teacher).
7. Avoidance of the conditions that caused the offense, perhaps even to the point of moving to a new locale.
8. Acting differently when confronted with the same situation in which the offender sinned the first time.[35]

Maimonides stressed earnest public contrition, public repentance, and a transformed lifestyle—even to the point of recommending that the penitent say, "I am a different person, not the same person who committed those deeds."[36]

Some sociological and psychological approaches to being forgiven are useful for the development of Christian forgiving and its processes. Beverly Flanigan suggests eight everyday activities we can do to promote forgiveness:

1 Admit speedily and openly when you are wrong.
2. Apologize to people you have wronged. If possible, issue your apology in the presence of others to demonstrate that you are not afraid to return power to those you have hurt.
3. Praise those close to you when they express regret about hurting someone. Encourage them to admit wrongdoing and apologize to the injured person.
4. Respect the attempts of others to forgive someone.
5. When it is true, tell people who have modeled forgiveness to you that you respect their achievements. By the same token, when other people's nonforgiveness contaminates you, tell them.
6. Avoid litigation until you have heard each other's views of the injury. Forgiveness is more likely when people are not adversaries.
7. Teach that life is not fair. One person will have more gifts and opportunities than another person and fewer than others. Envy or greed should never be the basis of nonforgiveness.
8. To forgive is to choose to move forward into the future. Show others that you choose the future, not the past, as the focus of aspirations in your daily life.[37]

These guidelines will certainly promote the practice of forgiveness and bring ripple effects of peace into your community. Yet the practice of seeking forgivingness Flanigan describes omits the role of the divine. In Christianity, divine forgiveness is intricately connected with human forgiveness. When we are forgiven by those who are against us, our relationship with God will be right: "So when you are offering your gift at the altar, if you remember that your brother or sister has something against you, leave your gift there before the altar and go; first be reconciled to your brother or sister, and then come and offer your gift" (Matt 5:23-24).

Christian forgiven-ness is part of Christian worship. The core of Christian forgiven-ness is repentance and restoration of relationships with God and with the offended. As we pursue the restoration of the double relationship, we receive forgiven-ness in the process. We have dealt with repentance as contrition and confession (*metanoia*), the beginning of the forgiven-ness process. The next steps are repentance as the change of behavior (*epistrephō*), the act of recompense, asking for forgiving, and seeking reconciliation.

1. Repentance results in a change of one's behavior. If the changed heart does not lead to a changed lifestyle, it is not true repentance. The term *epistrephō* denotes turning to God (Acts 3:19) and turning from darkness to light (Acts 26:18). It also signifies the life of repentance proven by deeds: people "should repent and turn to God, and do works meet for repentance" (Acts 26:20*b*). John the Baptist urges us to "bear fruits worthy of repentance" (Luke 3:8*a*). After repentance, a thief must stop stealing, an exploiter must stop exploiting, and an oppressor must stop oppressing. Changing one's wrong action itself is to receive forgiven-ness from God and the wounded.

2. Repentance is the act of recompense. When accompanied by recompense, a sinner's repentance is genuine. For Bonhoeffer, forgiveness without repentance is a cheap grace. When Zacchaeus promised Jesus that he would give away half of his possessions and pay back four times more than what he had defrauded (Luke 19:8), his work of contrition started. Only when he came to fulfill his words (I surmise that he did), did his forgiven-ness transpire.

Based upon an actual occurrence, Tolstoy's last major novel, *Resurrection* (1899), recapitulates the idea of forgiven-ness through recompense. In the story, Nobleman Dmitri Nekhludov approaches middle age burdened by guilt. His seduction ten years earlier of the maid, Katusha Maslova, leads to her degradation and acceptance of the life of a prostitute. When Maslova is unduly condemned for murder, Nekhludov decides to intervene on her behalf. He seeks to make amends for his sin and his privileged life by challenging the wrongs of the criminal justice system. When Maslova is convicted, he follows her all the way to Siberia, leaving in his wake all his old material wealth and privilege. His journey into Siberia becomes a heartwarming journey of repentance. *Resurrection* is a beautiful story of forgiven-ness. Recompense means more than making financial compensation to the injured for his or her loss; it means restoring his or her human dignity as well.

In feudal society, an offender was required to make recompense to the offended according to his or her status. A wrong or crime against a king would require more recompense than a crime against a baron or a commoner. For Anselm, since God is infinite, we do not possess the power to fully make recompense for our sins against God's holiness and honor. But contrary to this line of thought, what God requires of the offender is to compensate the human victims of his or her offense. This compensation does not depend on the status of the one offended. Rather, we need to attend, heal, and recompense the injuries of the offended with all our hearts, as if we were making restitution to God. In fact, as we offend our neighbor, we injure God. By restoring our neighbor's dignity, we restore God's dignity as well.

3. Forgiven-ness can be achieved through the act of asking for forgiveness. The offender needs to ask forgiveness from God first and then from the wronged. Having done works of repentance, and while admitting his or her wrong openly to the offended, the offender should implore in humility the forgiveness of the offended. To ask forgiveness is not to ask that those we have offended forget the wrong we have done. We do ask, however, that the cease remembering it with resentment and a heart of vengeance. The offended can forgive the offender, or delay forgivingness at this juncture. If the offended is not ready to forgive the offender, the offender must patiently wait for his or her forgiving in due course. Even if the offended decides to forgive, the offender needs to seek one more step.

4. Forgiven-ness becomes consummated in reconciling with the offended. A genuine act of asking for forgiveness may lead the offended and the offender to reconcile. There is little the offender can do if the offended does not wish to be reconciled. Nonetheless, the offender has to seek reconciliation. In reconciliation, both parties genuinely may feel goodwill toward each other and wish to build their relationship again.

Collective Forgiven-ness

A group, community, or nation sometimes seeks forgiveness. It is necessary for a corporate organization to receive a collective forgiveness from individuals or groups it has oppressed. As in the case of individual procedures, a collective unit needs to undergo the processes of forgiveness. According to Shriver, forgiveness entails four elements. It "begins with a remembering and a moral judgment of wrong, injustice and injury."[38] Both parties to an offence must agree about the wrongs committed. Second, forgiveness demands the renunciation of vengeance, although it does not require the abandonment of justice. Third, forgiveness makes necessary an empathy with the enemy's humanity. It acknowledges that an enemy is a human being like us. Finally, a genuine forgiveness seeks "the renewal of a human relationship."[39]

In South Africa, the South African Truth and Reconciliation Commission (TRC) administered the process of forgiveness after the apartheid era. The TRC Act gave amnesty to those who openly admitted to having committed human rights violations for political reasons during apartheid. According to Charles Villa-Vicencio, national director of research for the South African Truth and Reconciliation Commission, the TRC Act had four basic tasks within its two year mandate: "The fullest and most complete disclosure of past gross human rights violations, preparation for the reintegration of perpetrators of gross human rights violations, an authentic historical record of human rights abuse, and a penetrating and empathetic understanding of the 'motives' and 'perspective' of perpetrators."[40] These are just the beginning of the reconciliation process.

A number of people are dissatisfied with the TRC's intentions and outraged that justice has not served apartheid's victims. Chris Ribeiro, the son of the murdered parents, resists anyone "pushing reconciliation down my throat."[41] Marius Schoon, who lost his wife and a daughter in a South African Army raid, protests at "the imposition of a Christian morality of forgiveness."[42] For many victims, the TRC Act is not enough. Villa-Vicencio views the commission as a necessary step to heal the wounds of apartheid at the present stage of restoration and suggests more comprehensive theological steps that are necessary to accomplish true reconciliation:

- Acknowledgment or confession of the truth.
- Contrition and repentance (a willingness to live a different kind of life).

- A willingness, where possible, to make restitution or reparation for past wrongs.
- The extending and receiving of forgiveness.[43]

Collective forgiven-ness is similar to individual forgiven-ness except in its public dimension and ambiguity. Unlike personal forgiven-ness, the line between victims and their perpetrators blurs in collective forgiven-ness. Although the TRC Act has been positively received, many victims have rejected its work. Collective forgiven-ness inevitably depends on an official declaration of an authorized institution and public opinion. With this understanding, we can review the procedures of collective forgiven-ness:

1. A group of wrongdoers has to publicly acknowledge that they have sinned and have done wrong. Collective forgiven-ness begins with a communal memory in which a group of aggressors admits its sin, injustice, and injury. Japanese history books omit references to Japan's role as aggressor in the Pacific War and as perpetrator of great atrocities against the peoples it conquered. But, remembering history accurately is an important element because of the need to morally assess the past. Japanese refusal to apologize to Asian nations, as well as to the United States, derives from its desire to transmit an honorable past to posterity and to avoid historical responsibilities for what the nation has done. Contrary to their present belief, however, their moral integrity will be preserved only as they gain a deep awareness of their past.

2. The wrongdoers need to express remorse and repent of their wrong publicly. Accompanied by genuine repentance, German national remorse since World War II has been sincere and open. Japan, on the other hand, has satisfied itself with remorse bereft of acts of repentance. National remorse is not enough for a fresh beginning; only national remorse and repentance can open a door to a new beginning of relationships.

3. Wrongdoers need to compensate for what they have done wrong. Recompense is not about restoring exactly what has been lost, but rather the sign of a commitment to fully right the wrong. Most of the time, it is impossible to restore what has been lost, since the most important things are irreplaceable. Nonetheless, the German public apologies and large monetary compensation of Jewish survivors, the nation of Israel, and other non-Jewish victims of German belligerence have produced many positive results.

4. Wrongdoers need to seek reconciliation with the injured. After compensating for what they did wrong, the sinned need to repair damage in their relations to the sinned-against. It is a renewal of relationship between opposite parties, restoring justice and a new cooperative walk toward a common future. After reconciling with the sinned-against, the sinned need to reconcile with God.

Justice by Faith and Justification by Faith

I n receiving prayers, God has to listen to two sides. The sinned against, placing their trust in God's justice, pray for that justice to be made manifest in human affairs—especially their own. The sinner prays for her or his justification, having faith in God's grace. God's grace works to restore both groups to wholeness. The Bible shows us, however, that God's grace is not impartial. God is more concerned about the victim than the victimizer.

Listening to the Wounded

In his article "The Shrill Voice of the Wounded Party," Walter Brueggemann finds three players in the Hebrew Bible. In the exodus narrative, he finds Yahweh, Pharaoh, and Israel. Israel under the power of Pharaoh was "in a situation of wretchedness where it is ruthlessly abused, and from which it is helpless to extricate itself." Yahweh plays a third role—advocating on behalf of Israel as the sinned against. The prophetic traditions also reveal three players, but this time in a different grouping: Yahweh, the urban elite of the Jerusalem establishment, and the marginalized. Yahweh as the third player once again stood "in transformative solidarity precisely with the sinned against." He notices that God always sides with the sinned against in a conflict.

Brueggemann, however, affirms that God's love is abundant even for sinners. But if this is the case, how much more compassionate and gracious God will be for the innocents against whom sin has been committed! Therefore, God is merciful toward all humans, but especially to the sinned against.[1]

In the New Testament, Jesus declared that he came to call sinners. Does Jesus care more about sinners than the sinned against? As we remember, when the scribes and the Pharisees criticized Jesus for his association with tax collectors and sinners, Jesus said, "Those who are well have no need of a physician, but those who are sick; I have come to call not the righteous but sinners" (Mark 2:17). It is worth noting that Jesus put sinners side by side with the sick. The sick need healing, not repentance. Bringing that healing to the sick (whom the religious establishment had labeled "sinners") was the reason Jesus came into the world.

The term "sinner" here is confusing. As we saw in chapter 1, the term *sinner* attached itself not to offenders and criminals, but rather to the marginalized, the oppressed, and the poor who could not afford to observe sabbatical laws and religious regulations. Shepherds who had to tend sheep on the Sabbaths; tanners who had to deal with the smelly skins of the dead animals; the sick who could not carry out religious duties—these are examples of sinners in Jesus' day. Most of these so-called sinners were religiously unclean, socially isolated, and economically exploited.

In short, the sinners with whom Jesus associated were not real sinners in the modern sense (although they were not without sin). Rather, they were the downtrodden who needed solace, healing, and liberation. Jesus promised the healing or deliverance of these sinned against (the so-called sinners) from their oppression and affliction. God cares about their well-being and the restoration of their rights.

Two Meanings of Faith

When we read the Bible, we see at least two different expressions of faith: the faith of sinners and the faith of the sinned against. The faith of sinners rests on God's mercy; the faith of the sinned against trusts in God's fairness. If sinners have faith in God, God will justify them. If the sinned against have faith in God, they can know that God's justice will be done. The faith of the sinners aims at divine acceptance and validation, while the faith of the sinned against points to divine verdict and vindication.

Faith in Justification: The Faith of the Sinners

The phrase the faith of the just surfaces from Paul's Epistle to Romans: "For in it the righteousness of God is revealed through faith for faith; as it is written, 'The one who is righteous will live by faith'" (1:17). Paul quotes from the prophet Habakkuk, applying the quotation to his own context. To Paul, this faith means believing in Jesus; more specifically, it means trusting in Jesus' redeeming power. This faith is connected to justification. Thus, faith in Paul's theology is developed for sinners. For the sinner, faith means trusting in God's pardoning mercy through Jesus Christ. In the centuries since Paul wrote, the church has further developed this idea of faith and justification of sinners. The church has further developed this faith-justification type alone. Such faith makes the sinners righteous through God's grace (Roman Catholics) or causes them to be regarded as righteous through God's grace (Protestants). This type of faith concerns the righteousness of the sinners.

Faith in Justice: The Faith of the Sinned Against

The phrase the faith of the just derives from Habakkuk. In the book of Habakkuk, faith meant waiting. Habakkuk lived in a time when evil prospered. His main complaint was why a just God would be "silent when the wicked swallow those more righteous than they" (1:13). At his watchtower, he stood and kept watch to see what God would say to him. Finally, God answered him and said: "Write the vision; make it plain on tablets, so that a runner may read it. For there is still a vision for the appointed time; it speaks of the end, and does not lie. If it seems to tarry, wait for it; it will surely come, it will not delay. Look at the proud! Their spirit is not right in them, but *the righteous live by their faith*" (2:2-4).[2] For Habakkuk, faith is to wait for God's vindication for the wronged. Faith is also patiently waiting for God's judgment upon the wicked. Trusting in the faithfulness of God for the restoration of justice is the gist of Habakkuk's faith. Waiting signifies trusting in God's fair treatment of everyone—the divine justice. To him, faith is connected to justice, not justification. His concept of faith is developed for the sinned against.

This faith concerns the rights of the sinned against. Since the church has treated the faith of the sinners, it needs to balance the view by lifting up the faith of the sinned against in the Bible. For the sinned against, faith denotes trusting in God's grace that reinstates God's justice by restoring their rights—human rights and civil rights.

In the New Testament, we see the faith of heroes in the Letter to the Hebrews. By faith Moses refused to be called a son of Pharaoh's daughter, opting to share ill treatment with his people rather than to enjoy the momentary pleasures of sin. Even the hope of resurrection derives from faith: "Women received their dead by resurrection. Others were tortured, refusing to accept release, in order to obtain a better resurrection" (Heb 11:35). Ultimately Jesus was "the pioneer and perfecter of our faith, who for the sake of the joy that was set before him endured the cross" (Heb 12:2). Jesus' faith endured, not so that he might secure his own justification, but that he might achieve the vindication of the sinned against: "Consider him who endured such hostility against himself from sinners, so that you may not grow weary or lose heart" (Heb 12:3). Their faith was the "assurance of things hoped for, the conviction of things not seen" (Heb 11:1). Like Jesus, they did not seek their own justification; rather, their faith gave them courage to trust in the verdict and justice of God. For the injured, faith in justice pursues humanization. Such a faith is the foundation of resistance for the wounded.

Justice by Faith for the Wounded

When we look at the doctrine of justification from a victim's perspective, the exoneration of the guilty party without a proper procedure is not good news. That is an act of injustice, which causes resentment in the victim. Oppressors readily embrace the doctrine of justification by faith, since it benefits them. The Protestant doctrine of justification may doubly grieve the victims of oppressors: In addition to suffering at the hands of those who oppress them, they must also witness God's refusal to treat their oppressors with justice.

Can God pardon and justify oppressors apart from the work of their repentance? Is that justice? If God forgives and justifies a murderer without restitution, is God fair? Julian Pleasants points out that human rights precede divine rites in Jesus' teaching.[3] Before we bring our offering to God, we need to reconcile with our victims first (Matt 5:23-24). When God's forgiveness of offenders concurs with the offenders' restoration of their victims' rights, justice has transpired. Justification by faith does not mean that sinners can be justified without the work of repentance. Rather, it means that they are justified in order to do the work of restoration. Justification occurs not when God lets sinners off the hook but when God's grace convicts and empowers sinners to work for the rectification of their wrongs.

Biblical Justice

In the Bible, justice is characterized by divinely granted commandments. Biblical justice is much involved in victims' rights. The biblical laws mandate the restitution of victims' losses. "When someone steals an ox or a sheep, and slaughters it or sells it, the thief shall pay five oxen for an ox, and four sheep for a sheep. The thief shall make restitution, but if unable to do so, shall be sold for the theft. When the animal, whether ox or donkey or sheep, is found alive in the thief's possession, the thief shall pay double" (Exod 22:1-4).

When thieves can restore the original ox, or sheep, they pay double. If they cannot, they pay fivefold or fourfold, in consideration of the trouble they have caused their victims. These ordinances also deter possible crimes. As seen here, the biblical writers were concerned with the well-being of victims, not with the rehabilitation of offenders.

If offenders make voluntary confession and restitution, they restore the value of the original goods plus a fifth of the loss: "Speak to the Israelites: When a man or a woman wrongs another, breaking faith with the LORD, that person incurs guilt and shall confess the sin that has been committed. The person shall make full restitution for the wrong, adding one fifth to it, and giving it to the one who was wronged" (Num 5:5-7). Zacchaeus voluntarily decided to give half of his possessions to the poor and to make fourfold restitution for fraud (Luke 19:1-10). He went far beyond what the law demanded. His determination shows his heart of repentance.

Biblical laws are concerned with the restoration of the victim's rights, not the punishment of his or her perpetrator. The victim has the right to make a more suitable offer to the perpetrator. In the Bible, civil law always holds up victims' rights, not the state's. It is the victim, not the state, which has the option of negotiating with the criminal.[4] The victim's right is a primary concern of biblical justice. When a wrong is done, God and the wronged are victimized together. Justice needs to be restored for God's and the victim's sake.

Justice In the Hebrew Bible

In the Hebrew Bible, God's essential nature is justice. Prophets such as Isaiah, Micah, Amos, and Hosea insist upon God's demand for justice. God's justice, however, appears to be in conflict with God's mercy. In reality, the Bible basically identifies God's justice as God's mercy. God is "a righteous God and a Savior" (Isa 45:21). So the psalmists praise God's justice and deliverance (Ps 7:17; Ps 35:23, 24, 28; Ps 36:6; Ps 140:12, 13; Ps 50:5, 6; Ps 94:14, 15; Ps 103:6; Ps 143:1).[5]

According to Kathleen Farmer, justice (*mishpat*) in Micah 6:8 ("To do justice, and to love kindness, and to walk humbly with your God") signifies God's action in a compassionate and merciful manner, not necessarily human "fairness or even-handedness."[6] The word *kindness* in the same verse is *hesed* in Hebrew. It can be translated into "mercy," "steadfast love," "loyalty," and "loving-kindness."[7] Farmer concludes that these two words, justice (*mishpat*) and kindness (*hesed*), are "two aspects of the same way of acting in the world."[8] When he pleaded with God to treat the people of Sodom justly, Abraham did so according to the idea of justice (*mishpat*) (Gen 18:17-33). Abraham's concept of justice is "closer to what we call 'grace' in English than it is to the concept of strict justice as we usually understand it."[9] Jonah wanted to see God's immediate judgment upon Nineveh, but God provided the city a second chance. By inducing Jonah to care about a bush that had given him shade, God taught him a lesson concerning the importance of the Ninevites: "You are concerned about the bush, for which you did not labor and which you did not grow; it came into being in a night and perished in a night. And should I not be concerned about Nineveh, that great city, in which there are more than a hundred twenty thousand persons who do not know their right hand from their left, and also many animals?" (Jonah 4:10-11). God's notion of justice concurs with Abraham's.[10] It consists of restorative grace and fairness.

Furthermore, for Farmer, Zech 7:9-10 articulates what actual justice is in our daily life: "Thus says the LORD of hosts: Render true judgments, show kindness and mercy to one another, do not oppress the widow, the orphan, the alien, or the poor; and do not devise evil in your hearts against one another." The spirit of Deuteronomy agrees with Zechariah's thoughts on being merciful and gracious toward the downtrodden: "(God) who executes justice for the orphan and the widow, and who loves the strangers, providing them food and clothing" (Deut 10:18). For the downtrodden, being treated humanely is not their special privilege but their basic right. It is also the core of divine justice.

Brueggemann affirms that God's love is copious for sinners and much more abundant for the innocently sinned against. To him, the God of mercy and grace is the foundation of the Old Testament theology. We should not, however, blur the difference between the oppressors and the oppressed. For him, the fact that God sides with the wounded party is God's judgment upon sinners.[11]

God in the Hebrew Bible is the God of justice. "Justice, and only justice, you shall pursue, so that you may live and occupy the land that the LORD your God is giving you," commands Deut 16:20.[12] God's justice is God's grace and fairness that restore human dignity, human rights, and civil rights.

Justice in the New Testament

It is our common misunderstanding to believe that the New Testament speaks little of justice. We often think that instead of speaking about justice and rights, the New Testament seems to discuss justification and righteousness.

In actuality, Jesus stresses justice in his teaching and ministry. The beatitudes of Jesus highlight the value of justice: "Blessed are those who hunger and thirst for righteousness, for they will be filled. . . . Blessed are those who are persecuted for righteousness' sake, for theirs is the kingdom of heaven" (Matt 5:6, 10). According to theologian Nicholas Wolterstrorff, the term *dikaios* should be translated as "justice" rather than "righteousness." It should be read as: "Blessed are those who hunger and thirst for justice, for they will be filled. Blessed are those who are persecuted for the sake of justice, for theirs is the kingdom of heaven."[13] This translation connects the social concern of the Hebrew Bible with that of the New Testament. The term *righteousness* connotes individual piety, while justice possesses social dimensions as well.[14]

Bringing good news to the poor, proclaiming release to the captives, recovering sight to the blind, letting the oppressed go free, and proclaiming the year of Jubilee—these occupied the heart of Jesus' mission (Luke 4:18-19).

The song of Mary shows the role of the Messiah as a justice worker. He was expected to bring social and economic transformation so the people of whatever socioeconomic status might share equality.

And Mary said,
"My soul magnifies the Lord,
  and my spirit rejoices in God my Savior,
for he has looked with favor on the lowliness of his servant.
  Surely, from now on all generations will call me blessed; . . .
He has brought down the powerful from their thrones,
  and lifted up the lowly;
he has filled the hungry with good things,
  and sent the rich away empty." (Luke 1:46-53)

In the Messiah's presence, the lowly and the poor would be lifted up, while the rich and the powerful would undergo a fall. These passages indicate that it is not religious, but rather social and political changes that set the agenda for the messianic tasks. In line with the spirit of the Hebrew Bible, he cared for the well-being of the poor, the sick, the widows, and the aliens. Jesus' mission focused on justice for the oppressed, not the justification of the oppressor.

It is true that we find the idea of retributive justice in the New Testament: The Son of Man "will repay everyone for what has been done" (Matt 16: 27). But God's mercy embraces God's justice. The parable of the Lost Son (Luke 15:11-32); the laborers in the vineyard (Matt 20:1-16); and the generous reward of the master (Matt 24:47) speak to the convergence of God's justice and grace, debunking the idea of solely retributive justice. God's justice is not simply retributive, but gracious and redemptive.

The Definition of Justice

What is justice? Whose justice are we talking about? Can we define it apart from God's justice?

Socrates defines justice as "doing one's own." It means that everyone pursues the occupation in the community to which she or he is best fitted.[15] In the *Republic*, the philosophical thug Thrasymachus contends that justice is nothing else than the advantage of the stronger.[16] For Plato, justice is a matter of social harmony. Aristotle divides the concept of justice into two types: general and particular. General justice concerns itself with lawfulness, while particular justice focuses on fairness and equality in the treatment of others. He further subdivides particular justice into distributive and rectificatory forms. While distributive justice involves what people deserve, rectificatory justice cares for equality and numerical proportion.[17] Like his teachers, Aristotle prefers commutative justice, the idea of a fair exchange. With him, justice shifts from retribution and vengeance to the domestic virtues.[18]

Roman Catholic moral theology defines justice as the virtue that advocates on behalf of human beings for the rights that belong to them. For Thomas Aquinas, "justice signifies equality—to adjust something is to make it equal to some standard—and equality is a relationship to something other."[19] He distinguishes communal justice from individual justice. Communal justice serves the common good, while individual justice concerns private goods.[20] Individual justice has two types: distributive and commutative. Distributive justice divides the common goods according to the status in the community of the person receiving. An aristocracy judges this status by virtue, oligarchies by wealth, and democracies by freedom. Commutative justice regulates exchanges between two people. The act of restitution characterizes commutative justice.[21]

For Martin Luther, justice is a form of faith. Faith is an unshakeable trust in God. Justice is founded on God because God is our ultimate judge through Christ our Mediator. Justice influences a person to give to people what she or he owes them.[22] Expounding on the book of Romans, Luther contends that the law makes no one live without sin and that no one becomes just through the works of the law. The right way to be virtuous and to be saved is to be justified through faith in Christ, who has earned our rights by his blood, who has become a mercy seat for us (Exod 25:17; Lev 16:14), and who has forgiven us of all our previous sins.

For Luther, it is nothing other than God's justice that justifies us in spite of our sinfulness: "In so doing, God proves that it is his justice alone, which he gives through faith, that helps us, the justice which was at the appointed time revealed through the Gospel and, previous to that, was witnessed to by the Law and the Prophets."[23]

Today, American philosophy has revisited the issue of justice. Harvard philosopher John Rawls seeks to find a proper ordering between liberty and equality in light of the needs of the least advantaged in society. He has developed two principles:

> First, each person participating in a practice, or affected by it, has an equal right to the most extensive liberty compatible with a like liberty for all; and second, inequalities are arbitrary unless it is reasonable to expect that they will work out for everyone's advantage, and provided the positions and offices to which they attach, or from which they may be gained, are open to all. These principles express justice as a complex of three ideas:

liberty, equality, and reward for services contributing to the common good.[24]

Rawls asserts that people choose principles of justice, first, by supporting the maximum amount of liberty compatible with the same liberty for others and, second, by requiring that wealth be distributed to make the worst-off members of the society as well off as possible. Concerning the ethical principle of distribution, he closely follows Gandhi. While rejecting the Western idea of utilitarianism that focuses on the greatest good for the greatest number in society, Gandhi upheld the idea of social justice as fairness to the individual, with priority to the disadvantaged.[25]

Rawls's younger colleague, Robert Nozick, tries to defend a strong notion of entitlement, which allows everyone to have what he or she is entitled to, without alluding to inequalities. He insists on private property rights and virtually ignores any concept of community.[26]

In contrast to the idea of justice as equality and impartiality, liberation theology has undergirded a definition of justice in which God sides with the poor. God is not neutral, but opts for the poor. It understands justice as a "preferential option for the poor." For liberation theologians, true justice is based on the idea of equity, not equality. They insist that to practice justice is more important than to define it. To do justice is to know God.

Restorative and Retributive Justice

We have defined justice in diverse ways. In terms of distributing justice in society, there can be two different directions: retributive and restorative.

Retributive justice focuses on retribution for a crime. It is based on the idea of the *lex talionis*: "If any harm follows, then you shall give life for life, eye for eye, tooth for tooth, hand for hand, foot for foot, burn for burn, wound for wound, stripe for stripe" (Exod 21:23-25). This law of lex talionis sounds pitiless and malicious, but in reality it is grounded in the law of mercy. Since the injured have the tendency to retaliate more than they were hurt, the law sets a limit to retribution: "tooth for tooth, eye for eye." Without this boundary, retaliation will only continue to escalate. Retribution is different from revenge. For Robert Nozick, "Retribution sets an internal limit to the amount of the punishment, according to the seriousness of the wrong, whereas revenge internally need set no limit to what is inflicted."[27] In this sense, retribution emerges from benevolence. Deviating from its intention, the law of *lex talionis* has been abused in the absence of mercy. It has been translated into a theology of retaliation or reprisal. Its focus has been on sin-punishment, rigidly attributing all suffering to sin and even interpreting the suffering of the victim as the consequence of sin. This is the reason why on seeing a man blind from birth, Jesus' disciples asked Jesus whose sin had caused his blindness (John 9:1-41).

The critical issue in justice is whether we focus on perpetrators or their victims. Retributive justice centers on the perpetrators. In this justice, punishment is used to deter future crimes. It is always unsatisfying and unsettling to fit punishment for a crime. Unfortunately, there is little room for caring for victims in the retributive system of criminal justice. When justice becomes primarily retribution, the victims of crimes have even been excluded altogether from the criminal justice process.

Our present criminal system is parallel to church doctrines on the retributive dimension of justice. First, both legal and church systems focus on offenders, neglecting victims. In the criminal system, crime is regarded as an offence against the state while in the religious system sin is basically against God. The victims are on the sidelines, called when considered necessary as witnesses in litigation or used for the process of offenders' sanctification in the religious system.

Second, criminal justice aims to place blame and dispense punishment. In the legal system, the primary purpose of justice is to retaliate against and incarcerate criminals, while in the ecclesiastical system, the purpose of divine justice is to punish the sin of humanity. According to this view (best expressed in Anselm's satisfaction theory), even God cannot forgive sinners without punishing them because of God's own principle of justice. Justice demands retribution one way or another.

Third, our criminal justice system pits offenders against the state. The offender and the state are in an adversarial, antagonistic, and impersonal relationship. In the ecclesiastical system, God needs to blame somebody for sin. Those upon whom this blame falls—human beings—are rendered incapable of redeeming the world, due to the God's condemnation of them as sinners. For that reason God chooses the one person innocent of sin—Christ—and shifts the blame and punishment for sin onto his shoulders. Hence, just as in the criminal justice system, this substitutionary view of the atonement rests on an adversarial relationship between God who judges and Christ who takes upon himself the judgment.

In contrast to these three components of retributive justice drawn from the criminal justice system and Christian theology, let us look at three aspects of restorative justice. In what follows I have relied heavily on the work of Howard Zehr, a prominent sociologist who has played a midwife's role in the birth of the concept of restorative justice.

First, restorative justice draws attention to victims. Victims' needs, desires, and rights come first, not last. According to this view, in the criminal justice system victims, not the state, become active in the process of restoring justice. In the ecclesiastical system, victims and God work together equally and inseparably toward the goal of restoring justice. Second, restorative justice seeks "to identify responsibilities, meet needs, and promote healing."[28] Offenders face their victims to see how much harm they have inflicted, and to take responsibility for that harm. In criminal justice, offenders become responsible for what they have done to their victims. In the ecclesiastical system, offenders become responsible to their victims as much as they are to God. Third, restorative justice involves victims, offenders, and community. It campaigns for the healing of individuals and the community. The criminal-justice system identifies the needs of victims, the accountabilities of offenders, and community's role in enabling the conversation between the two. The church system works on reconciliation between victims, offenders, community, and God. Its nature is participatory, cooperative, common, and communal.[29]

Restorative justice highlights the well-being of the victim. Jesus' parable of the Good Samaritan teaches us how we should respond to a victim's need, not our own needs (Luke 10:25-37). Note that, even though the parable is named after the Samaritan, it is not him, but rather the victim, on whom the parable focuses. We are the victim's neighbors, not the robber's. In the parable, without the victim, there would not be any notion of neighbor. The church needs to turn its attention to how to restore the victim, not how to forgive the robber. Julian Pleasants points out that in the parable a robbery victim lies bleeding by the side of the road while the government starts the process of capturing and punishing the robber to save the honor of the law and deter future robberies. At the same time the church goes on to maintain the rites by which the robber can be saved from the wrath of God, without any consideration of whether the robber must also go back to save the victim. [30] For Pleasants, the government and the church pass by the victim. Restorative justice involves the robber and all of us in healing the victim and restoring his or her human dignity.

The philosophy of restorative justice embraces apology, healing, compassion, mercy, forgiveness, and reconciliation. Victims can take advantage of meeting their offenders and receiving support from other victims. They are freed to see that their own feeling of victimization is only intensified by retributive actions against the offenders.

In civil law, restitution works. The state of Minnesota experimented with a method of restitution. In the experiment, restitution became the condition to be met in one-fourth of all probation cases. In these cases the court ordered the offender to make full cash restitution to the victim more than nine out of ten times.[31] This program was basically applied to nonviolent criminal offenders who were deemed able to pay. Most judges, probation officers, and victims favored the use of restitution, and most offenders considered the restitution required of them fair.[32]

In *Restorative Justice: An Ancient Approach to Improve Today's World*, Elmar Weitekamp argues that the punitive approach is counterproductive and detrimental and that restorative justice is a better method for developing sensible justice policies that work to improve the quality of community life. According to him, more primitive societies used monetary compensation to the victim, rather than the punishment of the criminal, as the basis upon which they dispensed justice.[33]

Restorative justice highlights the restoration of a broken relationship over retaliation for a crime. The following story epitomizes restorative justice:

A sixteen-year-old youth is standing before a judge in a court. The judge doesn't mince words. "Well done, Jimmy. You've achieved all you promised and more. I wish you well. Your record is clean. You can go now. Good luck," says he.

It is a common sight in New Zealand where the marvelous piece of 1989 legislation called "The Children, Young Persons and Their Families Act" has been effective. It is the law that brought Jimmy to court four months ago for joyriding in stolen cars. After his arrest, a trained mediator convened a family group conference: the car owners, Jimmy and his family, his teacher and football coach, and a police representative. At the conference, Jimmy first had to admit his guilt and apologize for his offense and the group worked toward consensus as to what they would recommend as a suitable package to the judge. Since Jimmy had a drinking problem, he had to attend a program for three months, pay some compensation to the car owners and perform 100 hours of community service, all within a four-month period. After having done all these, he has just started with a clean slate.[34]

In addition, a victim-offender mediation program brings a wrongdoer and the wronged face to face, if both agree to do so. The mediation program creates a place where both stories can be heard and provides a mediator to facilitate discussion of material, emotional, and psychological injuries. It lets the wronged and the wrongdoer negotiate a restitution agreement that delineates both the damage done to the victim and the offender's responsibility. Victim-offender mediation programs with juvenile offenders have led to the following findings:

1. During a two-year period, 3,142 cases were referred to the four study-site programs. Ninety-five percent of the mediation sessions brought forth a successfully negotiated restitution agreement to restore the victim's financial losses.

2. In the presence of a trained mediator, victims met with their offenders and were more satisfied (79 percent) with the justice system than similar victims who went through a regular court process (58 percent).

3. After meeting their offenders, the fear level of victims for revictimization substantially subsided.

4. Offenders who met their victims more successfully completed their restitution obligation (81 percent) than similar offenders without mediation (58 percent).

5. Offenders (18 percent) who met their victims relapsed less than similar offenders without mediation (27 percent).[35]

Family group conferencing began in New Zealand as a way to address the failures of traditional juvenile justice and to integrate indigenous Maori values that underscore the role of family and community in addressing wrongdoing. Through a process that uses a facilitated meeting and dialogue, a family group conference meets the needs of crime victims and their families and offenders and their families. Institutionalized in the law of New Zealand in 1989, family group conferences are now the norm for processing juvenile cases. As a result, judges report drops in caseloads of up to 80 percent.[36]

Jesus' Death and Resurrection

From a victim's perspective, Jesus was killed by the injustice of his time. He opposed the power of injustice. He healed the sick on the Sabbath, freed the poor from the sabbatical ordinances, fed hungry crowds, taught new laws, and proclaimed the coming reign of God. He broke the dietary law of the elders and preached against the legalism of the Jewish authorities. Finally, the Jewish and Roman authorities collaborated to execute him, seeing him as a threat to the Jewish religious establishment and Roman political stability.

Their unjust execution of Jesus ripped open the veil of the religious and political leaders' evil. His message of the impending reign of God defied the Jewish teaching of the political kingdom and denied the existing rule of the Roman Empire. He did not abandon or compromise his message, but stuck to it up to his execution. His was the voice of the downtrodden and the cry for religious and political justice. He contradicted the evil and injustice of the power that had produced the han of the downtrodden. His death was not a natural one, but a han-filled one that found voice in his outcry, "My God, my God, why have you forsaken me?" He worked for the arrival of God's kingdom and was murdered by the unjust powers for doing so. His death signifies his solidarity with the victims of injustice, oppression, abuse of power, and violence. Jesus could not just simply be murdered and then buried. Having been cut down too soon to complete the establishment of God's reign, his han was too ardent to pass quietly into the grave. He had to rise to proclaim the kingdom of God again. He did not lay down his life in order to forgive either those who executed him or those who oppressed and exploited others. The power of injustice killed him, robbing him of the opportunity to live longer and to deliver the han-ridden from the bondage of legalism and the abuse of power. He did not aspire to shed his blood to redeem his oppressors; he tried to avoid his death but came to realize that his death was in God's circumstantial will. (See chapter 7.) If he had been convinced that his blood would redeem all human beings generation after generation, he would not have struggled so much that his sweat became like drops of blood falling down on the ground (Luke 22:44). He struggled with an agony much more profound than simply fear of his own death. Instead, he suffered with the fact that his premature death would cut him off from fulfilling his mission (Luke 4:16) on earth. However, Jesus chose to face crucifixion because he trusted in God's ability to fulfill his mission even through death, and wanted to confront the power of injustice and evil with justice and truth. For him, nothing was more important than realizing the mission God had given him—including his own impending death.

No power in the universe can defeat God's mission in the world. Jesus' resurrection denotes the inevitable triumph of justice and truth over the rule of injustice. His resurrection is not a mere proof of his supernatural power but is the unstoppable consequence of the strength of his truth and his trust in God's will. One thing we should notice is that the resurrected Jesus goes before his disciples to Galilee where the downtrodden lived: "But go, tell his disciples and Peter that he is going ahead of you to Galilee; there you will see him, just as he told you" (Mark 16:7). After hearing this, Mary Magdalene, Mary the mother of James, and Salome fled from the tomb in terror (Mark 16:8). It is at this point in the story that the Gospel of Mark originally ended. At that time Galilee (home of the poor and marginalized) was in conflict with Jerusalem (home of the rich and powerful). Jesus, who came from Nazareth, never sided with Jerusalem and never stayed voluntarily in the city overnight. Even after the resurrection, he went down to Galilee first. This indicates that we can meet the risen Christ in Galilee where the downtrodden live. His going to Galilee shows that he rose to complete his mission for the downtrodden. For those who feared the principalities and powers, the doers of injustice and evil, Jesus' resurrection to do God's mission among the least and the lost was good news. His resurrection was necessary if he were to complete the mission with which God had entrusted him.

And so, the church needs to work with the resurrected Jesus in Galilee for carrying out his mission. The Bible (e.g., in Exod 21 and 22; and Matt 5) informs us of God' concrete ordinances for the civil rights of victims. It is more concerned that the offended see justice than that offenders be justified. The church's doctrinal systems have shifted this focus, concerning themselves with different ways of assuring sinners of forgiveness. While that forgiveness was important to Jesus, far more crucial to his ministry was the well-being of the downtrodden. His death and resurrection proved that his heart was set to work with the victims of injustice. Jesus spent most of his time for the sick and the poor who were the victims of religious, economic, and social oppression. It is time for the church to develop a way of restoring justice for victims, reinstating the priorities of Jesus' mission.

Collective Justice

The Israelites stressed the idea of solidarity, de-emphasizing the idea of individual sin. When a person committed a sin, the whole family, his or her tribe, or the whole nation was punished for it. When Achan committed the sin of keeping to himself certain spoils from the fall of Jericho, God was offended and Israel lost its battle against Ai because Achan's sin was that of the nation (Josh 7). As sin is collective in the Hebrew Bible, so is justice. Victims are fully restored only in the restoration of social justice beyond individual justice. If individual justice for a victim is restored alone, then she or he may be victimized again in the structure of social injustice.

In his book *Moral Man and Immoral Society*, Reinhold Niebuhr explains why individuals are more morally sensible in their ability to consider the interests of others than are groups. While individuals can be self-giving in terms of choosing the benefits of others, a group of individuals becomes selfish in its decision-making because it pursues the volition of each person's selfish inclinations rather than their generous consideration for others. This collection of individuals' egoism creates a society immoral at heart: "In every human group there is less reason to guide and to check impulse, less capacity for self-transcendence, less ability to comprehend the needs of others therefore more unrestrained egoism than the individuals, who compose the group, reveal in their personal relationships."[37]

Numerous good Christians work as managers and executives of companies in the world. There are generous people, but when they go to work, they operate under the principles of proficiency (profit) and efficiency, showing little generosity in their practice. They have to prove to their owners and stockholders that they can maximize profits for their companies. Peter Drucker asserts that this is why business schools require courses on ethics: The business world is, at its core, heartless.[38] Without addressing collective injustice, it will be very difficult to implement justice for individuals. This is because justice is social.

In the world where the wealthiest 20 percent of the world's population controls almost 83 percent of the world's resources, while the poorest 20 percent survives with less than 2 percent,[39] social justice is threatened and jeopardized. Those poor who inherit poverty will not experience justice in their lives within such a structure of the world. Christians are to commit themselves to bringing social and global justice to the world beyond the narrow limits of their own family, their own company, their own gender, their own race, and their own nation. They do so because their loyalties reside in the reign of God. To do so, however, they need more than good intentions. They must be wise enough to know how to redeem the institutions, systems, and structures in which they participate. Doing so will require reforming their institutions and groups to do more than play on narrowly defined group interests.

Justification by Faith for the Offender

In the Christian system of belief, the doctrine of justification by faith means salvation for sinners. Any sin we commit not only hurts our victims but also deeply wounds God (Matt 25:45). So, before we talk about "justification by faith," it is necessary to define the meaning of salvation. The term salvation derives from Latin *salvus*, "unharmed," ancestor of the English term "safe." A dictionary meaning of the term is "the saving of the soul; the deliverance from sin and its consequences, and admission to eternal bliss, wrought for man by the atonement of Christ" (*Oxford English Dictionary*). Yet in spite of this definition, salvation is not a matter of the spiritual realm alone. Salvation is not something we can put into our pocket as a possession. Nor does salvation mean securing a ticket to paradise or heaven. Salvation is the restoration of a loving relationship with God and neighbors. It is not a place or a possession, but rather a relationship. The absence of relationships turns an island paradise or a place of rest into a living hell. Salvation brings about true fellowships with God and others.

Justification by Grace

The story of the thief who was crucified along with Jesus (Luke 23) shows a clear case of justification by faith through grace. He has done nothing to deserve his salvation except show penitence for his wrong and confess faith in Jesus. Jesus was gracious to him. Our relationship with God may be compared to our relationship with our children. Regardless of their defective characters, there is no way that we can deny the fact that they are our children. On the same ground, God cannot deny the fact that we are God's creation. Nothing in the universe can sever our fundamental relationship with God. Faith affirms that we are God's no matter what happens to us. God embraces us unconditionally. God's unconditional acceptance of us is grace, and our acceptance in turn of God's unconditional acceptance is faith. In Tillich's term, salvation means to accept the fact that we are accepted. In the parable of the Lost Son, we assume that upon returning home the son changed his self-indulgent lifestyle. In fact, his return was itself the core of his changed attitude and lifestyle, restoring his relationship with his father. Justification is our initial entry into this restoring relationship with God. However, that justification will not endure unless it gives rise to a warm relationship between ourselves and God, just as the lost son's return would have meant little unless a change in his attitude and actions had made an ongoing restored relationship with his father possible. Thus justification is not our possession, but rather the process of our relationship to God.

The Pauline Epistles highlight the justice of God that justifies the sinner. Paul repeatedly proclaims that the just lives by faith in Jesus, not by the law. He understands justification as a renewal of the covenant through the redeeming grace of Jesus Christ.

The idea of justification is deeply embedded in prophetic reading of God's covenant with Israel, particularly in Deutero-Isaiah where God promises God's faithfulness to Israel, and also provides the hope of salvation to the Gentiles.[40] The early Christian church understood the Jesus event as the fulfillment of God's covenant with Israel and with the Gentiles. Paul centered his theology on the graciousness of God through Jesus Christ, extending it to the justification of Jews and Gentiles.

The Letter of James, however, contains a seemingly contradictory statement to Paul's understanding of justification by faith: "You see that a person is justified by works and not by faith alone"(2:24). It rebuts the idea of "justification by faith alone." Siding with James, Paul in fact validates "faith" manifest in action and never mentions the phrase "justification by faith alone." James rightly teaches against a misleading doctrine of faith that Paul himself denies strongly (Rom 3:8; 6:1-2).[41] The early church forgot Paul's clear understanding of justification until it rediscovered justification's importance through Augustine's theological controversies. His perspective on God's grace was similar to that of the Reformers who came after him: "But the grace of God is always good; and by it it comes to pass that a man is of a good will, though he was before of an evil one."[42] To him, God justifies us so that our justice may not be our own.

However, Augustine still reserved Catholic elements in his belief that justification grows and counts our merits (although they are God's merits), and justifying faith works by love: "Then faith without works can save a man, and what his fellow-apostle James says must be false. . . . For if those who persevere in these wicked courses shall nevertheless be saved on account of their faith in Christ, how can it be true that they shall not inherit the kingdom of God?"[43] He stood on a bridge between the principle of justification by faith alone and the belief of justification by faith that works through love.

For Thomas Aquinas, justification is attained by faith but is informed by love; the faith is a gift of grace infused into the soul, which leads to good works and thus makes us righteous before God: "He (God) so infuses the gift of justifying grace that at the same time He (God) moves the free-will to accept the gift of grace, in such as are capable of being moved thus."[44] He believed in the integration of four factors for justification: "the infusion of grace," "the movement of the free-will towards God by faith," "the movement of the free-will towards sin," and "the remission of sins."[45] Thomas reminds us of the gift of grace that makes us righteous in faith by transforming us from sin to justice.

Protestants

The early Luther believed that the righteousness of God as mercy transforms a person to be actually made righteous. This is accomplished by God's grace alone and not by any human action, merit, or good works. He feared the term *justice of God* because of its wrathfulness against sinners. But later on Luther came to realize that God's justice or righteousness regards a person as righteous regardless of the person's actual state of life. God's grace in Christ treats us as righteous, and faith is the reception of this grace. Faith, however, is not something we ought to try to achieve or for which we should strive. He understood that God does not demand faith from us, but that both faith and justification are the work of God. To him, the justice of God was no longer a threat, but the sweet good news of a free gift that saves sinners like him. At first he feared the anger of God that condemns him, but later he affirmed the love of God that justifies such a sinner as he. For Luther, faith is trust in the grace of God through Christ, and justification is God's declaration of us as righteous for Christ's sake, which is followed by a real life of righteousness.

It is a common misunderstanding to believe that Luther replaced the merits of Roman Catholic doctrine with faith. To him, faith is the realization of justification, God's gift, not its condition. In the *Small Catechism,* he states, "I believe that I cannot come to my Lord Jesus Christ by my own intelligence or power. But the Holy Spirit calls me by the Gospel, enlightened me with His gifts, made me holy and kept me in the true faith, just as He calls, gathers together, enlightens and makes holy the whole Church on earth and keeps it with Jesus in the one, true faith."[46] He could not obtain faith by his own efforts because it is a free gift of the grace of God.

The sixteenth-century Catholics repeatedly raised the question of whether Luther's doctrine of justification is entirely passive. Luther answered this with the paradox of a dual human nature: spiritual and corporeal.[47] With our spiritual nature, we cling to faith alone that makes us pious, free, and blessed: "One thing and only one thing, is necessary for Christian life, righteousness, and freedom. That one thing is the most holy Word of God, the gospel of Christ."[48] With our corporeal nature, we subject ourselves to work: "Here the works begin; here a man cannot enjoy leisure; here he must indeed take care to discipline his body by fastings, watchings, labors, and other reasonable discipline and to subject it to the Spirit so that it will obey and conform to the inner man and faith and not revolt against faith and hinder the inner man, as it is the nature of the body to do if it is not held in check."[49] Luther presented the passive aspect of faith as a matter of our spiritual nature; the active aspect related to our corporeal existence. In Luther's system, the true meaning of justification by faith is that we are justified by God's grace alone. For Luther, faith is trusting in God's grace.

In contrast to Luther, John Wesley underpinned justification by faith with accountability. He increasingly upheld the importance of repentance, and works of righteousness that followed repentance, following works for repentance, as the prerequisite for justifying faith:

> We have received it as a maxim, that "a man is to do nothing in order to justification." Nothing can be more false. Whoever desires to find favor with God, should "cease from evil, and learn to do well." So God himself teaches by the Prophet Isaiah. Whoever repents, should "do works meet for repentance." And if this is not in order to find favor, what does he do them for? . . . (4.) Is not this salvation by works? Not by the merit of works, but by works as a condition.[50]

"Works as a condition" refers to repentance. He reiterated this position in the 1774 *Minutes*. Repentance is not the work by which we will be saved, but the precondition of faith. To Luther and Calvin, repentance occurs after one receives faith because repentance is itself a work of faith. For Wesley, repentance takes place before justification. In his theology, faith has two phases: repentance faith (the faith of a servant) and justifying faith (the faith of a son or daughter). While the faith of a servant obeys God out of fear, the faith of children obeys God out of love. The faith of a servant is the initial faith before justification, preparing a sinner for justifying faith through repentance. The faith of children is a trust in Christ with a loving and obedient heart, which is justifying faith proper.[51]

Modern Thinkers

For Paul Tillich, the doctrine of justification by faith applies not only to the life of ethics but also to the life of the intellectual realm. In spite of our doubt about God, we can be saved by God's grace: "You cannot reach God by the work of right thinking or by a sacrifice of the intellect or by a submission to strange authorities, such as the doctrines of the church and the Bible."[52] Neither right action nor right belief nor right thinking will save us, but God's grace alone can save us. Faith means to accept the fact that we are accepted: "But man must accept just this. He must accept that he is accepted."[53]

Bultmann compares his method of demythologizing with the principle of justification by faith: "Like the doctrine of justification it (the method of demythologizing) destroys every false security and every false demand for it on the part of man, whether he seeks it in his good works or in his ascertainable knowledge. Security can be found only by abandoning all security, by being ready, as Luther put it, to plunge into the inner darkness."[54] For Bultmann, justification by faith points to giving up all we have except God—an abandon and trust that is itself faith.

Joint Declaration on the Doctrine of Justification

The Lutheran World Federation and the Roman Catholic Church pronounced a joint statement on justification on October 31, 1999.[55] In what follows I will provide a brief summary of its contents.

The Joint Declaration (JD) underscored justification by grace in faith alone: "By grace alone, in faith in Christ's saving work and not because of any merit on our part, we are accepted by God and receive the Holy Spirit, who renews our hearts while equipping and calling us to good works." First, justification denotes the transformation of our lives, making us just: "Justification is forgiveness of sins and being made righteous, through which God imparts the gift of new life in Christ" (JD 22).[56] Second, we are justified by grace alone, not by works; and this grace precedes faith: "Justification takes place by grace alone" (JD 15 and 16), "by faith alone, the person is justified apart from works" (Rom 3:28, cf. JD

25). "Grace creates faith not only when faith begins in a person but as long as faith lasts" (Thomas Aquinas, S. Th. II/II 4, 4 ad 3).[57] Third, grace empowers us to live the life of faith, hope, and love: "Grace as fellowship of the justified with God in faith, hope, and love is always received from the salvific and creative work of God" (cf. JD 27).[58] Fourth, justification is connected with sanctification. We will be responsible for our works: "By justification we are unconditionally brought into communion with God. This includes the promise of eternal life. . . . We face a judgment in which God's gracious sentence will approve anything in our life and action that corresponds to his will."[59]

The true meaning of justification by faith is to describe the fact that our salvation wholly depends on God's grace. Our salvation is a gift entirely from God, not a consequence of our work. Neither moral works nor intellectual works can save us.

Many Christians believe, however, that they are justified by the faith of knowing Jesus as the savior or by the faith of believing biblical doctrines. This is a form of Gnosticism, in which we are saved or justified by knowledge. Many others believe that by doing various types of ministry or by obeying various types of authorities—including the Bible or the church—they are justified. This is a form of justification by works. The idea of *sola fide* (faith alone) debunks all these false securities of salvation, highlighting the grace of God that saves us freely and liberally. The true meaning of *justification by faith* signifies that not even our faith can save us; rather, it is God who saves through the gift of faith. Furthermore, it signifies that God saves us, not as a result of Jesus' death, but because of God's grace, a grace demonstrated by Jesus' identification with victims as seen in his death. To accept this paradox is faith in the totality of divine grace.

Moreover, the true meaning of justification by faith is not merely being saved by believing in Jesus Christ, but loving God through Jesus Christ. Justification by faith is not some sort of test we check off the list when we have finished; it is partaking of the abundant and ongoing life of God through Jesus Christ. Faith is not only trusting God who saves but also loving God who cares. That is, faith is to accept the God who accepts us (passive) and to love the God who loves us (active). This justification means not only freedom from sin, guilt, and their consequences but also the freedom to love God. Our faith in God signifies the act of loving God.

The relationship between God and us is unending and unbreakable.

To understand this and accept this is the act of faith. In this notion of justification, we do not see God as a judge but as our mother or father who cares for us all the way to the end. The relationship between God and us is unbreakable throughout eternity.

Jesus' Death

It has been said that Jesus died for the sins of the world. Many Christians believe in that Jesus' death is a literal blood atonement, while others reject the idea of blood atonement altogether. Both interpretations tend to apply literalistic understandings to the idea of Jesus' death as an atonement, and for that reason have proved themselves irrelevant to a number of Christians. We need to interpret this blood atonement from a symbolic point of view. Symbols point beyond themselves in describing something deeper than human words are able to articulate. Jesus was killed by the Jewish religious leaders and the Roman rulers. For them, Jesus caused religious and political headaches, threatening their establishment and stability. Although killed by the authorities, Jesus had some control over the situation. In other words, he was not totally helpless because he could escape the arrest but chose not to do so.

Jesus' death was not, however, completely voluntary. Probably, he realized that he could not hide for a long time or that he could not accomplish his mission by hiding himself. Not desiring to go to the cross, he nonetheless discerned God's will in doing so. Having found God's will, he submitted his own will to it. In this sense, his death was in God's providence (not predestination).

But why was it necessary for Jesus to suffer such a death? Was his crucifixion the will of God? He did not have to die to appease God, but he could not avoid his death because of the religious and political situation in Judea. In spite of the evil plot of the rulers, God's providence was able to use the unacceptable cruelty of the crucifixion to achieve the ultimate will of God (see chapter 8) to renew humanity. Under the circumstance, the crucifixion was the best option for Jesus to accomplish his original mission. The crucifixion and the resurrection have become the means by which God was able to achieve the mission of Jesus: to vindicate the downtrodden and victimized, and restore our human dignity and lost humanity. Jesus saw the limit of his earthly mission at the physical level. His crucifixion was allowed to him so that he could carry out his mission more effectively through the resurrection. We have used diverse metaphors to explain the effect of his death: "ransom," "Christ as Victor," "substitution," "moral influence," and "scapegoat." These metaphors point to the fact that his death reveals God's undying grace as available for the salvation of oppressors in spite of their sins, cruelties, and evil.

Did Jesus have to die in the way and at the time that he did? Yes, it was inevitable that he should die under those circumstances because the political situation under the rules of the Romans and Jewish authorities could not allow Jesus' revolutionary ministry. If had he not died, a national calamity might have occurred because of the confusion he had created, since people regarded him as a political messiah. His death was better than the death of many; as Caiaphas said, "it was better to have one person die for the people" (John 18:14).

To understand Jesus' death more accurately, we might need to draw a bigger picture of why Jesus came into this life. If we had lived the life of love and harmony that God intended in creation, there would have been no need for the coming of Jesus. The sin of humanity necessitated Jesus' birth, service, and death. In this sense, Jesus lived and died for giving his life to humanity, which is traditionally referred to as the expiation of the sin of the world. He sacrificed his life to redeem humanity, not to appease God's anger or God's violated sense of justice. God does not need one more sacrifice to forgive the sins of the world. The symbolic expression of Jesus' sacrifice has been misconstrued at the literal level. If God forgives people's sin by requiring a human sacrifice, God is not a God of forgiveness and grace but a God of retribution. Thus, we need to understand that his blood was shed because of the violence of the offenders or sinners.

To offenders, Jesus' death points to the suffering of the oppressed and victims, calling the offenders to repentance and restitution. For the wounded, Jesus' crucifixion signifies God's woundedness with them. It shows God's love for both the oppressed and the oppressors. To the oppressed, it shows God's solidarity with their suffering. To oppressors, it demonstrates God's love in calling them to repent of their sins and thus reclaim their humanity.

To present Jesus' death as God's punishment for human sin is to mislead. The Hebrew Bible records that God had forgiven sin before Jesus' birth, life, and death. If sacrifice could cleanse our sins apart from our repentance, all we would need to do to live forgiven lives would be to offer a daily sacrifice to God. As God spoke through Amos, we must do away with such sacrifices: "I hate, I despise your festivals, and I take no delight in your solemn assemblies. Even though you offer me your burnt offerings and grain offerings, I will not accept them; and the offerings of well being of your fatted animals I will not look upon. . . . But let justice roll down like waters, and righteousness like an ever-flowing stream" (Amos 5:21-24). If sacrifice is all it takes to cleanse us from sin, if God can declare us righteous without actually effecting our transformation in any way, then God cares little for us. Amos's God demands the restoration of justice and fruits worthy of repentance, instead of ritualistic sacrifices.

We must not think that the penal substitutionary view—God's punishment of Jesus for human sin—is the only way to understand the atonement. To do so is to paint God as bloodthirsty and capricious, cutting shady deals with the devil. We need a new understanding of the atonement. Before Jesus' death, God forgave the Israelites' sins when they repented of their sins. Jesus' own parable of the Lost Son (Luke 15) speaks to the same reality: God as the father forgives the sin of the lost son without reference to the blood of Jesus Christ. It was not because the sin of Israel and the rest of the world were so enormous that Jesus had to come into the world to placate God by his death, but because he wanted to transform the world of injustice and violence through God's love. God wants to forgive our sins if we repent of them. Without repentance, God's forgiveness through the crucifixion does not mean much. The power of God displayed in the crucifixion challenges oppressors to cease their abuse of power. The oppressors crucify God whenever they oppress others. The cross is the profound emblem, both of God's suffering and God's redemption, because it shows God's solidarity with victims and God's rejection of the oppressors' violence. The cross does not wipe out the oppressors, but negates their sins and wrongs. It symbolizes God's never-give-up love toward those who victimize their fellow human beings. Jesus on the cross negates their negation of God's love (Tillich). Justification by faith transpires when the sinners or oppressors accept the fact that Jesus died on the cross because of their sin and that Jesus challenges them to become the people God created them to be.

Collective Justification

The term "justification" derives from Israel's covenantal relationship with God in the Hebrew Bible. God validates Israel collectively on the basis of the covenant that binds them to mutual faithfulness. In some cases (Ps 143), regardless of Israel's worthiness, God will comes to help Israel on the grounds of the covenant. God will not only judge but also vindicate God's people for the honor of God's name (Ps 135:13-14; cf. Ps 43:1).[60] God's nature is righteous, merciful, and truthful so that God justifies the house of Israel (Ps 98:3). Although being victimized by Israel's injustice, God justifies it collectively on the basis of God's mercy and covenant.

In the conversation with Abraham, God said that God would not destroy Sodom if there were ten righteous people in the city (Gen 18:16-33). Ten people could save the city. God could justify the preservation of Sodom for the sake of ten people. We can see the collective dimension of God's grace in treating cities and nations in the Hebrew Bible.

In the New Testament, the church becomes God's people alongside Israel. God anoints and pours the Holy Spirit into the church by grace (Acts 2). On the day of Pentecost, about 120 disciples were all together in one place. They were all filled with the Spirit and spoke in other languages (vv. 1-4). The Spirit collectively infused these different people with the ability to speak in other languages. Regardless of their degree of righteousness, the Holy Spirit anointed them collectively as the instruments of God's message. This experience of the collective immersion in the Spirit engendered the church that is justified by God's redemptive love. The church is not justified by its own merit but by God's grace. That is why it is called the redemptive community. The work of the church is to engender more redemptive works in the world through God's grace.

As a concrete example, the United States has never seriously attempted to make up for the wrong of slavery.[61] Of course, there is no way the United States can fully compensate the victims of slavery. But, it is critical to try to recompense the victims of slavery, even if it is only symbolically. Some Euro Americans say they are not responsible for their ancestors' wrongs regarding slavery. They try to ignore the fact that contemporary African Americans are the real victims of the past system of slavery. But, by some symbolic attempts to make up for the injustice of the slavery, Euro Americans in the United States may be justified by grace, although it will never restore full justice concerning this matter. The example of Germany to the Jewish survivors under the Nazi atrocity shows a way of being "justified" by mercy.

It took seven years from the end of World War II for Germany to begin making reparations payments to Israel to help with the absorption of one-half million survivors of the Holocaust. The 1952 Luxemburg Agreement brought a total of $715 million in German money and goods to Israel, and an additional $107 million to the Conference on Jewish Material Claims for the rehabilitation of Jewish survivors and institutions worldwide.

Some on the political left viewed the Luxemburg Agreement as an insult—$1,500 per murdered Jew!—and a capitulation to America's post-war recruitment of the Nazi-ridden West German government to the anti-Communist cause. But the fact is that the moral currency of Israel and the Jewish people received a boost from the reparations agreement that has yet to be fully spent. The very concept of the Zionist state as an "affirmative action" for Jews and the recent efforts by survivors and their allies to press claims against corporations, banks, and other beneficiaries of Jewish suffering were given lasting credibility by Germany's payment of reparations.[62]

The authors of the above statement made it clear that even though the amount paid to each recipient was not large, the reparations had an effect that was far more than financial. There is still a way by which Euro Americans can receive their justification by God's grace in racial relations; that is, to try to recompense the descendants of the slaves who have not received any compensatory education, monetary assistance, or humane treatment. Since the emancipation, they have been left alone without property, education, and social networks to compete with the educated, established, and socially advantaged; they have been abandoned alone either to swim by themselves or be swept by the strong torrent. Too many have succumbed to the current because they never had the opportunity to learn to swim. There is a great need to establish social funds for their own and their children's education. African Americans have never been treated properly and justly in U.S. history. As the U.S. has paid $20,000 to each survivor of the Japanese American internment, so must it do something equivalent for African Americans, even if what it does is largely symbolic. Through the grace of God and the mercy of African Americans, Euro Americans' efforts to right the past wrongs of slavery might yet become the starting point of their justification. The same principle of collective recompense must be applied to the descendants of Native American massacre victims and other groups of collective victims in the United States.

CHAPTER SEVEN

Healing (Wholeness) and Holiness (Sanctification)

Healing (Wholeness)

Justice will bring forth peace and sacred contentment to the sinned against and naturally lead to healing. Healing means "to make whole or sound in bodily condition," "to restore to health or soundness," "to free from disease or ailment" (*The Oxford English Dictionary*). There are two ways to heal han: transformation and transcendence. Some hans can be healed by transforming their sources, while other hans can be assuaged by transcending their depths. In general, conscious han can be resolved by eradicating han-causing factors; unconscious han will be dissolved by working through the han of others, rising in turn above our own han. Although these two dimensions of han are distinguishable, they are also intertwined, making it difficult to separate the ways in which they can be healed. Some conscious hans can be transcended, and some unconscious hans can be transformed.

Healing is an ongoing process, transpiring gradually under the guidance of the Holy Spirit. Prayer is a vital instrument in healing han. Prayer is significantly effective in healing psychosomatic ills and social evil. Since prayer is foundational in Christian life, I will not treat it separately in our discussion of healing.

Healing includes three aspects. First, it occurs when victims allow the healing stream of the Spirit to flow through them. By letting the Spirit work through them, victims become cleansed from han and experience healing, a gift of God. This in turn transforms them into agents of grace in healing others. Second, healing occurs through self-denial. This involves denying distorted self-images and restoring the image of God in them. Third, as wounded healers they partake in transforming the collective or structural levels of han, making the fragmentary world whole.

The Wounded Healer: The Work of the Paraclete

Han is compressed energy. This energy of han can be used constructively or destructively. When the wounded are preoccupied with their own han, working for the destruction of their enemies, their han will grow more bitter in its agony. When the wounded see others' han beyond their own, moving toward the God of healing, their han will burn as the energy to unravel others' han and han-causing sources.

Mircea Eliade used the term "wounded healer" to describe the function of shamans. The shamans-to-be undergo divine sicknesses when they are initially called by the spirits that have possessed them.[1] Through such experiences of the divine sicknesses they come to heal others. Henry Nouwen in his book *The Wounded Healer* articulates how the wounded can use their hurt and imperfection as an avenue of grace in working for the healing of others. Their own need for healing leads into the healing of others' wounds. The han-ridden can use their own han as the channel of God's healing stream to flow into the healing of others' han. Jesus is the ultimate wounded healer. Through his own woundedness, he heals the wounded. Peter says, "By his wounds you have been healed" (1 Pet 2:24). Jesus embraces the wounded and touches their wounds through his wounds, nursing the wounds of the suffering to healing. Jesus' woundedness is God's han, the ultimate paradigm for the healing of the wounded.

Jesus used the parable of the Good Samaritan (Luke 10) to point out that the robbed was helped by the wounded. The Samaritan used his experience of woundedness to extend his care for the robbed. The priest and the Levite simply passed on by, perhaps because of a lack of wounded experiences. But the Samaritan stopped to assist the injured traveler because of his experience of han. While helping him, the Samaritan must have experienced the healing of his own han vicariously.

Healing takes place in relating to God and others, for it is relational in nature. Being made whole is the natural consequence of deepening our spiritual fellowship with the God of wholeness. The Bible tells us: "Strive first for the kingdom of God and his (God's) righteousness (*justice*), and all these things will be given to you as well" (Matt 6:33).[2] Seeking God's reign and God's justice first, not our own healing, will result in the healing of our wounds. Those victims who strive first for God's reign in other victims' lives can experience God's reign in the present through the work of the Holy Spirit. The Holy Spirit is the One who touches and heals the victims by leading them step by step to their wholeness.

The Holy Spirit had been active before Jesus promised to send the Advocate, the Paraclete: "But the Advocate, the Holy Spirit, whom the Father (God) will send in my name, will teach you everything, and remind you of all that I have said to you" (John 14:25-26). After Jesus' crucifixion and resurrection, the Advocate came. Why did Jesus promise the coming of the Advocate additionally? Is the Advocate different from the Holy Spirit? The Advocate and the Holy Spirit are the same, but the Advocate (Paraclete) can be distinguished from the Holy Spirit. After the crucifixion of Jesus, the Holy Spirit, *pneuma hagion*, was called the Paraclete in the Johannine writings. It is certain that the Holy Spirit who had been with Jesus before the crucifixion went through the excruciating experience of the cross with Jesus. The Holy Spirit was wounded with Jesus and was called the Paraclete, the Comforter, after Jesus' departure (John 16:7, 8, 13). Thus, this Paraclete is the wounded Holy Spirit.

Since the Holy Spirit was wounded through Jesus' crucifixion, she knows the depths of unjust suffering and advocates victims' rights. The Paraclete, the wounded Healer, makes victims well through by empowering them to become wounded healers. She wastes no experience of victims and makes use of their hurt for the healing of the world.

> Blessed be . . . the God of all consolation, who consoles us in all our affliction, so that we may be able to console those who are in any affliction with the consolation with which we ourselves are consoled by God. For just as the sufferings of Christ are abundant for us, so also our consolation is abundant through Christ. (2 Cor 1:3-5)

Here the term "consolation" in Greek is *paraklēsis*. God can console us because Jesus represents God's suffering with us in history. The way God comforts us is the way the Holy Spirit undergoes suffering within us. Consoling is the attribute and work of the Holy Spirit, the Paraclete, the Crucified One in our suffering. The Paraclete is the Spirit that knows the han of human beings: "Likewise the Spirit helps us in our weakness; for we do not know how to pray as we ought, but that very Spirit intercedes with sighs too deep to words" (Rom 8:26).

The God who has undergone the crucifixion understands our affliction. Found only in the Fourth Gospel and in 1 John 2:1 in the New

Testament, the Paraclete is the Spirit who continues the work of consoling the wounded. Some translations use "Comforter," "Helper," "Advocate," yet the term *Paraclete* can hardly be translatable in a single word. The Greeks employed the word in diverse situations. In a court, a paraclete might be an advocate called in to speak on behalf of another, support, intercede for another, or defend another.[3]

The word *comfort* comes from the Latin *fortis*, "brave" or "strong," and a comforter was the one who makes dispirited people brave (or strong). The comforter in this sense is different from our common usage, which usually refers to the one who sympathizes with people in sorrow. The Comforter is the Spirit that is at work in the community.[4] Through our experience of han, we may not just suffer from it, but also receive the opportunity to understand others' han. We are not wounded meaninglessly. *In the Voice of a Child* by Judy Emerson takes us into the experience of a survivor of child sexual abuse and helps us see how she discovered freedom and wholeness. The sexual abuse generated a festering wound that could not heal in a milieu of family secrecy and denial. Breaking the silence of the secret and bringing her wound into the open were the gates for her to release the poison of sexual abuse. Ten years later, Emerson was working as a child and family therapist, specializing in child sexual abuse.[5]

To comfort others in affliction is to partake of the Spirit's work. To heal others' han is the way we let the Paraclete work in us and through us. As we work for the healing of others' han, the Spirit touches our own han and works through it. As we become healed, we become more involved in healing others.

Once, Peter's mother-in-law was in bed with fever. Jesus healed her, and she immediately attended to the needs of others. She might have needed a little time to resume her energy, but she worked for Jesus and his disciples immediately. She was healed to help others and was fully healed in the process of helping others. We will be healed in the midst of comforting, working for, and strengthening others. Healing is not our work, but the Spirit's. As we open ourselves to the Holy Spirit, the Spirit moves into our hearts, opens our han, and sublimates it into transforming energy.

Self-denial

Self-denial is another way to heal our han. Jesus says, "If any want to become my followers, let them deny themselves and take up their cross daily and follow me" (Luke 9:23). Self-denial is an essential step in following Jesus. The wounded have already experienced the denial of their worth by the offender. Thus, for them, self-denial means negating, not their true selves, but the false construction of who they are created by those who have victimized them.

Self-denial is self-emptying in reality. There are two selves: the inauthentic (false) self and the authentic (true) self. An inauthentic self is the self projected by the offender, and the authentic self is the self created by God. Self-denial is to empty our inauthentic self and to let our authentic self live. It is an act of negation of the negated self, followed by affirmation of the true self in Christ. This authentic self is the image of God in us. Emptying is not merely an act of ridding ourselves of our inauthentic self, but also an act of allowing the fullness of the image of God in us to become real.

This self-emptying process will help the wounded transcend the aspects of han that cannot be resolved or overcome. Tragic events are irrevocable, and the loss of loved ones is irreplaceable. Those irresolvable dimensions of han can be transcended by emptying our han-filled self. By emptying the self, we can touch the depth of the self where God dwells because God is closer to our self, even than we are (Luther). Emptying our false self is to find the authentic self that God created in us.

Structural Healing

Individual healing is closely interwoven with structural healing. It is difficult to heal individual hans apart from structural hans.

The parable of the Good Samaritan (Luke 10:29-37) can illustrate this point. If we pay attention only to the one who was robbed, we will improve the safety of travelers around Jericho little. To help travelers on the road to Jericho, we need to deal with the problem of robbers. Otherwise, there will be more victims. It is also necessary to learn why robbers flourish in the region, if we desire to fundamentally help travelers. If regional poverty and unemployment are the reasons for the spread of robbers, these issues need to be addressed. Since structural changes will fundamentally remove the dangers that the travelers face, good Samaritans will invest their time and energy into the change of social structures in addition to attending on victims. Christians are called to be good Samaritans in this world. Being Christians involves the wisdom of knowing how to transform the han-causing structures of our society such as sexism, racism, plutocracy, handicappism, empire building, and the postcolonial expansion of transnational corporations.

If a woman's han of racial discrimination is healed at the personal level while the society remains racist, the healing of her han means little because she will be hurt again by its racist structures. If a battered wife's han is healed at the personal level, yet the family structures that caused the abuse remain, it is a certainty that upon returning to her family she will be battered again. Her family structure of abuse and the patriarch of the culture need to be changed for the full healing of spousal abuse.

Deeper healing transpires if the wounded can get involved in transforming the systems that cause social han. For instance, many victims of child abuse often work for the preventions of child abuse, victims of hate crimes for hate crimes prevention bills, victims of violent shootings for gun control, battered wives for a change in the patriarchal system behind abusive relationships, and victims of racial violence for the change of a racist society and culture. Victims' commitments to social transformation will stop turning the wheel of the vicious cycle of violence that reproduces systemic evil.

The following illustration further points to the indispensability of structural change for the well-being of individuals.

> One day, people in a township noticed several persons screaming for help as they were being floated downstream by the river's rapid currents. The villagers immediately rescued the victims from the turbulent waters. As time went on, they, however, found more people carried downstream by the river. Research revealed that the bridge farther up the river had been partially broken.
>
> As more people were carried downstream, the villagers increased their annual budget to the problem. They hired permanent rescue teams, developed more sophisticated rescue equipment, trained more volunteers, and even built a hospital. Every one was so busy with his or her rescue work that the bridge repair was not considered. Thus, more bodies kept floating down.[6]

This story teaches us the significance of systemic changes in the wholeness of society. The church has paid a great deal of attention to individual victims, building hospitals to heal their wounds. Yet it has done little to prevent such victimization in the future. It has been busy with saving individuals but has neglected in seeing why so many victims fall into open holes and float down the river. The church urgently needs to focus its energy on how to prevent the causes of victimization, without neglecting the needs of current victims.

A problem caused by han is not a mere occasion of its cure, but a God-given opportunity to improve a regrettable condition in which we find ourselves and expand the reign of God around us. It can be compared with a sickness. When we catch a cold, it is a warning for us to slow down, pointing possibly to a deeper problem. It is time for us not only to treat the cold symptoms but also to rest and strengthen our weakened immune system, a real cause of the cold. Through a sickness, we can locate the deeper problems of our health and use the opportunity to improve our health beyond treating its symptoms.

Likewise, healing han is a good opportunity to improve the condition of our lives and our society simultaneously. Fundamental healing for wounded individuals transpires if they are involved in a worthy and higher cause for changing the system that injures people. As they realize the greater meaning of their mission in building the community of God, they will experience deep satisfaction.

The Holy Spirit uses the wounded to attend the injured and to bring forth structural changes through them. The Holy Spirit orchestrates the works of the wounded to heal individuals, a society, a nation, and the world. The Holy Spirit searches all things, even the depths of God (1 Cor 2:10), and searches the culprits of han and treats them at fundamental levels.

Holiness (Sanctification)

After being justified, sinners pursue their life according to the will of God. That life of following the will of God is the process of sanctification, being made holy.

On one level, sanctification means being set apart, made separate from the world. Yet at a deeper level holiness is simply about being made whole. The idea of holiness comes from the practice of animal selection for cultic rituals. "If the offering is a sacrifice of well-being, if you offer an animal of the herd, whether male or female, you shall offer one without blemish before the LORD" (Lev 3:1). Wholesome and flawless animals were selected to be sacrificed. The origin of holiness can be seen in the case of setting wholesome animals apart for sacrifices. Holiness emerges not only from set-apartness but also from unity, purity, completeness, and perfection.[7] Holiness is unity, entirety, and wholeness. Thus, being a holy person or a saint means being a whole person—not unilateral, not fragmented, and not exclusive.

For Martin Luther, being holy meant depending on the grace of God alone for our Christian life. We are justified by God's grace alone and are sanctified by the same. We are not really righteous, but God ascribes righteousness to us. In the same manner we are unholy, but God's grace makes it possible for God to treat us as though we were holy. Thus, we remain sinners as well as saints (*simul justus et peccator*) even after being justified and sanctified. This paradoxical existence of Christians brings forth gradual transformation into righteousness in a life of ups and downs. We become holy, but slowly, because of our persistent sinfulness. Luther said:

> And such faith, renewal, and forgiveness of sins is followed by good works. And what there is still sinful or imperfect also in them shall not be accounted as sin or defect, even (and that, too) for Christ's sake; but the entire man, both as to his person and his works, is to be called and to be righteous and holy from pure grace and mercy, shed upon us (unfolded) and spread over us in Christ.[8]

Consequently, holiness signifies the state of being covered by God's grace. It is not far off from justification because we remain sinners even in our holiness.

Calvin understood sanctification in line with justification. Those who are justified become sanctified, not by their own efforts, but by God's irresistible grace. To him, election is the key to understanding our sanctification: "In the additional statement that they were elected that they might be holy, the apostle openly refutes the error of those who deduce election from prescience, since he declares that whatever virtue appears in men is the result of election."[9] Using Paul's theology, he concludes that sanctification takes place by God's election.

To Calvin, true sanctification produces good works, connected to justification through election. Good works are the fruits of election given to us in Jesus Christ before the world began. The believers are called to be holy and blameless before God in love.

For Wesley, after justification we become holy in actuality by God's grace. While Luther and Calvin focused on justification, treating the transformed life of believers as secondary, Wesley emphasized the life of sanctification based on justification as its foundation. He desired to strive to be holy, not resigning into a nonprogressive and passive Christian life. So he made a logical distinction between justification and the new birth.

> But though it be allowed, that justification and the new birth are, in point of time, inseparable from each other, yet are they easily distinguished, as being not the same, but things of a widely different nature. Justification implies only a relative, the new birth a real, change. God in justifying us does something for us; in begetting us again, he does the work in us. The former changes our outward relation to God, so that of enemies we become children; by the latter our inmost souls are changed, so that of sinners we become saints.[10]

Wesley understood justification as a form and the new birth as its content. In other words, justification is going home and the new birth is the beginning of a new life at home. The new birth is the beginning of sanctification, without which justification is empty:

> What is justification? This was the Second thing which I proposed to show. And it is evident, from what has been already observed, that it is not the being made actually just and righteous.
> This is sanctification; which is, indeed, in some degree, the immediate fruit of justification, but, nevertheless, is a distinct gift of God, and of a totally different nature. The one implies what God does for us through his Son; the other, what he works in us by his Spirit. So that, although some rare instances may be found, wherein the term justified or justification is used in so wide a sense as to include sanctification also.[11]

Although justification depends on the work of Jesus Christ and sanctification counts on the work of the Holy Spirit, we need both Jesus and the Spirit for our turning and growing. For Wesley, the new life, which is synonymous with "conversion," is instantaneous, while sanctification is gradual in believers' lives.

Differentiating itself from the Protestant Reformers, the Roman Catholic Church highlights the actuality of holiness by sanctifying grace. The Council of Trent declared that justification involves not only forgiveness of sin but also holiness and renewal of a sinner by means of willingly receiving sanctifying grace and other supernatural gifts (Trent, l. c., cap. vii). A single act of God effects freedom from sin and holiness. For, just as light dispels darkness, so does the infusion of sanctifying grace drive out original and mortal sin from the soul (Cf. Trent, sess. VI).

Sanctification slowly occurs, according to the teaching of the Roman Catholic Church, as we proceed on a gradually upward path.

Collective Holiness

Israel is a nation pursuing a collective holiness. Israel is a holy nation. God made it holy through the covenant: "Now therefore, if you obey my voice and keep my covenant, you shall be my treasured possession out of all the peoples. Indeed, the whole earth is mine, but you shall be for me a priestly kingdom and a holy nation" (Exod 19:5-6). Isaiah relates the reality of holiness to the character of Yahweh, and Ezekiel explains how the God of the covenantal relationship acts for the purpose of God's holiness and urges Israel to follow God's holiness.[12]

In the New Testament, Paul was convinced one moment that nothing in creation, including death or life, can separate him from the love of God in Jesus Christ (Rom 8:38-39). In the next moment, he confessed that if he could save his own people, he would not mind being cut off from Jesus: "I have great sorrow and unceasing anguish in my heart. For I could wish that I myself were accursed and cut off from Christ for the sake of my own people, my kindred according to the flesh" (Rom 9:2-3). This spirit of laying down one's own salvation for her or his own people is the essence of Paul's missionary theology, the spirit of collective holiness.

When Peter experienced the Holy Spirit, he preached the gospel of Jesus Christ, and then about three thousand people repented of their sin, creating a new community of fellowship. It is incredible that all believers were together and had all things in common (Acts 2:44). They sold their possessions and shared the proceeds with all according to each individual's need. Day by day, they spent time together in the temple and praised God with the goodwill of all the people, sharing their food with generosity (2:44-47). This community of the believers was practicing collective holiness until the time of the Jerusalem persecution (Acts 8). The church is *ecclesia*, a community called out to meet together for holy or holistic missions. It is the community of faith that ought to elevate the holiness of its various members and pursue their common holiness. Pursuing individual holiness has its place in the church, but must be balanced with collective holiness. Until we achieve community holiness, individual holiness will remain abstract. As Wesley said, there is no other holiness than social holiness. Since holiness involves wholeness, holy people seek community holiness.

CHAPTER EIGHT

Jubilee and Christian Perfection

Jubilee

The wounded need to live their lives to the full in spite of the trouble in their lives. The life of joy is the best life there is; it is the kind of life God desires that we should live, contrary to our unfavorable circumstances. If the wounded miss the opportunity to live their lives fully and joyfully, that is the great loss of true precious life to God and to them.

This concluding chapter highlights exalting God as the definitive way to maximize our potential in life. Exalting God must transpire in each step of our journey to liberation, not only in its last step. It is the most excellent way to live the liberation of life.

Exalting God

Why do we exalt God in the midst of a troublesome life? The reason is that God is deeply present there with specific plans for us. Paul holds that all things work together for good in God (Rom 8:28). God has concrete plans or providence for each of us. To exalt means to welcome God's plan for us. It entails two acts: rejoicing and thanking. Paul exhorts us: "Rejoice always, pray without ceasing, give thanks in all circumstances; for this is the will of God in Christ Jesus for you" (1 Thess 5:16-18). To him rejoicing comes even before praying. In fact, rejoicing is a potent form of prayer. We should rejoice in God and be thankful in all circumstances, not only in some.

Frank Foglio, author of *Hey, God!* had one daughter who was involved in an automobile accident. Her brain was severely damaged, and her condition deteriorated rapidly in spite of thousands of prayers for her recovery. She was finally transferred to the ward of a mental institution for hopeless patients.

> Seven years passed and there was no glimpse of hope. One day he was on the way to the institution, angry at God: 'How could you be a God of love? I wouldn't permit such a thing to happen to my daughter if I had the power to prevent it. You could heal her. But You won't. Don't You love people as much as even I do? You must not.' 'Praise me,' a voice spoke to him. 'What for?' he retorted. 'Praise Me that your daughter is where she is.' 'Never!' he spit out. 'I would rather die than do that.' He remembered, however, listening to a tape about thanksgiving in all things. The Voice repeated the command. He replied, 'God, I couldn't praise You if I tried. And I'm not going to try, because I don't believe I should.' A little later, he confessed, 'I would praise You, but You would have to help me.' After arriving at the institution, he wondered why he would come to see her who could not recognize him at all. When he heard the Voice of God the third time, his heart of stone, anger, bitterness, and resentment began to melt. Choked with emotion, he surrendered to the Voice, whispering 'Okay, God. I thank You that my daughter is where she is. I know that You love her more than I do.' That day his daughter could recognize him for the first time after the accident. He says, 'Tell everyone our daughter is home now with us. We know that God always wants us to praise Him (God), regardless of how things look.'[1]

This story shows us that it is God's will for us to praise God in a heartbreaking situation. But why do we have to praise God in tragedies? Isn't Folio right when he said that he should not praise God for his daughter's accident? I believe that he is right in terms of refusing to praise God because of the accident. It does not make any sense to offer our praise to God for a tragic event. Yet we must praise God because of God's presence with us and God's plan for us. In the midst of tragedy, God is there with us, for us, and in us. God suffers alongside victims and works for their healing and for the restoration of justice. This is the reason why we exalt God even in tragedies.

In the time of trouble, we need to focus on God, not on the trouble itself. When a tragic event happens to us, we naturally focus on the event. It is not easy for us to see God beyond the tragedy. When we see God even in the midst of such han-producing tragic events, we may find the strength to transcend and heal the pain of our injuries. Understanding God's providence for our lives provides a fundamental foundation for our healing, hope, and bliss. God's providence is not the same as God's predestination or fate; it is God's plan. Providence is an open plan while predestination is a closed, predetermined plan. God has a plan for each person and each group. If we realize that God has a benevolent providence for each of us, we will be joyful and will more willingly partake of God's plan for us.

Then, why do unfair tragedies happen to us? Isn't God all-powerful? Why can't God stop or eradicate evil from our world? Is it the will of God that we suffer? It is clear in the Bible that our suffering from evil is not the will of God. However, God allows us to suffer from evil in certain circumstances because God created people with freedom. In spite of all human evil, God seeks to bring good out of all situations.

In his little book *The Will of God*, Leslie Weatherhead presents three wills of God: the intentional will of God, the circumstantial will of God, and the ultimate will of God. God has ideal plans for us and does not desire us to suffer from evil (the intentional will of God). God does not use force to restrain people's abuse of freedom with which they hurt others, causing evil in the world, yet God has plans within given situations (the circumstantial will of God). God, nevertheless, will not abandon God's intentional will but fulfills it through God's circumstantial will. "No evil is finally able to defeat God or cause any 'value' to be lost."[2] God finally realizes God's purpose (the ultimate will of God).

I differ slightly from Weatherhead. I believe that our response can either fulfill or foil God's purpose. If we exalt God's will, God's power is free to act upon us. Yet by rejecting God's will in favor of our own desires, our refusal to trust in effect limits the divine will. Although there is no guarantee that the intentional will of God will be realized at the end, God's ultimate will is to make the most of tragic events for our own good. God is mighty in accomplishing God's will toward us. God's mightiness, however, has been misunderstood for ages. It is not the arbitrary or one-sided power with which God is able to do anything God wants. Rather, it is the strength with which God cares for us and actualizes our potential. God is all powerful, not in controlling or forcing us, but in caring for and loving us. God's cogency will win over our hearts and make everything beautiful or meaningful in the end (the ultimate will). Thus, we trust in God and exalt God for all things, including tragic or unfair incidents because of God's presence in them.

When Paul and Silas were wrongly accused, beaten, and thrown into a prison in Philippi, they were "praying and singing hymns to God" at midnight (Acts 16:11-40). Then an earthquake happened, opened all the doors, and unfastened all the chains of the prisoners. Paul and Silas, the victims of injustice, exalted God, instead of complaining to or blaming God and others for their agony. False accusations, illegal beatings, unjust incarceration; none of these could define Paul and Silas's state of mind. Their exaltation of God shook the foundation of the prison and opened the doors. Their adoration based on their love of God could not be suppressed by external conditions and opened all the doors and unfastened everyone's chains in the prison.

Exalting God unleashes the power of the Spirit freely to do the work of God in us and for us. Our thanksgiving opens all the doors of our frozen prison of affliction, and our elation releases us from all the harsh chains of pain and oppression.

Joseph's story is inspirational because of his life of exalting God. Although his own brothers sold him into Egypt, Joseph did not seek vengeance on them but instead saw God's invisible hand behind all the tragedies he had suffered. He forgave them when he had total control over their lives and comforted them by saying, "And now do not be distressed, or angry with yourselves, because you sold me here; for God sent me before you to preserve life. For the famine has been in the land these two years; and there are five more years in which there will be neither plowing nor harvest. God sent me before you to preserve for you a remnant on earth. . ." (Gen 45:5-7). He believed in and lived in God's providence by focusing on God's generous ultimate plan, not on his brothers' evil plot. A deep joy can gush from us when we understand that we are in God's providence and act according to God's gracious plan.

I have seen in my own experience that exalting God in spite of hardship has not only released me from suffering and agony, it has revitalized my energy and joy in life. On a number of occasions, I have transcended the power of injustice and absurdity of the world by the strength of exulting in God. My reluctant move from California to Ohio was one of those occasions.

My teaching career started in Southern California. Because of various circumstances, I had to look for a job elsewhere. This entailed selling my house in California just as housing prices there had hit rock bottom. When we sold the house, we lost the down payment plus two years of subsidy for renting it. Fortunately, I soon found a teaching position in a school in Dayton, Ohio. Although I had no initial enthusiasm for moving to Dayton, Ohio, I held on to my life of exalting God, keeping my inner joy alive and believing in God's providence. Rendering exaltation to God sustained and strengthened my grateful and joyful life in the midst of a difficult transition.

As soon as our family moved to Ohio, the severe cough from which I had suffered in California—almost certainly caused by the polluted air there—cleared up. In hindsight, I can see God's careful plan clearly: If I had stayed in California, my body could not have survived the harsh environment for many more years. I realized why God moved our family to Dayton. I regained my health, which I had lost in California, and God's grace restored our financial loss. Furthermore, I have really enjoyed teaching students in my present school. Moreover, Jane, my spouse, who had to quit her tenured position in a California college because of my move, found a teaching position (an internally publicized position) in a local community college even before we moved to Dayton. My experience is that God has provided according to our needs and has closely cared about us. Since Jane and I realized God's providence in our life, we have had deeper elation inside in spite of difficult circumstances. This story is one of several occasions in which we have experienced the unmistakable presence of God. Many times we have experienced either no change in circumstances or changes into worse circumstances through our practice of exalting God; yet we have increased our joyful life in exalting God. We exalt God regardless of our conditions.

Whenever Jane and I were in intense distress because of unfairness, injustice, exclusion, failures, and sickness, we encouraged each other to exalt God for God's providence. Indeed, we have experienced the healing stream of the Holy Spirit that surrounds us and reinvigorates our energy of life. Exalting God always brought forth transformation—sometimes a transformation of the external circumstances that created the hardship in the first place, and other internal transformation, allowing us to respond to those situations out of hope and joy rather than bitterness and despair. Whether God changes the external circumstances or our inner response to them, we are called to exalt God, the ultimate expression of trusting and loving God. This confession itself wells up from an attitudinal change. Habakkuk articulates this attitudinal transformation best:

Though the fig tree does not blossom,
and no fruit is on the vines;
though the produce of the olive fails
and the fields yield no food;

145

though the flock is cut off from the fold
and there is no herd in the stalls,
yet I will rejoice in the LORD;
I will exult in the God of my salvation. (3:17-18)

Victims need not despair at seeing injustice and tragedies, but must rejoice and thank God because of God's plan. God does not despair. Thus, we must not despair, either. This is the reason why Paul exhorted his fellow Christians: "Finally, my brothers and sisters, rejoice in the Lord" (Phil 3:1). He said this in a prison. In any circumstance, we do not look at a tragedy only, but see God who is there in the form of the crucified.

Exalting God consists of two things: thanksgiving and joy. It is the act of approving, honoring, and glorifying God.

Thanksgiving

Thanksgiving is to express gratitude, especially to God. It is a genuine recognition and celebration of God's goodness. Thanksgiving arises from our trust in God. It is an act of full trust in God's gracious plan for us.

A sage said that if she had to choose between pain and nothingness, she would take pain. It is better to experience something than nothing. Even pain itself becomes a source of gratitude. Whenever I feel despair or loss, I reduce myself to nothing. Then everything I experience becomes something. The meaning of life is to choose to experience something, rather than nothing. Between to be and not to be, thanksgiving to God means to choose "to be."

Job suffered tragedies, and his wife counseled him to curse God and die. Instead, he confessed that he would put his trust in God although God may slay him (13:15). Our full trust in God affirms that God's justice and truth will be fulfilled in this life and beyond. God is benevolent and generous. For those who are called by God and who love God, everything works for good in the end (Rom 8:28).

Even in crises, we are grateful because of God's intimate presence with us. An ungrateful heart blocks the flow of a healing stream, but a grateful heart lets it run. Sometimes we feel that gratitude to God seems to be a duty rather than a joy; sometimes we think that it represents an attempt to curry favors with God. When we fix our eyes upon our own self—our success, prosperity, and achievement—gratitude turns into an obligation. However, when we grow beyond our self-centered life into a life that centers itself on God, our gratitude becomes overflowing. Expressing thanks to God cannot be a manipulation to get what we want from God, but it can and must express our trust in the divine goodness and faithfulness to us. By thanking God, we open the door of our hearts to God so that God may dwell in us.

God appreciates the appreciation we express to God. My two sons frequently voice their gratitude for their mother's cooking dinner—and once in a while my cooking of breakfast. Whenever they display their appreciation this way, how it gladdens us! God is grateful when we are grateful for God and God's work. The depths of our gratitude and our trust in God grow together.

In an interview, poet and writer Maya Angelou shared a poignant story about an experience she had in the early 1950s. She had returned to the United States from Europe, leaving behind a child. She said:

> One day I was very frightened for my sanity. . . . So I went to my voice teacher and told him I was going mad. He said, 'Here's a yellow pad. Write your blessings.' I said, 'Oh, please, I don't want to even hear that. I'm going crazy.' He said, 'Start with the fact that you can hear me, that you can see the page, that you can hold the pen.' Before I reached the end of the page I was transformed. So, everything I have written, every book, every stage play, every screenplay, was written on a yellow pad. As soon as I pick it up, I am reminded of my blessings.[3]

Thankfulness is like a tree. If we plant it in our hearts, it grows slowly toward heaven, raising up its branches, flourishing its green leaves, and bearing fruit to enrich our lives. "*Gratitude* may begin as a pinprick of light, but soon its light dissolves a roomful of darkness."[4] As our hearts are filled with thankfulness, praise gushes from them in joy. The more we thank God for our lives, the profounder we become *to be*. Thankfulness deconstructs our unconscious and conscious han, and reconstructs our lives in trusting God.

Joy

Bud Osborn, a Canadian poet and a street activist, e-mailed me after reading my book *The Wounded Heart of God*. "How can I resolve so much han in me?" he asked. Reading his life story and his poetry was a moving experience for me.[5] His life epitomizes the essence of han. His request for help was urgent. My reply was: "Joy is the most effective way to resolve han."

Joy is the inward experience and outward expression of thankful ela-tion. It is a source of satisfaction. A jubilant joy springs from delighting in somebody or something. Furthermore, a deep joy wells up from a rela-tionship with somebody—for Christians, from our loving relationship with God.

Albert Camus said that neither human beings nor the world is absurd, but for human beings to be in the world is absurd because we are strangers in the world. We cannot build a world that denies or surpasses the absurdity and limits of our existence in the world, but we can revolt against absurdity of the world. "Rebellion" was his way of constructing a society of moderation, truth, and justice through a human solidarity.[6] Likewise, Christians need to resist injustice, absurdity, and evil in the world, but we ultimately overcome the world of injustice and absurdity by rejoicing, not by resisting alone. It is the best way to transcend and surmount this absurd world.

"Rejoice always, pray without ceasing, give thanks in all circumstances; for this is the will of God in Christ Jesus for you" (1 Thess 5:16-18), instructs Paul. Rejoicing is the will of God. Paul places it even before praying. In fact, rejoicing is the most effective way of praying to God. Rejoicing, praying, and thanksgiving will fulfill the will of God in our life.

Joy is the way of Christian discipleship. Our existence centers on the joy of God. Regardless of our situations, we do not lose our joy in God. We are privileged to express the joy in God in life. Joy in God cannot be defeated. The psalmist declares, "Because he (God) is at my right hand, I shall not be moved. Therefore my heart is glad, and my soul rejoices; my body also rests secure. . . .You show me the path of life. In your presence there is full-ness of joy; in your right hand are pleasures forevermore" (Ps 16: 8, 9, 11).[7] Where God is, there is the fullness of joy. Joy is the unambiguous mark of God's presence. Nehemiah declares that the joy of God is our strength (Neh 8:10). Joy is God's vigor to surmount han in life, and it is God's energy to replenish our heart. Joy is dynamic. It has the power that trans-forms and refreshes us and the people around us. Thus, the most important fruit of the Holy Spirit is love, while the second is joy (Gal 5:22).

The Joy of the Sabbath in Creation

Healing by the strength of the Holy Spirit brings wholeness to the wounded. As healing takes place, the Holy Spirit invites the wounded to the Spirit's table of Sabbath.[8]

The universe is the manifestation of God's joy. God completed the creation of the universe in seven days. The Sabbath symbolizes God's joy of creation. God worked for the creation of the universe for six days and on the seventh God rested. Without this seventh day, God's creation never completes. The Sabbath, the day of rest, crowns God's creation (Gen 2:1-4). Even before the seventh day, God looked at God's own creation every evening and said that it was good. That means that God enjoyed God's own work every night. In the evening God stopped working and enjoyed God's own creation. Every evening was a little Sabbath for God. On the sixth day God created human beings according to the image of God and enjoyed them. And then God fully rested on the seventh day.

Was God really tired when God chose to rest on the seventh day? Of course not. Isaiah said that God does not faint or grow weary (Isa 40:28). On the seventh day God *truly* rested. This true rest means that God delighted in all the beings and things God created. The Sabbath does not denote doing nothing, but rather genuinely enjoying God's work. By introducing the Sabbath to us, God asks us to enjoy our own lives as God's creation. Enjoyment does not mean to attain whatever we desire, but to use the gifts that God has given us for others and for ourselves. Enjoying signifies to appreciate and celebrate what God has done for us, in us, with us, and through us, and to place the fruition of that work at the feet of God and neighbor. As God creates us in God's own image, God asks us to complete God's creative work by resting well. The best rest is rejoicing. The image of God is joy, pointing to the fact that we are the face of God's joy.

We are too busy with our lives to stop to appreciate God and God's joy in creating us. We rush all the time. "Time is too precious to waste by rushing it."[9] We need to learn to rest in God's joyful plan for us. Even the healing of our wounds should not be the focal point of life. Nothing should preoccupy our lives except God. The Sabbath arises with the understanding that we honor the aim of God's creation by partaking of God's joy through love. The wounded really need to rest in the joy of God in creation. The Sabbath is home for the wounded and for the tired in this restless world. Sabbath transpires whenever we find true rest in the Spirit of joy. After the Sabbath we do not face "Monday" in the creation story.[10] True rest knows no Monday and no anxiety about our being and doing.

Sabbatical God made the seventh day holy by separating it from all other days. Resting is interpenetrated with holiness by the divine designation. It is the will of God for us to keep our rest holy. The Sabbath and

Jubilee are God's will toward us so that we can enjoy God's world by recreating and rejuvenating ourselves.

The Joy of the Sabbath in the Midst of Trouble

The Sabbath points to the fact that victims celebrate God's triumph in the midst of their struggle against injustice and evil. The Sabbath does not happen at the end of the week only, but transpires with our deep awareness of God's presence in trouble. In this sense, the Sabbath is not a particular day, but rather awareness. While resolving han and transforming the life of han, we savor gratitude, joy, peace, and eternal feast in observing the holy Sabbath. Sabbatical joy overflows from God's blessed creation when we celebrate adversities with God's care.

Jesus freed the Sabbath from human control by declaring that he is the ruler of the Sabbath. While the scribes and the Pharisees tried to chain people by forcing them to "rest" on the seventh day, Jesus freed them by having them enjoy their Sabbath. He said that the Sabbath exists for people, not the other way around.

To the victims of religious and social oppression, Jesus declared, "Come to me, all you that are weary and are carrying heavy burdens, and I will give you rest" (Matt 11:28). Jesus promised them a Sabbath. More accurately speaking, Jesus is himself the Sabbath for the victims! Jesus means repose in the midst of a storm, freedom in the midst of oppression, and gusto in the midst of sorrow. With Jesus we cannot afford to live under the despondence and despair of life, but experience full joy even in the midst of our han. A wise rabbi once said that on the judgment day God would ask us about unutilized joys that we could have enjoyed.

Most victims of sin or crime suffer from the pang of wounds and rarely actualize the joy of life because of God. They hardly find the Sabbath in their wounded lives. One goal for them might be that they find some kind of joy by the time their life's journey has come to its end. A better way, however, would be for the wounded to begin to live joyful lives now by embracing their own wounds. Christian joy can be experienced in the middle of every life journey, particularly in crises and tragedies.

Joy of a Feast and the Last Supper

In the Bible, joy is connected to a feast. Heavenly joy is expressed as a banquet. According to the book of Job, the universe starts with joy:

"Where were you when I laid the foundation of the earth? . . . when the morning stars sang together and all the heavenly beings shouted for joy?" (38:4, 7). According to the New Testament, the world will end with a banquet of marriage, which will be filled with joy: "And the angel said to me, 'Write this: Blessed are those who are invited to the marriage supper of the Lamb' " (Rev 19:9).

Jesus performed his first miracle at a wedding banquet. The banquet is the place in life where the miracle of God transpires. It is the symbolism of God's joyous presence. The banquet that the father threw for the son who returned home epitomizes the joy of Jubilee (Luke 15). The son rejoiced with his father, yet the father's joy was exceeded his son's; it was an overwhelming joy because his son restored his joy of life once again. No sooner had his son come back home than his shame, unbearable burden, and wound were all immediately uplifted and resolved, and he burst into joy. The feast points to a time of Jubilee when forgiveness transpires, reconciliation takes place, and joy fills the house.

The most important symbol of Christian banquet is the Eucharist. The Passover is the most important Jewish celebration, while the Last Supper is the Christian equivalent. The Last Supper signifies a deep joy for Christians. For the early church, it was a joyous celebration, not a somber ceremony. Inferring from Acts 2:46-47: "Day by day, as they spent much time together in the temple, they broke bread at home and ate their food with glad and generous hearts, praising God and having the goodwill of all the people." Lietzmann contends that the Jerusalem church celebrated its Lord's Supper with festive joy and as a continuation of the daily fellowship at meals with the earthly Jesus.[11] The early church gave to this recurring feast the name *Eucharist*, which derives from the Greek *eucharistia*, meaning gratefulness or thanksgiving. The Eucharist symbolizes the heavenly banquet of thanksgiving on earth (Calvin and Wesley). It renders thankfulness to God in spite of the heartbreak of life. Jesus celebrated his Last Supper on the eve of the crucifixion.

It was a Jewish custom to render praise to God for each dish and to end the meal with a benediction. Mark 14:23 ("Then he took a cup, and after giving thanks he gave it to them, and all of them drank from it.") shows the act of praise at the end of the meal. This is a stylistic variant for the act of praise (*eulogeō*) mentioned at the beginning of the meal.[12]

The Eucharist affirms joy and thanksgiving in this fragmentary life, indicating that we are united with Christ, the joy of God. Jesus gave thanks to God for the supper that they were about to receive, even as the crucifixion lay immediately ahead of him. The dinner was an occasion of celebration, in spite of the han that Jesus' impending death had created. Before the event of the crucifixion, Jesus declared, "But take courage; I have conquered the world!" (John 16:33). The Eucharist is not only the visible sign of invisible grace but also the visible symbol of thankfulness and victory in time of sorrow, agony, and uncertainty.

The Joy of the Sabbath Faith

The Sabbath does not arise from something we have accomplished by the end of a week, but arrives at our decision of faith. It is freely given to us. We don't have to claim it after our hard work, but it is something that we take from God with thankfulness. It is the banquet graciously prepared by God to which we are invited. This idea of the Sabbath as a gift corresponds to the Sabbath by faith, which is compatible with the doctrine of "the justification by faith." We usually assume joy as a result of our own sweat. The acronym "TGIF" (Thank God It's Friday) represents this cultural ethos.[13] Can we say "TGIM"? Is it too early to celebrate Monday since we do not deserve it? Do we really have to wait until the weekend to celebrate? In this culture of earning joy as the reward of our hard work, we need to celebrate joy as God's gift freely given to us.

Joy as Relationship

Joy is intense and exuberant happiness. True joy is our awakening to the fact that God is intensely present where we are. It is an intense, overwhelming desire for us to know the ultimate beyond our grasp. Joy comes from a relationship. When two lovers meet, joy occurs between them. Then, joy is the outcome of love (St. Thomas). Love requires the other. Joy takes place as we are related to the other. Lasting true joy wells up when we are related to our own Creator, who has infused our lives with purpose. When the mother is around her child, the child will be joyful. From the beginning we are molded to be with God, our Creator. Only our intimate relationship with God engenders genuine joy.

There is a story about a genuine joy that derives from a relationship. During the gold rush, a group of forty-niners went to a small town in Oregon. Tired from a long futile journey, they were unhappy, depressed, and irascible. Their behavior in the tavern—cursing and fighting with one another—displayed their ill temper. The next day they disappeared from the town.

A week later they came back to the tavern with mysteriously joyful faces. Their attitudes were changed; no one caroused, cursed, or fought. They calmly drank, talking little but regarding the world with happy smiles. After purchasing a few things, they quietly left the town again.

Before long the forty-niners discovered that a large group of townspeople were following them, picks and shovels in hand. The forty-niners looked at one another and raised the question of who leaked the secret. They soon concluded that no one had let the information slip, so they confronted their pursuers and asked, "Why are you following us?" "We know you found gold," they answered. "How did you find that out?" replied the forty-niners. "We are not dumb. Think about it. When you first came to town, you were unhappy, cursing, and fighting amongst yourselves. When you came back, you could not hide your joy and happiness; your faces were radiant and blissful. That is how we knew you found gold."[14]

When we find something important in our lives, that discovery changes us. When we find God, the Ultimate Being, we become totally new beings and our joy overwhelms us. The ultimate joy of life flows from our relationship with the Ultimate Being in Jesus Christ. We cannot hide the evidence of such a genuine joy.

Types of Joy

How can we rejoice always? Sometimes we are sad, we grieve, we weep, and we despair. Wasn't Paul disappointed, sad, and annoyed? How could he command us to be joyful always? What is the secret to this constant rejoicing?

There are several types of joy. All can coexist simultaneously. For Christians, it is desirable to have them all.

Responsive Joy: This is the joy to respond to joyful circumstances. It is a passive joy that interacts with an external, active joy. On hearing jokes and humor, we crack up; when we perceive something as funny, we respond with outbursts of laughter. Others' smiles and laughter set off our joy. Responsive joy displays an empathy with the joy of others. When we meet those whom we long to see, we experience this exuberant joy of response. This joy is a circumstantial delight.

Active Joy: This joy arises from the inside. As time goes by, we learn how to be joyful beyond our circumstances and how to take the initiative in generating joy. Through positive thinking and a creative mind, we make others and ourselves merry and joyful. Lending helping hands to someone also increases our energy level and boosts our immune system by releasing endorphin, a group of peptide hormones that are found mainly in the brain.[15] Research shows that even the simple act of watching someone help others triggers immediate and measurable enhancement of the immune system.[16] This joy is contagious and regenerative.

Easter Joy: After the resurrection of Jesus, his disciples drastically changed their outlooks on life. They went from despair to exuberant joy. His resurrection transforms the world of hopelessness into the world of joy. Easter represents the joy of hope. This joy arises from our relationship with God. Thus, Easter joy is a receptive joy. As we open ourselves to God, we invite the Spirit of God into our emptied heart and experience the joy of the Spirit. We do not earn this joy, but receive it as a heavenly gift. It is the joy that stays with us even in time of trouble and sorrow. It comes with peace. We don't possess this joy, but we partake of it.

The source of Easter joy is enduring because it is unconditional and infinite. If Easter joy were no more than the sum of transient joys, it would be destructible. But Jesus overcame the crucifixion and death, engendering Easter joy. This victory guarantees the ultimate triumph of truth and justice and supports a joy that can coexist even with suffering.[17] The source of joy is not others or ourselves, but the Spirit of God. This extraordinary joy does not depend on our intellectual decisions, but relies on our spiritual receptivity. It is a relational joy with the Spirit beyond the joy this world can offer.

People of Easter joy enjoy the life of *eternal now*. Eternity is not quantitative time (*chronos*), but qualitative time (*kairos*). When we join the God of Sabbath, we experience this eternity, *kairos*. We enjoy this eternity now in life. In the midst of a fitful Sea of Galilee, we repose with Christ. In the midst of crucifixion, we experience the resurrection of Christ. According to the Greek teaching of the immortality of the soul, we will enjoy rest after passing through the fitful sea of life. But in the Christian teaching of eternity, we experience the joy of the resurrection in the midst of suffering and being crucified. Our eternal joy starts *now* with God in whom the past and the future are all rolled up in the present. It means that we taste Sabbaths and heavenly bliss in spite of the heart of han. By God's Sabbath and joy, we transcend the power of han in our lives: "For I am convinced that neither death, nor life, nor angels, nor rulers, nor things present, nor things to come, nor powers, nor height, nor depth, nor anything else in all creation, will be able to separate us from the love of God in Christ Jesus our Lord" (Rom 8:38-39). Nothing can disrupt our joy eternal in God's love. In the life of joy and thanksgiving, we overwhelm injustice, bitterness, resentment, despair, and the threat of death. We fear no death but delight in our joy now to the fullest: "Very truly, I tell you, anyone who hears my word and believes him who sent me has eternal life, and does not come under judgment, but has passed from death to life" (John 5:24). No more death! We have moved from death to life. Eternal life is the eternal Sabbath in which we feast on the divine joy and gratuitousness.

Collective Jubilee

The Year of Jubilee

"You shall count off seven weeks of years, seven times seven years, so that the period of seven weeks of years gives forty-nine years" (Lev 25:8). The Sabbath is connected to the sabbatical year, the seventh year, and the sabbatical year is connected to the Jubilee, which is in effect a big Sabbath. Jubilee is the Sabbath of Sabbaths, the fiftieth year right after year forty-nine (seven years times seven years). Richard Lowery surmises that seventh-year debt release brought forth the Sabbath. The Sabbath gave rise to the conceptual model for the "Priestly Sabbath Year" and "Jubilee," which differ from the older "seventh-year" release laws in Deut 15 and Exod 21 and 23. He calls the Sabbath a "little Jubilee."[18]

The Hebrew Bible

According to Jacob Milgrom, the basic thrust of the Jubilee is from Lev 25:23-24: "The land shall not be sold in perpetuity, for the land is mine; with me you are but aliens and tenants. Throughout the land that you hold, you shall provide for the redemption of the land."[19] Regardless of whether it has been sold to someone, a piece of land can be reclaimed. Every fiftieth year, it must be redemptively restored to its original owner, based on the ownership of God. Return of foreclosed land and cancellation of debts were practiced in the ancient Near East.[20] The intent of these practices was to prevent the collapse of the economy under the unbalanced weight of private indebtedness.[21] The Jubilee in its core calls for remission of debts, restoration of land, sabbatical rest for land and human beings, and release from economic slavery.[22]

The Jubilee had three main elements: liberty or release, restoration or return, and justice. Liberty means, "Do not control or use other people. Set them free." Restoration includes "returning land to its family, and people to their land." Justice means "fairness when calculating the price for a temporary sale."[23] These two images point to the transition of the idea of Jubilee from a literal sense to a wider metaphoric relevance. The later Isaiah reflects this move. The Servant of Yahweh in Deutero-Isaiah (Isa 42:1-7, the Servant, a light to the nations) includes strong parts of the curative plan of God for Israel, particularly for the weak and oppressed. Isaiah 58 (false and true worship) calls for liberation of the oppressed while criticizing cultic rituals with no social justice. Furthermore, Isaiah 61 (the good news of deliverance) uses Jubilee images to portray the Anointed One as the messenger of Yahweh to bring good news to the poor, to proclaim liberty to the captives, and to announce the year of Yahweh's favor, almost unquestionably a reference to a Jubilee year. The ideas of return and restoring redemption are united in the future vision of Isaiah 35 (the return of the redeemed to Zion). Thus, in the Hebrew Bible the Jubilee involves an eschatological imagery while espousing an ethical challenge for justice to the downtrodden in the contemporary world.[24]

The New Testament

The "Nazareth manifesto" (Luke 4:16-30) is the clearest statement of Jesus' own mission. Jesus quotes directly from Isaiah 61, which is strongly formed by Jubilee concepts. His proclamation shows the fulfillment of the messianic hopes in him.

> The Spirit of the Lord is upon me,
> because he has anointed me
> to bring good news to the poor.
> He has sent me to proclaim release to the captives
> and recovery of sight to the blind,
> to let the oppressed go free,
> to proclaim the year of the Lord's favor. (vv. 18-19)

In spite of the fact that they disagree on what he meant by it, most scholars agree that Jesus made use of the imagery of Jubilee. Some have argued that Jesus was a Jubilee practitioner and called for a literal enactment of the Levitical Jubilee.[25] Others have spiritualized this mission statement, based on the fact that Jesus used the prophetic texts (Isa 61) and not the Levitical law (Lev 25). They have argued that he simply used the language of Jubilee that was required to announce the arrival of God's kingdom, with no intention to call for an actual Jubilee.[26]

Sharon Ringe contends that the Jubilee traditions served as a source for early Christian ethics and Christology, and confessing Jesus as the Christ is to get involved in acts of liberation. She highlights the two factors that impact the Jubilee language as entering the gospel tradition:

> First, images that began in social, political, or economic spheres are associated with God's eschatological reign. Just as that reign is at once physical and spiritual, social and individual, political and personal, so the Jubilee declared at its inception touches all of human life. . . . Second, the Jubilee traditions become sources for the language of Christology as well as of ethics. Jesus as the Anointed One (Christ/Messiah) of God is presented as the herald announcing the beginning of God's new reign, and proclaiming liberty to all who participate in it. To portray Jesus as the herald of God's reign is to emphasize Jesus' intimacy with God, for a royal messenger would be accorded the same dignity as the sovereign who is represented. To portray Jesus as the proclaimer of the Jubilee links recognition of Jesus as the Christ with response to the Jubilee message itself: to confess Jesus as the Christ is to participate in acts of liberation.[27]

Ringe points out the five issues related to the Jubilee images of the Synoptic Gospels: christological imagery, the agenda of justice, forgiveness and liberation, the affirmation of divine sovereignty, and eschatology and human responsibility.[28]

The Jubilee is a great institution. The notion of the Jubilee has shaped the direction of the world economy for the first time in the world history by swaying the World Bank, International Monetary Fund, and rich countries to forgive the debts of the poor countries.

Jubilee 2000, the highly successful international debt campaign pressure group, was established in 1996 with the definite aim of a debt-free start to the new millennium for a billion of the world's poorest people. Part of Jubilee 2000's plan was for Britain to scrap the debts of twenty of the world's poorest countries. Around £1 billion ($1.43 billion) of debt was going to be written off and another twenty-one countries were to be encouraged to qualify for similar relief. Jubilee 2000's pressure has brought action from the G7, the IMF, and World Bank, the world's main creditors. The G7 in 1999 agreed to overhaul the Heavily Indebted Poor Countries (HIPC) initiative and pledged to get twenty of the worst affected countries into it by the end of 2000. Jubilee 2000 says fifty-two countries need cancellation of a total of $376 billion of debt. By 2000, creditors promised to write off $110 billion, but by the end of 2000 only $1 billion was going to be cancelled.[29] During the annual meetings of the World Bank and IMF in Washington, D.C., on September 28 and 29, 2002, fifteen creditor countries committed themselves to providing the $1 billion of additional debt relief to the HIPC Trust Fund.[30]

Here we have used the term *Jubilee* as a way of relieving the heavy debts of poor nations. It is the collective dimension of the Jubilee. The present practice of the debt release of the HIPC approaches the original intention of the Jubilee. The Jubilee also can go beyond its literal meaning.

The manna story is a symbol of Jubilee economy. The manna was the daily bread provided by God to the Israelites during their forty years of wilderness wandering. They were able to gather it daily with the exception of the Sabbath. If they gathered beyond the needs of their families, with the exception of the sixth day when they gathered a double portion for the Sabbath, the surplus manna would rot and breed worms (Exod 16:1-30). This bread from heaven symbolizes the equal distribution of the daily bread and prohibition of the excessive accumulation of wealth. According to Ched Myers, the manna was a test to see if Israel would follow instructions on how to "gather" this gift.[31] The Sabbath code of the accumulation concerns the fairness of the economic system of Israel. The code is related to the seventh-year debt release. The debt release of the Sabbath year aims "to safeguard both social justice—'there will be no one in need among you'—and sound fiscal policy—'creditor nations will not rule over you'" (Deut 15:4-6).[32]

Twenty percent of the human family currently possesses almost 83 percent of the world's resources, while the poorest 20 percent receive less than 2 percent.[33] The Jubilee points to the economy of grace, the politics of liberation from any bondage, and ecological cares for even wild animals (Exod 23:10-11). Preceded by the bread from heaven, the Jubilee frees us from all straitjackets of laissez faire capitalism, sociopolitical oppression, and ecological abuses. Jesus is our bread from heaven (John 6:41-51) in this hungry and unfair world. Our Jubilee in this world of han is Jesus, the Messiah of justice and grace.

Christian Perfection

After being justified, sinners need to pursue a holy life toward its perfection. In the eighteen century, most Protestants lived a life of little progress in holiness. Lutherans were resigned to a debilitated lifestyle because they remained sinners no matter how hard they strived to be holy, and Calvinists totally ascribed their holiness to the will of God, not to their own efforts.

Reacting to the incapacitated lifestyle of Christians, John Wesley spearheaded a movement of what he called "scriptural holiness" by asserting the possibility of Christian perfection on earth. For him, it was closer to the will of God for us to strive to be perfect than to become resigned to our inabilities. He believed that we are able to perfect in this life. To him, unless we can be perfect, Jesus would not command us to be perfect (Matt 5:48); the Scripture asks us to be holy, too, because God is holy (1 Pet 1:16). His understanding of perfection is different from the common understanding of the term. Perfection means neither faultlessness nor the completion of a Christian journey. From the perspective of what it negates, Christian perfection or entire sanctification denotes freedom from pride, unbelief, and a self-centered life. In terms of what it affirms, Christian perfection signifies the state where pure love fills our heart and our souls.

> It is thus that we wait for entire sanctification; for a full salvation from all our sins,—from pride, self-will, anger, unbelief; or, as the Apostle expresses it, 'go on unto perfection.' But what is perfection? The word has various senses: Here it means perfect love. It is love excluding sin; love filling the heart, taking up the whole capacity of the soul. It is love 'rejoicing evermore, praying without ceasing, in every thing giving thanks'.[34]

Wesley described Christian perfection as a process of growing in grace, not the end of growth. He denied any concept of absolute perfection where no further grace was needed. Christians in the state of perfection make mistakes and sometimes commit sins; however, they do not sin intentionally: "Indeed it is said, this means only, He sinneth not willfully; or he doth not commit sin habitually; or, not as other men do; or, not as he did before."[35] Using First John, "Whosoever is born of God does not commit sin," Wesley affirmed the loving and sinless state of entire sanctification by God's grace in contrast with an absolute sinless state.[36]

For Wesley, the state of perfection is well expressed in Paul's saying:

" 'I am crucified with Christ: Nevertheless I live; yet not I, but Christ liveth in me.'—Words that manifestly describe a deliverance from inward as well as from outward sin. This is expressed both negatively, I live not; (my evil nature, the body of sin, is destroyed;) and positively, Christ liveth in me; and, therefore, all that is holy, and just, and good."[37] The death of sin and the life of Christ's holiness simultaneously work for our entire sanctification in Christ's crucifixion.

Holiness is not a status, but a dynamic relationship. The perfect Christian is perfect because she or he has an unbroken relationship with Christ, not because she or he has reached an objective moral standard of perfection.[38] The holiest need Christ. Separated from Christ, no one is perfect.

In his "Brief Thought on Christian Perfection," Wesley says that a perfect Christian loves God with all his or her heart, and mind, and soul. Perfection embraces "the humble, gentle, patient love of God, and our neighbor, ruling our tempers, words, and actions."[39] A simple act of faith works perfection in the soul in an instant. But a gradual work of sanctification must precede the instant perfection and ensue it. This instant perfection usually takes place many years after justification, although Welsey does not exclude the possibility of it occurring within "five years or five months." Wesley believes that "this instant generally is the instant of death, the moment before the soul leaves the body" without excluding the possibility of happening "ten, twenty, or forty years before."[40]

Whether it is called entire sanctification, perfection, or something else, sinners are bound to pursue the highest level of Christian maturity. In this final stage of Christian life, the sinner does not intentionally cause the sinned-against by avoiding a deliberate sin. Christian perfection is the state of love reigning in their hearts. It happens when they are connected to Christ.

Collective Perfection

Wesley was not the first of the church's teachers to employ the idea of Christian perfection. Many before him, especially among the mystical tradition, saw perfection as the central goal of the Christian life. While some of these approached the idea of perfection in ways similar to Wesley,[41] others defined it in much more individualistic and privatistic terms. For them, perfection comes from meditation and contemplation, and by ceasing outward works. They practiced religion in a solitary place.

Wesley rejected any idea of perfection in a cessation of service. For him, Christian perfection is relational and social. Solitary perfection is an oxymoron:

> Directly opposite to this is the gospel of Christ. Solitary religion is not to be found there. 'Holy solitaries' is a phrase no more consistent with the gospel than holy adulterers. The gospel of Christ knows of no religion, but social; no holiness but social holiness. 'Faith working by love' is the length and breadth and depth and height of Christian perfection. This commandment have we from Christ, that he who loves God, love his brother also.[42]

To Wesley, holiness is social holiness. The love of God needs to be understood in a community. An individual cannot fully grasp the meaning of faith apart from a community. He elevated this doctrine of entire holiness to a social level, since a society is interwoven with the sins of individuals. God's power transforms social evil so that someday the world may grow into its full harmony and serenity of social holiness. Furthermore, Wesley dreamt of a Christian world where we see justice, peace, and mercy prevailing. He believed that Satan's plot against God will fail and that evil people would disappear from the earth.

> But shall we not see greater things than these? Yea, greater than have been yet from the beginning of the world. Can Satan cause the truth of God to fail, or his promises to be of none effect? If not, the time will come when Christianity will prevail over all, and cover the earth. Let us stand a little, and survey (the Third thing which was proposed) this strange sight, a Christian World.[43]

In such a Christian world, people hear kind words and wise words, and see truth, transparent hearts, love, and God—no unkind words, no contention, no strife, and no railings. Destruction will be destroyed, and war will be dismantled. In such a world, justice is met with mercy and cruelty will diminish and fail.[44]

Furthermore, institutions and corporations will be regenerated. Transnational corporations have destroyed local economies, engendering hostile and fearful business environments by swallowing up smaller companies. They give their loyalties to no community or nation but only to their own greed. They have little plan to build up those communities among whom they do business, but exploit them for their own aggrandizement alone.

In their influential book *For the Common Good*, John Cobb and Herman Daly eloquently articulate the need to enhance the local economy in such a way that it undermines the transnational structure of the global economy.[45] They advocate a local economy that encourages the self-sustenance and self-governance of local people. To improve the quality of people's life and the conditions of local communities, it is necessary for us to support local commerce over the trade of transnational corporations.

By enhancing local businesses, we can subvert the structure of transnational corporations that have escalated world poverty, have moved the globe toward a monoculture, have stirred up racial conflict, and have disrupted our natural environments. For instance, for a carrot to end up on our dinner table, it has to travel an average of 1,300 miles. Shipping a truckload of produce across the country costs up to $4,500, polluting the air with fossil fuel combustion. By buying local producers' carrots, we stop unnecessary trucking and vitalize our local economy. A dollar used on local foods goes around in the local economy, generating $1.81 to $2.78 in other business.[46]

In the state of collective perfection, local communities, supported by robust local economies, will achieve self-sustenance and self-reliance. Local businesses and corporations will thrive on caring about the quality of their community life and on making their decisions based on the well-being of their community in addition to efficiency and proficiency. Such blossoming of local businesses and corporations will even nudge transnational corporations to be dissolved or change themselves into local corporations, which truly build up their communities. Collective perfection will raise the morality of businesses and corporations up to the level of moral individuals. By elevating the corporate, systemic, and structured immorality of society to a personal level of Christian perfection, we may realize its collective perfection.

NOTES

Introduction

1. The name of such a psychosomatic symptom is *sok-ah-ree*, the affliction of the inside.

2. David A. Clark, "Letter From Prison," *Psychology Today* no. 1 (January/February 1993): 12-15.

3. Ibid., 15.

4. Every year, state child protective service agencies in the United States receive reports on more than three million cases of suspected child abuse and neglect. Child neglect is the single most commonly reported and substantiated form of maltreatment of children in the United States, with many of the injuries more severe than those from other forms of abuse. A recent national survey shows that neglect represented 60 percent of confirmed cases; physical abuse, 23 percent; sexual abuse, 9 percent; emotional abuse, 4 percent ; and other forms of maltreatment, 5 percent. Dave Paulk, "Recognizing Child Abuse, Child Abusers, and Individuals Who Are Likely to Abuse," *Physician Assistant* 23 (1 May 1999): 38, 40, 42.

5. Kathy Spatz Wisdom, "Victims of Childhood Sexual Abuse—Later Criminal Consequences," part 2 of 2, Contemporary Women's Issues Database (1 March 1993): 1, 1993 United States Government.

6. Gustavo Gutiérrez, *A Theology of Liberation* (trans. Caridad Inda and John Eagleson; Maryknoll, N.Y.: Orbis Books, 1973), 36-37.

7. Ibid., 177.

8. Ibid., 149-78.

9. Joyce Murray, "Liberation for Communion in the Soteriology of Gustavo Gutiérrez," *Theological Studies* 59 (March 1998): 60.

10. Amanda Garrett, "When Priests Commit Suicide Sexual Abuse Allegations Often Spur Decision," Cleveland, Ohio newspaper *The Plain Dealer*, 25 May 2002, AI.

11. Ibid.

1. Wounds (Han) and Sin

1. *Han* is a term that Korean *minjung* (downtrodden) theologians began to employ in the 1970s. See Yong Bock Kim, ed., *Minjung Theology* (Singapore: The Christian Conference of Asia, 1981).

2. Richard Meryhew, "Battered Woman in Rural Areas Have Unique Problems Escaping Cycle of Abuse," *Minneapolis-St. Paul, Minnesota Star Tribune*, 19 March 2000.

3. Leslye Orloff, *Brief Facts: Battered Immigrant Women Protection Act of 1999*. Hearing. (Washington, D.C.: GPO, 2000), 60.

4. Robert A. Underwood, Congressional Record. 150 (2 November 2001): E1980.

5. Charles N. Jamison, "Racism," *Essence* 7 (November 1992): 64.

6. Kevin Lamb, "Lasting Effects of Abuse," *Dayton (Ohio) Daily News*, 25 June 2002, C1.

7. Ibid.

8. Ibid., C3.

9. Ibid., C1.

10. Me Ra Koh, "My Boyfriend Raped Me," *Campus Life* 60 (September 2001): 61.

11. Ibid., 62.

12. Underwood, Congregational Record.

13. Peter Marks, "A Skyline Is Conspicuous by an Absence" (24 October 2001, *The New York Times*).

14. See *The Wounded Heart of God* (Nashville: Abingdon, 1993), chap. 2.

15. Although tragedies and natural catastrophes can create han, our focus will be on han caused by human actions.

16. See also Matt 9:12-13 and Luke 5:31.

17. Cf. Bill Moyers, "The First Murder," *Genesis: A Living Conversation*, PBS series, 16 October 1996.

18. Most scholars believe someone inserted the speeches of Elihu between the dialogues and God's answer later. This is why God refers only to the three friends, and mentions no name of Elihu. Solomon B. Freehof, *Book of Job: A Commentary* (New York: Union of American Hebrew Congregations, 1958), 235.

19. A number of scholars consider the original author wrote only part of God's speeches and most of chapters 40 and 41 were later additions. The two descriptions of the behemoth and the leviathan were independent nature poems and were added later to the original divine speech. Ibid.

20. Gustavo Gutiérrez, *On Job: God-talk and the Suffering of the Innocent* (trans. Matthew J. O'Connell; Maryknoll, N.Y.: Orbis Books, 1987), 82.

21. Owen Thomas and Ellen Wondra, *Introduction to Theology* (3rd ed.; Harrisburg, Pa.: Morehouse, 2002), 158.

22. "See, he will kill me; I have no hope (the consonantal text)," or "Though he kill me, yet I will trust in him (the traditional)" (NRSV).

23. Simone Weil, "From Random Thoughts on the Love of God," *The Soul Is Here for Its Own Joy: Sacred Poems from Many Cultures* (ed. Robert Bly; Hopewell, N.J.: Ecco, 1995), 112.

24. Friedrich Schleiermacher believed that. See Ted Peters, *Sin* (Grand Rapids: W. B. Eerdmans, 1994), 7-9.

25. Elie Wiesel, *Messengers of God* (trans. Marion Wiesel; New York: Random House, 1976); Richard Rubenstein, *The Cunning of History* (New York: Harper Colophon Books, 1978).

26. G. Tyler Miller, *Living in the Environment: Principles, Connections, and Solutions* (8th ed; Belmont, Calif: Wadsworth, 1994), 10.

27. Joachim Jeremias, *Jerusalem at Jesus' Time* (Philadelphia: Fortress, 1969), quoted in

Byung-mu Ahn, "Jesus and the Minjung," in *Minjung Theology: People as the Subjects of History* (ed. Commission on Theological Concerns of the Christian Conference of Asia; Maryknoll, N.Y.: Orbis Books, 1981), 143.

28. Joachim Jeremias, *New Testament Theology* (New York: Charles Scribner's Sons, 1971), 112.

29. Herders were believed to drive their herds onto others' land and steal the produce of the herd. The publicans were particularly outlawed; they were *toll* collectors (*mōkᵉsāh*), different from *tax* collectors (*gabbāyāh*). While tax collectors as state officials took in the direct taxes, the toll collectors were subtenants of the rich toll farmers who had to extract the agreed amount plus their additional profit. They often capitalized on public ignorance of the scale of tolls to bring money into their pockets during the tax season (Luke 3:12*f*). The civil rights of the publicans were denied, and they were deprived of their rights to be witnesses. Jeremias, *New Testament Theology*, 109-10.

30. Byung-mu Ahn, "Jesus and the Minjung," 144.

31. Ibid.

32. Jeremias, *New Testament Theology*, 112.

33. Byung-mu Ahn, "Jesus and the Minjung," 150.

34. Jeremias, *New Testament Theology*, 113.

35. Joachim Jeremias, *The Lord's Prayer* (trans. John Reumann; Philadelphia: Fortress, 1964), 10-12.

36. Eduard Schweizer, *The Good News According to Matthew* (trans. David Green; Atlanta: John Knox Press, 1975), 153. He further explains that when the prayer was said at an early hour, "daily bread" meant the bread of the same day; otherwise, it referred to tomorrow. According to Jerome, the Gospel of the Nazareans, which is lost, used the term *mᵃhar*. Foerster concludes that *mᵃhar*, tomorrow, is the Aramaic express standing behind the Greek *epiousios*: [W. Foerster, "*Epiousios*," in Kittel, *Theological Dictionary of the New Testament*, II (1964), 590-99]. To Jerome, the "bread for tomorrow" was not earthly bread but the bread of life. In the early church the eschatological understanding of "bread of life," "heavenly manna," "bread of the age of salvation" was familiar, if not the leading interpretation of "bread for tomorrow" [Jeremias, *The Lord's Prayer*, 25]. We cannot exclusively spiritualize or materialize the petition for tomorrow's bread, but include both. However, its primary intention was to ask daily bread for tomorrow.

37. Jeremias, *New Testament Theology*, 192.

38. Considering Jesus' teaching that focuses human relationships before our relationship with God (Matt 5:23-24), we can see that oppressors need to ask forgiveness from their victims before asking God's forgiveness.

39. This part echoes an ancient Jewish evening prayer.

> Lead me not into the power of transgression,
> And bring me not into the power of sin,
> And not into the power of iniquity,
> And not into the power of temptation,
> And not into the power of anything shameful. [Jeremias, *The Lord's Prayer*, 30]

The meaning of this evening prayer was to protect early Christians from the power of sin, temptation, and anything shameful.

40. Ralph Knierim, *Die Hauptbegriffe für Sünde im Alten Testament* (Gütersloh, 1965), cited by Robin Cover in "Sin," *The Anchor Bible Dictionary*, Logos Library System, 2000.

41. Ibid.

42. Ibid.

43. E. P. Sanders, "Sin: New Testament," *The Anchor Bible Dictionary*, Logos Library System, 2000; William Barclay, *The Gospel of Matthew* (2 vols.; Philadelphia: Westminster, 1975) 1: 221.

44. Augustine, "A Treatise on the Merits and Forgiveness of Sin and on the Baptism of Infants," Anti-Pelagian Writings First Series, *The Nicene and Post-Nicene Fathers* (ed. Philip Schaff, vol. 2, bk. 2; Albany, Ore.: AGES Software, 1996), 249.

45. Walter Rauschenbusch, *A Theology for the Social Gospel* (New York: Macmillan, 1917), 60.

46. Ibid., 50.

47. Reinhold Niebuhr, *The Nature and Destiny of Man,* vol. 1 (New York: Scribner's, 1941-43), 178-240.

48. Valerie Saiving, "The Human Situation," *Womanspirit Rising* (eds. Carol Christ and Judith Plaskow; New York: Harper & Row, 1979), 37.

2. Shame and Guilt

1. Cf. Lewis B. Smedes, *Shame and Grace: Healing the Shame We Don't Deserve* (San Francisco: HarperSanFrancisco, 1993), 9-10.

2. J. P. Tangney, "Moral Affect: The Good, the Bad, and the Ugly," *Journal of Personality and Social Psychology* 61 (1991): 598-607.

3. Ibid.

4. Christopher Lasch, "Shame," *New Republic* (10 August 1992): 30.

5. Gerhart Piers and Milton B. Singer, *Shame and Guilt* (New York: Norton, 1971), 23-24.

6. Christopher Lasch, "Shame," 30.

7. Gloria Steinem, *Revolution from Within: A Book of Self-esteem* (Boston: Little, Brown and Co., 1992).

8. Lasch, "Shame," 29-35.

9. Jerome H. Neyrey, *Honor and Shame in the Gospel of Matthew* (Louisville: Westminster John Knox, 1998), 14-68.

10. Hans Betz, *The Sermon on the Mount* (Minneapolis: Fortress, 1995), 289.

11. Ulrich Luz, *Matthew 1-7* (Minneapolis: Fortress, 1989), 325.

12. Jerome H. Neyrey, *Honor and Shame in the Gospel of Matthew*, 205.

13. Gerald G. O'Collins, "Crucifixion," *Anchor Bible Dictionary*, Logos Library System, 1998.

14. Andrea Dworkin, "The Third Rape," *Los Angeles Times*, 28 April 1991, m1, m6.

15. *The International Standard Bible Encyclopaedia*, s.v. "Shame," by Charles M. Stuart.

16. *Manchester Guardian*, 7 November 1996, p. 9.

17. Julia Martinez, "The Conspicuous Comeuppance," *Atlanta Journal Constitution*, 15 December 1996, R2.

18. *The International Standard Bible Encyclopaedia*, s.v. " Shame."

19. Erik Erikson, "Autonomy v. Shame and Doubt," *Childhood and Society* (2nd ed.; New York: Norton, 1963), 156.

20. Carl Schneider, *Shame, Exposure and Privacy* (Boston: Beacon, 1977), 37.

21. Ibid.

22. *The New Bible Dictionary*, s.v. "Crime and Punishment."

23. Herbert Morris, ed., introduction to *Guilt and Shame* (Belmont, Calif.: Wadsworth, 1971), 1.

24. Donald Capps, *The Depleted Self: Sin in a Narcissistic Age* (Philadelphia: Fortress, 1993).

25. See Ty C. Colbert, *Why Do I Feel Guilty When I've Done Nothing Wrong?* (Nashville: Thomas Nelson, 1995).

26. Piers and Singer, *Shame and Guilt*, 15-16.

27. *The International Standard Bible Encyclopaedia*, s.v. "Guilt," by Harris F. Rall.

28. Charlie LeDuff, "Squad I on Holiday Shift, Gratitude at the Firehouse," *The New York Times* (23 November 2001).

29. Piers and Singer, *Shame and Guilt*, 45.

30. Karl Jaspers, "Differentiation of German Guilt," in *Guilt and Shame* (ed. Herbert Morris), 51.

31. Ibid., 50.

32. Elisabeth Schüssler Fiorenza, "Wartime as Formative," *Christian Century* (16 August 1995), 778.

33. Jeffery L. Sheler, "The Era of *Collective* Repentance," *U.S. News & World Report*, 119 (3 July 1995): 10.

34. Ibid.

35. George F. Will, "The Journey up from Guilt," *Newsweek* 25 (18 June 1990): 68.

3. Shame Anger and Guilt Anger

1. Brown University, "Teaching Children Healthy Responses to Anger with Assertiveness Training," *Brown University Child and Adolescent Behavior Letter* (7 July 1999): 1.

2. J. P. Tangney et al., "Shamed into Anger? The Relation of Shame and Guilt to Anger and Self-reported Aggression," *Journal of Personality and Social Psychology* 62 (1992): 669-75.

3. Research News, "Low Social Support and Anger Accelerate Hardening of Arteries," *Heart Disease Weekly*.

4. Ibid.

5. American Heart Association National Center, "Anger Triggers Heart Attacks In Some, But Aspirin May Reduce Risk," *News Release* (28 September 1995).

6. Carlos F. Mendes de Leon, "Psychosocial Characteristics and Recurrent Events After Percutaneous Transluminal Coronary Angioplasty," *American Journal of Cardiology* 77 (February 1996): 252-55.

7. "Anger," *University of Michigan News and Information Services* (13 March 1986), 1-2.

8. William Barclay, *The Gospel of Matthew* (2 vols.; Philadelphia: Westminster, 1975), 1:96.

9. Gary Hankins, *Prescription for Anger: Coping with Angry Feelings and Angry People* (Beaverton, Ore.: Princess, 1988), 28-29.

10. Bill DeFoore, *Anger* (Deerfield Beach, Fla.: Health Communications, 1991), 38.

11. Henri Parens, "Rage Toward Self and Others in Early Childhood," *Rage, Power, and Aggression: The Role of Affect in Motivation, Development, and Adaptation* (eds. Robert A. Glick and Steven P. Roose; 2 vols.; New Haven: Yale University Press, 1993), 2: 123-47.

12. Otto Kernberg, "The Psychopathology of Hatred," in *Rage, Power, and Aggression*, 2: 61-79.

13. Mary Baures, "Letting Go of Bitterness and Hate," *Journal of Humanistic Psychology* 36 (Winter 1996): 75-90.

14. *The Six Version Parallel New Testament* (Wheaton: Christian Life Publications, 1974), 12 FN.

15. "Anger, Depression Tied to Heart Attacks, Strokes," *Corporate Detroit* (8 August 1994): 22.

16. Thomas D. Hanks, *God So Loved the Third World: The Biblical Vocabulary of Oppression* (Maryknoll, N.Y.: Orbis Books, 1983), 115.

4. Resistance and Repentance

1. Howard Clinebell, *Growth Counseling: Hope-centered Methods of Actualizing Human Wholeness* (Nashville: Abingdon, 1979).

2. Walter Wink, *Engaging the Powers: Discernment and Resistance in a World of Domination* (Minneapolis: Fortress, 1992), 186.

3. James W. Douglass, *The Non-violent Cross* (New York: Macmillan, 1968), 193.

4. Walter Wink, *Engaging the Powers*, 176.

5. Ibid., 179.

6. Ibid., 182.

7. Ibid.

8. Ibid., 186-89.

9. Ibid., 189.

10. Richard A. Horsley, "Response to Walter Wink," in *The Love of Enemy and Nonretaliation in the New Testament* (ed. Willard M. Swartley; Louisville: Westminster/John Knox, 1992), 126-32.

11. Richard Horsley, "Ethics and Exegesis," in *The Love of Enemy and Nonretaliation in the New Testament*, 86-87. Contrary to Horsley's position, Gerd Theissen refers to first-century Jewish precedents for the effective use of nonviolent strategies as a means of social resistance against the Romans. Theissen, "Gewaltverzicht und Feindesliebe (Matt 5, 38-48; Luke 6, 27-38) und deren sozialgeschichtlicher Hintergrund": 160-97, cited by Dorothy Jean Weaver, "Transforming Nonresistance: From *Lex Talionis* to Do Not Resist the Evil One," in *The Love of Enemy and Nonretaliation in the New Testament*, 34.

12. Ibid., 130.

13. Walter Wink, "Counterresponse to Richard Horsley," in *The Love of Enemy and Nonretaliation in the New Testament*, 133-36.

14. Jimmy Carter, "I Cannot Forgive That Jerk," *Christianity Today* (5 February 2000), http://www.christianitytoday.com/moi/2000/001/feb/5.5.html.

15. Ibid.

16. Ibid.

17. According to Joachim Jeremias, it is improbable that on the basis of the Q-saying, Matthew expanded Luke 17:3 in 18:15-17, since Matt 18:15-17 is not a unity in itself. Matthew 18:16 is his later addition grounded on Deut 19:15 ("A single witness shall not suffice to convict a person of any crime or wrongdoing in connection with any offense that may be committed. Only on the evidence of two or three witnesses shall a charge be sustained") because of his inclination to the Hebrew Bible. Günther Bornkamm, Gerhard Barth, and Heinz Joachim Held, *Tradition and Interpretation in Matthew* (trans. Percy Scott; London: SCM, 1963), 84.

18. Eduard Schweizer, *The Good News According to Matthew* (trans. David E. Green; Atlanta: John Knox Press, 1975), 370.

19. During the lifetime of Jesus, there was no church. These steps must be an anachronistic teaching and practicing of the Matthean church using the authority of Jesus.

20. Ibid.

21. *The New International Dictionary of New Testament Theology*, s.v. "Conversion, Penitence, Repentance, Proselyte," by J. Goetzmann.

22. A. Boyd Luter, "Repentance," *Anchor Bible Dictionary*, Logos Library System, 1998.

23. *The New International Dictionary of New Testament Theology*, s.v. "Metamelomai," by F. Laubach.

24. A. Boyd Luter, "Repentance," *Anchor Bible Dictionary*, Logos Library System, 1998.

25. *The New International Dictionary of New Testament Theology*, s.v. "Epistrephō," by F. Laubach.

26. *The Jewish Encyclopedia*, s.v. "Repentance."

27. Cf. Joseph P. Hearley, "Repentance," *Anchor Bible Dictionary*, Logos Library System, 1998.

28. Cf. Joseph Haroutunian, "Repentance," in *A Handbook of Christian Theology* (London: A Meridian Book, 1958), 321-23.

29. Shimon Apisdorf, *Yom Kippur Survival Kit* (Columbus, Ohio: Leviathan, 1992), 99-106.

30. Thomas Aquinas, *Summa Theologiae: A Concise Translation* (ed. Timothy McDermott; Westminster, Md.: Christian Classics, 1989), 590.

31. Ibid., 600.

32. Ibid.

33. Ibid., 591.

34. Bernhard Lohse, *A Short History of Christian Doctrines* (trans. F. Ernest Stoeffler; Philadelphia: Fortress, 1966), 160.

35. Jeffery L. Sheler, "The Era of *Collective* Repentance," *U.S. News & World Report* (3 July 1995): 10.

5. Forgivingness and Forgiven-ness

1. Quoted in William H. Willimon, "Our Kind of Crowd," in *Reflections on Forgiveness and Spiritual Growth* (ed. Andrew Weaver and Monica Furlong; Nashville: Abingdon, 2001), 85.

2. William Klassen, *The Forgiving Community* (Philadelphia: The Westminster Press, 1966).

3. Ibid., 31-32.

4. *The New International Dictionary of New Testament Theology*, s.v. "Forgiveness," by H. Vorländer.

5. Klassen, *The Forgiving Community*, 31-32.

6. Karen S. Peterson, "Victim of Betrayal Must Learn How to Forgive," *USA Today* (18 August 1998), n.p.

7. Ibid.

8. Gary S. Shogren, "Forgiveness," *The Anchor Bible Dictionary*, Logos Library System, 1998.

9. Marjorie Suchocki, *The Fall to Violence: Original Sin in Relational Theology* (New York: Continuum, 1994), 146-49.

10. L. Gregory Jones, *Embodying Forgiveness* (Grand Rapids: Eerdmans, 1995), 218.

11. Ibid.

12. John Patton, *Is Human Forgiveness Possible?: A Pastoral Care Perspective* (Nashville: Abingdon, 1985), 184.

13. Ernest Kurtz and Katherine Ketcham, *The Spirituality of Imperfection: Modern Wisdom from Classic Stories* (New York: Bantam Books, 1992), 213-29.

14. Punishment is not retaliation. Withholding resources is the most common form of punishment. Loading the scales means that when your resources are taken, you must purposely replace them so that it is your own accomplishments that give you a sense of personal power. Forgivers should join support groups, start new relationships, perhaps find a new or renewed enthusiasm for a job, make new friends, and reacquaint themselves with their own strengths. Whichever way it is done, by deriving new advantages from the injury itself you are no longer at the mercy of someone else's will. The creation of opportunity takes work, but the payoffs in self-esteem and restored balance are enormous.

15. Beverly Flanigan, *Forgiving the Unforgivable* (New York: Macmillan, 1992), 69-170.

16. Ibid., 72.

17. Richard Fitzgibbons, "Forgiveness Boosts Health and Self-Esteem, Research Shows," *Jet* 6 (11 January 1999): 39.

18. Fred Luskin, *Forgive for Good: A Proven Prescription for Health and Happiness* (San Francisco: HarperSanFrancisco, 2002).

19. PERT has three steps. First, dust off our remote control so we can find what is playing on our beauty, gratitude, love, and forgiveness channels. Second, practice the "Breath of Thanks" a couple of times every day. The Breath of Thanks is a breathing exercise of saying "thank you" ten times. Third, set aside about an hour each week to practice the "Heart Focus," which is a breathing exercise of focusing on re-experiencing peaceful and loving feelings. Beauty channel means to awaken ourselves to the beauty of our surroundings. Gratitude channel is to find grateful elements around us. Love channel is to look for people who are in love, smile at their bliss, and become a more loving person. Forgiving channel is to discover people's stories of forgiveness (Luskin, *Forgive for Good*, 114-19).

20. Ibid., 211-12.

21. Lewis Smedes, "Keys to Forgiving," *Christianity Today*, 15 (3 December 2001): 73. These words are directly from the article, but I abbreviated them and added inclusive terms to them.

22. Joram Graf Haber, *Forgiveness* (Savage, Md.: Rowman & Littlefield, 1991).

23. Kathleen Lawler, "*Forgive* to Live," *Health* 6 (July/August 2000): 28.

24. Karen S. Peterson, "Victims of Betrayal Must Learn How to Forgive," n.p.

25. Scott Peck, *Further Along the Road Less Traveled: Blame and Forgiveness*, audio (New York: Simon & Schuster, 1992).

26. Andrew Sung Park, *Racial Conflict and Healing: An Asian-American Theological Perspective* (Maryknoll, N.Y.: Orbis Books, 1996), 186.

27. Some modern Protestant theologians have questioned whether forgiveness has any different existence from reconciliation, or even whether it is a discrete aspect of a process. Both Karl Barth and Paul Tillich decline to give it the status of an independent event. See Karl Barth, *Church Dogmatics*, IV (2nd ed.; trans. G. F. Bromley and T. F. Torrence; Edinburgh: T. and T. Clark, 1975), 500-502; Paul Tillich, *Systematic Theology* (3 vols.; Chicago: University of Chicago Press, 1957), 2:177 and (Chicago: University of Chicago Press, 1963), 3:226-27.

28. Elliot N. Dorff, "The Elements of Forgiveness: A Jewish Approach" in *Dimensions of Forgiveness: Psychological Research & Theological Perspectives* (ed. Everett L. Worthington Jr.; Philadelphia: Templeton Foundation, 1988), 35.

29. Donald Shriver, *An Ethic for Enemies: Forgiveness in Politics* (New York: Oxford University Press, 1995).

30. Ibid., 166.

31. *New York Times*, "Letters" (6 October 1987), in *An Ethic for Enemies*, 166.

32. Frank H. Boehm, "Forgiveness: Another Kind of Medicine" [cited October 1997]. Online: http://dr-boehm.com/Forgiveness.htm. (October 1997). Boehm is a doctor and professor at Vanderbilt Medical Center, Nashville, Tenn.

33. *The Jewish Encyclopedia*, s.v. "Forgiveness."

34. "Yom Kippur," *Encyclopædia Britannica Online*, cited March 18, 1999. Online http://www.eb.com:180/bol/topic?eu=80094&sctn=1.

35. Elliot Dorff, "Forgiveness: A Jewish Approach," *Dimensions of Forgiveness* (ed. Everett L. Worthington Jr.; Philadelphia: Templeton Foundation, 1998), 43-44.

36. Ibid., 41.

37. Flanigan, *Forgiving the Unforgivable*, 256.

38. Shriver, *An Ethic for Enemies*, 7.

39. Ibid., 7-9.

40. Charles Villa-Vicencio, "The Road to Reconciliation," *Sojourners* (May/June 1997): 36-37.

41. Ibid.

42. Ibid.

43. Ibid.

6. Justice by Faith and Justification by Faith

1. Walter Brueggemann, "The Shrilled Voice of the Wounded Party," *The Other Side of Sin* (ed. Andrew Park and Susan Nelson; New York: SUNY Press, 2001).

2. Emphasis added.

3. He is professor emeritus in the Department of Biological Sciences at the University of Notre Dame. There he also studied theology. Julian Pleasants, "Religion That Restores Victims," *New Theological Review* (August 1996): 48.

4. Gary North, *Victim's Rights: The Biblical View of Civil Justice* (Tyler, Texas: Institute for Christian Economics, 1990), 219.

5. *Interpreter's Dictionary of the Bible*, s. v. "Justice" and "Righteousness."

6. Kathleen Farmer, paper presented at 1996 West Ohio School of Ministry, 11.

7. Ibid., 3.

8. Ibid., 15.

9. Ibid., 9.

10. Ibid., 11.

11. Brueggemann, "The Shrilled Voice of the Wounded Party."

12. Elizabeth Achtemeier, "Victimization and Healing: The Biblical View," *God and the Victim: Theological Reflections on Evil, Victimization, Justice, and Forgiveness* (ed. Lisa B. Lampman and Michelle D. Shattuck; Grand Rapids: Eerdmans, 1999), 94.

13. Nicholas Wolterstorff, "The Contours of Justice: An Ancient Call for Shalom," *God and the Victim* (Grand Rapids: Eerdmans, 1999), 124.

14. Ibid.

15. Plato, "From the *Republic*," in *What Is Justice?* (ed. Robert C. Solomon and Mark C. Murphy; Oxford: Oxford University Press, 1990), 35.

16. Ibid., 28.

17. Aristotle, "From *Nicomachean Ethics*," in *What Is Justice?* 38-48.

18. Solomon and Murphy, *What Is Justice?* 14.

19. Thomas Aquinas, *Summa Theologiae: A Concise Translation* (ed. Timothy McDermott; Westminster, Md.: Christian Classics, 1989), 382.

20. Ibid., 238.

21. Ibid., 388.

22. Martin Luther, *Preface to the Letter of St. Paul to the Romans*, The Ages Digital Library, 1997.

23. Ibid., 10.

24. John Rawls, "Justice as Fairness and a Theory of Justice," in *What Is Justice?* 306.

25. Tom Walz and Heather Ritchie, "Gandhian Principles in Social Work Practice: Ethnics Revisited," *Social Work* 3 (May 2000): 213.

26. Robert Nozick, "Anarchy, State and Utopia (1938—)," in *What Is Justice?* 6, 313-21.

27. Robert Nozick, "Retribution and Revenge" from Philosophical Explanations, in *What Is Justice?* 281.

28. I am indebted to Howard Zehr. Compare with his "Restoring Justice," in *God and the Victim*, 134.

29. Ibid., 132-36.

30. Julian R. Pleasants, "Religion That Restores Victims," *New Theological Review* (August 1996): 41.

31. *Summary Report: The Assessment of Restitution in the Minnesota Probation Service*, prepared for the Governor's Commission on Crime Prevention and Control (31 January 1976), 1.

32. Ibid.

33. Elmar Weitekamp, *Restorative Justice: An Ancient Approach to Improve Today's World* (Boulder, Colo.: Westview, 1997).

34. Jim Consedine, "A Justice Based on Healing," *Catholic Worker* (January-February 1996): 1.

35. *Restorative Justice Fact Sheet* is presented by a partnership among the Office of Justice Programs, National Institute of Justice, Office for Victims of Crime, National Institute of Corrections, and Office of Juvenile Justice and Delinquency Prevention, all within the U. S. Department of Justice, I US DoJ97A. See Mark S. Umbreit with Robert B. Coates and Boris Kalanj, *Victim Meets Offender: The Impact of Restorative Justice and Mediation* (Monsey, N.Y.: Criminal Justice Press, 1994).

36. Mark Umbreit and Howard Zehr, "Restorative Family Group Conferences: Differing Models and Guidelines for Practice," *Federal Probation* 3 (September 96): 24.

37. Reinhold Niebuhr, *Moral Man and Immoral Society* (New York: HarperCollins, 1932), xi-xii.

38. Peter Drucker, *Managing for the Future: The 1990s and Beyond* (New York: Truman Talley /Plume, 1993).

39. Ched Myers, *The Biblical Vision of Sabbath Economics* (Washington, D.C.: The Church of the Savior, 2001), 6.

40. Richard B. Hays, "Justification," *Anchor Bible Dictionary*, Logos Library System, 2000.

41. Ibid.

42. Augustine, "On Grace and Free Will," *The Nicene and Post Nicene Fathers*, The Ages Digital System, 1997.

43. Augustine, "On the Holy Trinity Doctrinal Treatises, Moral Treatises," *The Nicene and Post Nicene Fathers*, The Ages Digital System, 1997.

44. *Summa Theologica* (English Dominican trans.; New York: Benziger Bros., 1947), 1: 1145-49.

45. Ibid.

46. Martin Luther, *The Small Catechism*, The Ages Digital System, 1997.

47. Bernhard Lohse, *A Short History of Christian Doctrine* (trans. F. Ernest Stoeffler; Philadelphia: Fortress, 1996), 162.

48. Martin Luther, "The Freedom of a Christian," in *Luther's Works* (ed. Jaroslav Pelikan; vol. 55; Saint Louis : Concordia, 1955–1986), 31:345.

49. Ibid., 358-59.

50. John Wesley, "Minutes of Several Conversations Between the Reverend and Mr. John Wesley and Others: From the Year 1744 to the Year 1789," *The Complete Works of John Wesley*, The Ages Digital System, 1997.

51. Wesley, "On the Discoveries of Faith," in *The Complete Works of John Wesley*, The Ages Digital System, 1997.

52. Paul Tillich, *The Protestant Era* (trans., ed. James Adams; London: Nisbet, 1951), xiv.

53. Paul Tillich, *Systematic Theology* (3 vols.; Chicago: University of Chicago Press, 1951-63), 2:179.

54. Rudolf Bultmann et al., *Kerygma and Myth: A Theological Debate* (ed. Hans Werner Bartsch; New York: Harper & Row, 1962), 210.

55. *Joint Declaration of the Doctrine of Justification: The Lutheran World Federation and the Catholic Church*, Rev. Ishmael Noko of the Lutheran World Federation and Bishop Kasper, Secretary, Pontifical Council for Promoting Christian Unity, two of the signers of the Joint

Declaration on October 31, 1999. http://www.vatican.va/roman_curia/pontifical_councils/chrstuni/documents/rc_pc_chrstuni_doc_31101999_cath-luth-joint-declaration_en.html.

56. Ibid., 2A in "Annex to the Official Common Statement."

57. Ibid., 2C.

58. Ibid., 2D.

59. Ibid., 2E.

60. Hays, "Justification."

61. Even the civil war itself was fought for the preservation of the Union rather than the abolition of slavery.

62. Lawrence Bush and Jeffrey Dekro, "Jews and the Black Reparations Campaign," *Tikkun* 4 (July/August 2000): 12.

7. Healing (Wholeness) and Holiness (Sanctification)

1. Mircea Eliade, *Shamanism: Archaic Techniques of Ecstasy* (New York: Pantheon, 1964).

2. The inserts are added.

3. Robert Kysar, "The Gospel of John," *The Anchor Bible Dictionary*, Logos Library System, 2000.

4. Rudolf Bultmann, *The Gospel of John: A Commentary* (trans. G. R. Beasley-Murray; Oxford: Basil Blackwell, 1971), 561.

5. Judy Emerson, *In the Voice of a Child* (Nashville: Thomas Nelson, 1994). Author comments on her continuing growth ten years later, December 4, 1998 online at www.amazon.com.

6. Jack Canfield and Frank Siccone, *101 Ways to Develop Student Self-esteem and Responsibility* (2 vols.; Boston: Allyn and Bacon, 1993), 1:ix. I modified the story.

7. Nicholar Wolterstorff, "The Contours of Justice: An Ancient Call for Shalom," *God and the Victim: Theological Reflections on Evil, Victimization, Justice, and Forgiveness* (ed. Lisa Lampman and Michelle Shattuck; Grand Rapids: Eerdmans, 1999), 121.

8. Martin Luther, *The Smalcalt Articles*, The Ages Digital System, 1997.

9. John Calvin, *Institutes of the Christian Religion* (trans. Henry Beveridge; Grand Rapids: Eerdmans, 1989), bk. 3, XXII, 1: 214.

10. John Wesley, "The Great Privilege of Those Who Were Born of God," *The Complete Works of John Wesley*, The Ages Digital System, 1997.

11. John Wesley, "Justification by Faith," *The Complete Works of John Wesley*, The Ages Digital System, 1997.

12. Jo Bailey Wells, *God's Holy People* (Sheffield, England: Sheffield Academic Press, 2000), 14.

8. Jubilee and Christian Perfection

1. Merlin Carothers, *Praise Works* (Plainfield, N.J.: Logos International, 1973), 1-3.

2. Leslie Weatherhead, *The Will of God* (Nashville: Abingdon, 1944), 21.

3. *The Christian Science Monitor* (20 October 1993).

4. "Gratitude Heals," *Christian Science Monitor* (13 December 2002), 22.

5. Bud Osborn, *Hundred Block Rock* (Vancouver: Arsenal Pulp Press, 1999). I appreciate that he sent his short autobiography and other newspaper clips.

6. See his *The Stranger, The Plague,* and *The Rebel.*

7. The insert is mine.

8. I use this exclusive language to make up our long usage of the male pronoun in referring to the deity. My ultimate point is that God or the Holy Spirit is not a male or a female.

9. Paul Pearsall, *Super Joy: In Love with Living* (New York: Doubleday, 1988), 54.

10. Ched Myers, *The Biblical Vision of Sabbath Economics* (Washington, D.C.: The Church of the Savior, 2001), 11.

11. This is contrasted by the Pauline example from 1 Cor 11:23–26, in which the Lord's Supper is tied to the sacrificial death of Jesus on the cross and that is consciously linked to Jesus' Last Supper. Hans-Josef Klauck, "Lord's Supper," *The Anchor Bible Dictionary*, Logos Library System, 1997.

12. Christian Wolff, "Thanksgiving," *The Anchor Bible Dictionary*, Logos Library System, 1997.

13. Pearsall, *Super Joy,* 59.

14. The source of this story is uncertain.

15. Pearsall, *Super Joy,* 111-14.

16. Ibid., 72.

17. "Easter Joy," *America* 13 (16 April 2001): 3.

18. Richard Lowery, *Sabbath and Jubilee* (St. Louis: Chalice, 2000), 5.

19. Jacob Milgrom, "Jubilee: A Rallying Cry for Today's Oppressed," *Holy Land Hollow Jubilee: God, Justice and the Palestinians* (ed. Naim Ateek and Michael Prior; London: Melisende, 1999), 233.

20. M. Weinfeld, "The Sabbatical Year and Jubilee in the Pentateuchal Laws and Their Ancient Near Eastern Background," *The Laws in the Bible and Its Environment* (ed. T. Veijola; Göttingen: Vandenhoeck & Ruprecht, 1990: 39-62), cited in Milgrom, "Jubilee," 233.

21. D. O. Edzard, *The Near East: Early Civilizations* (ed. J Bottero, et al.; trans. R. F. Tannenbaum; Weidenfeld, Nicolson: London, 1965), 225, cited in Milgrom, "Jubilee," 233.

22. Milgrom, "Jubilee," 234.

23. Gordon Brubacher, "Principles of Jubilee in the Old Testament, and for the Enduring Community of Faith," *Holy Land Hollow Jubilee,* 35-36.

24. Christopher J. H. Wright, "Year of Jubilee," *The Anchor Bible Dictionary*, Logos Library System, 1997.

25. John Howard Yoder, *The Politics of Jesus* (Grand Rapids: Eerdmans, 1972).

26. Wright, "Year of Jubilee."

27. Sharon H. Ringe, *Jesus, Liberation, and the Biblical Jubilee* (Philadelphia: Fortress, 1985), xiv-xv.

28. Ibid., 92.

29. CNN, "Britain to Write Off Poor Nations' Debts," 2 December 2000.

30. Romilly Greenhill, "$1 Billion Committed at Annual Meetings, 'Not Enough'

Says Jubilee Research," 1 October 2002. Jubilee Research has calculated that at least another $2 billion to $3 billion of relief will be needed if the HIPC countries are to be given the additional relief that they deserve. http://www.jubilee2000uk.org/hipc/hipc_news/meetings011002.htm.

31. Ched Myers, *The Biblical Vision of Sabbath Economics*, 11.

32. Ibid., 15.

33. Ibid., 6.

34. John Wesley, "The Scripture Way of Salvation," *The Complete Works of John Wesley*, The Ages Digital System, 1997.

35. John Wesley, "Christian Perfection," *The Complete Works of John Wesley*.

36. Ibid., 2: 18.

37. Ibid., 2: 25.

38. Collin W. Williams, *John Wesley's Theology Today* (Nashville: Abingdon, 1960), 175.

39. John Wesley, "A Plain Account on Christian Perfection: Brief Thoughts on Christian Perfection," 1-3, *The Complete Works of John Wesley*.

40. Ibid.

41. For example, Gregory of Nyssa and the Macarian Homilies.

42. John Wesley, "List of Poetic Works," *The Complete Works of John Wesley*.

43. Wesley, "Spiritual Christianity," *The Complete Works of John Wesley*.

44. Ibid., 3: 1, 2, and 4.

45. Herman E. Daly and John B. Cobb Jr., *For The Common Good* (Boston: Beacon, 1989).

46. Ibid., 361.

BIBLIOGRAPHY

Achtemeier, Elizabeth. "Victimization and Healing." In *God and the Victim: Theological Reflections on Evil, Victimization, Justice and Forgiveness*. Grand Rapids: Eerdmans, 1999.

Ahn, Byung-mu. "Jesus and the Minjung." In *Minjung Theology: People As the Subjects of History*. Maryknoll: Orbis, 1981.

American Heart Association National Center. "Anger Triggers Heart Attacks in Some, But Aspirin May Reduce Risk." News Release. September 28, 1995.

"Anger." *University of Michigan News and Information Services*. March 13, 1986.

Apisdorf, Shimon. *Yom Kippur Survival Kit*. Columbus, Ohio: Leviathan Press, 1992.

Aquinas, Thomas. *Summa Theologiae: A Concise Translation*. Westminster, Md.: Christian Classics, 1989.

———. *Summa Theologica*. English Dominican trans. New York: Benziger Bros., 1947.

Augustine, *On Grace and Free Will* in *The Nicene and Post-Nicene Fathers*. The Ages Digital Library, 1997.

———. *On the Merits and Forgiveness of Sin and On the Baptism of Infants*. In *Anti-Pelagian Writings 1st Series* in *The Nicene and Post-Nicene Fathers*. The Ages Digital Library, 1997.

Barclay, William. *The Gospel of John*. Philadelphia: Westminster Press, 1976.

———. *The Gospel of Matthew*. 2 vols. Philadelphia: Westminster Press, 1975.

Barth, Karl. *Church Dogmatics*. IV. 2nd ed. Edited by G. F. Bromley and T. F. Torrence. Translated by G. F. Bromley. Edinburgh: T. and T. Clark, 1975.

Baures, Mary. "Letting Go of Bitterness and Hate." *Journal of Humanistic Psychology* 36 (Winter 1996): 75-90.

Betz, Hans. *The Sermon on the Mount*. Minneapolis: Fortress, 1995.

Bly, Robert, ed. *The Soul Is Here for Its Own Joy: Sacred Poems from Many Cultures*. Hopewell, N.J.: Ecco Press, 1995.

Boehm, Frank H. "Forgiveness: Another Kind of Medicine." Online at http://dr-boehm.com/Forgivenss.htm. October 1997.

Bornkamm, Günther, Gerhard Barth, and Heinz Joachim Held. *Tradition and Interpretation in Matthew*. London: SCM Press, 1963.

Bouvier, Paul. "Child Sexual Abuse: Vicious Circles of Fate or Paths to Resilience?" *Lancet* 9356 (8 February 2003): 446-48.

Brown University. "Teaching Children Healthy Responses to Anger with Assertiveness Training." *Brown University Child and Adolescent Behavior Letter* 7 (July 1999): 1-3.

Brubacher, Gordon. "Principles of Jubilee in the Old Testament, and for the Enduring Community of Faith." In *Holy Land Hollow Jubilee: God, Justice and the Palestinians.* Naim Ateek and Michael Prior, eds. London: Melisende, 1999.

Brueggemann, Walter. "The Shrill Voice of the Wounded Party," in *The Other Side of Sin: Woundedness from the Perspective of the Sinned-Against.* Edited by Andrew Sung Park and Susan L. Nelson. New York: SUNY Press, 2001.

Bultmann, Rudolph. *The Gospel of John: A Commentary.* Translated by G. R. Beasley-Murray. Oxford: Basil Blackwell, 1971.

————. *Kerygma and Myth: A Theological Debate.* New York: Harper & Row, 1962.

Bush, Lawrence and Jeffrey Dekro. "Jews and the Black Reparations Campaign." *Tikkun* 15, No. 4, (July/August 2000): 12-14.

Calvin, John. *Institutes of the Christian Religion.* Translated by Henry Beveridge. Grand Rapids: Eerdmans, 1989.

Canfield, Jack and Frank Siccone. *101 Ways to Develop Student Self-esteem and Responsibility.* 2 vols. Boston: Allyn and Bacon, 1993.

The Canons and Decrees of the Sacred and Documenical Council of Trent. Translated by J. Waterworth. London: Dolman, 1848.

Capps, Donald. *The Depleted Self: Sin in a Narcissistic Age.* Philadelphia: Fortress, 1993.

Carothers, Merlin. *Praise Works.* Plainfield, N.J.: Logos, 1973.

Carter, Jimmy. "I Cannot Forgive That Jerk." *Christianity Today* (5 February 2000), http://www.christianitytoday.com/moi/2000/001/feb/5.5.html.

Clark, David A. "Letter from Prison." *Psychology Today* (January/February 1993): 12-15.

Clinebell, Howard. *Growth Counseling: Hope-centered Methods of Actualizing Human Wholeness.* Nashville: Abingdon, 1979.

CNN. "Britain to Write Off Poor Nations' Debts." 2 December 2000.

Colbert, Ty C. *Why Do I Feel Guilty When I've Done Nothing Wrong?* Nashville: Thomas Nelson, 1995.

Consedine, Jim. "A Justice Based on Healing." *Catholic Worker* (January/February 1996): 1.

Cover, Robin. s. v. "Sin: OT." *The Anchor Bible Dictionary,* Logos Library System, 1998.

Daly, Herman E. and John B. Cobb Jr. *For the Common Good.* Boston: Beacon, 1989.

DeFoore, Bill. *Anger.* Deerfield Beach, Fla.: Health Communications, 1991.

Dorff, Elliot. "The Elements of Forgiveness: A Jewish Approach." In *Dimensions of Forgiveness: Psychological Research and Theological Perspectives.* Edited by Everett L. Worthington Jr. Philadelphia: Templeton Foundation, 1998.

Douglass, James W. *The Non-violent Cross.* New York: Macmillan, 1968.

Drucker, Peter. *Managing for the Future: The 1990s and Beyond.* New York: Truman Talley, 1993.

Dworkin, Andrea. "The Third Rape." *Los Angles Times,* 28 April 1991: m1, m6.

Eliade, Mircea. *Shamanism: Archaic Techniques of Ecstasy.* New York: Pantheon, 1964.

Emerson, Judy. *In the Voice of a Child.* Nashville: Thomas Nelson, 1994.

Erikson, Erik. *Childhood and Society.* 2nd ed. New York: Norton, 1963.

Ertem, Ilgi Ozturk, John M. Leventhal, and Sara Dobbs. "Intergenerational Continuity of Child Physical Abuse: How Good Is the Evidence?" *Lancet* 9283 (2 September 2000): 814-20.

Farmer, Kathleen. *1996 West Ohio School of Ministry.* Unpublished article.

Fiorenza, Elisabeth Schüssler. "Wartime as Formative." *Christian Century* 24 (16 August 1995): 778-80.

Fitzgibbons, Richard. "Forgiveness Boosts Health and Self-Esteem, Research Shows." *Jet* 6 (11 January, 1999): 39.

Flanigan, Beverly. *Forgiving the Unforgivable.* New York: Macmillan, 1992.

Freehof, B. *Book of Job: A Commentary.* New York: Union of American Hebrew Congregations, 1958.

Garrett, Amanda. "When Priests Commit Suicide Sexual Abuse Allegations Often Spur Decision." *The Plain Dealer* (25 May 2002): AI.

"Gratitude Heals." *Christian Science Monitor* 14 (13 December 2002): 22.

Gutiérrez, Gustavo. *On Job: God-talk and the Suffering of the Innocent.* Maryknoll: Orbis, 1987.

Haber, Joram. *Forgiveness.* Savage, Md.: Rowman & Littlefield, 1991.

Hankins, Gary. *Prescription for Anger: Coping with Angry Feelings and Angry People.* Beaverton, Ore.: Princess, 1988.

Hanks, Thomas D. *God So Loved the Third World: The Biblical Vocabulary of Oppression.* Maryknoll: Orbis, 1983.

Haroutunian, Joseph. *Repentance: A Handbook of Christian Theology.* London: Meridan Book, 1958.

Hearley, Joseph P. s. v. "Repentance: OT." *The Anchor Bible Dictionary,* Logos Library System, 1998.

Horsley, Richard A. "Ethics and Exegesis." In *The Love of Enemy and Nonretaliation in the New Testament.* Louisville: Westminster John Knox, 1992.

———. "Response to Walter Wink." In *The Love of Enemy and Nonretaliation in the New Testament.* Edited by Willard M. Swartley. Louisville: Westminster John Knox, 1992.

Jamison, Charles N. Jr. "Racism." *Essence* 7 (November 1992): 62-67.

Jaspers, Karl. "Differentiation of German Guilt." In *Guilt and Shame.* Edited by Herbert Morris. Belmont, Calif.: Wadsworth, 1971.

Jeremias, Joachim. *Jerusalem at Jesus' Time.* Philadelphia: Fortress, 1969.

———. *The Lord's Prayer.* Philadelphia: Fortress, 1964.

———. *New Testament Theology.* New York: Charles Scribner's Sons, 1971.

The Jewish Encyclopedia. s.v. "Forgiveness."

——— s.v. "Repentance."

Joint Declaration on the Doctrine of Justification: The Lutheran World Federation and the Catholic Church. 31 October 1999. http://www.vatican.va/roman_curia/pontifical_councils/chrstuni/documents/rc_pc_chrstuni_doc_31101999_cath-luth-joint-declaration_en.html.

Jones, L. Gregory. *Embodying Forgiveness.* Grand Rapids: Eerdmans, 1995.

Kernberg, Otto. "The Psychopathology of Hatred." In *Rage, Power, and Aggression.* New Haven: Yale University Press, 1993.

Kim, Yong Bock. *Minjung Theology.* Singapore: The Christian Conference of Asia, 1981.

"Yom Kippur." In Encyclopedia Britannica Online. http://www.eb.com:180/bol/topic?eu=80094&sctn=1>. 18 March 1999.

Klassen, William. *The Forgiving Community.* Philadelphia: Westminster, 1966.

Klauck, Hans-Josef. s. v. "Lord's Supper." *The Anchor Bible Dictionary,* Logos Library System, 1998.

Koh, Me Ra. "My Boyfriend Raped Me." *Campus Life* (September 2001: 60-64).

Kurtz, Ernest, and Katherine Ketcham. *The Spirituality of Imperfection: Modern Wisdom from Classic Stories*. New York: Bantam, 1992.

Lamb, Kevin. "Lasting Effects of Abuse." *Dayton Daily News* (25 June 2002): C1-3.

Lasch, Christopher. "Shame." *New Republic* 7 (10 August 1992): 29-35.

Lawler, Kathleen. "Forgive to Live." *Health*. Vol 14. No. 6, (July/August, 2000): 1-5, 28.

Lee, Sun-ai and Don Luce, eds. *The Wish: Poems of Contemporary Korea*. New York: Friendship, 1983.

Lohse, Bernhard. *A Short History of Christian Doctrines*. Translated by F. Ernest Stoeffler. Philadelphia: Fortress, 1996.

Lowery, Richard. *Sabbath and Jubilee*. St. Louis: Chalice, 2000.

Luskin, Fred. *Forgive for Good: A Proven Prescription for Health and Happiness*. San Francisco: HarperSanFrancisco, 2000.

Luter, A. Boyd. s. v. "Repentance: NT." *The Anchor Bible Dictionary*, Logos Library System, 1998.

Luther, Martin. *Luther's Works*. Edited by Jaroslav Pelikan. 55 vols. Saint Louis: Concordia, 1955–1986.

———. *Preface to the Letter of St. Paul to the Romans*. The Ages Digital Library, 1997.

———. *The Small Catechism*. The Ages Digital Library, 1997.

Luz, Ulrich. *Matthew 1–7*. Minneapolis: Fortress, 1989.

Martinez, Julia. "The Conspicuous Comeuppance." *Atlanta Journal Constitution* (15 December 1996): R2.

Mendes de Leon, Carlos F. "Psychosocial Characteristics and Recurrent Events After Percutaneous Transluminal Coronary Angioplasty." *American Journal of Cardiology* 77 (February 1996): 252-55.

Milgrom, Jacob. "Jubilee: A Rallying Cry for Today's Oppressed." In *Holy Land Hollow Jubilee: God, Justice and the Palestinians*. London: Melisende, 1999.

Miller, G. Tyler. *Living in the Environment: Principles, Connections, and Solutions*. 8th ed. Belmont, Calif: Wadsworth, 1994.

Morris, Herbert, ed. *Guilt and Shame*. Belmont, Calif.: Wadsworth, 1971.

Moyers, Bill. "The First Murder." *Genesis: A Living Conversation*. PBS Series, 16 October 1996.

Murray, Joyce. "Liberation for Communion in the Soteriology of Gustavo Gutiérrez." *Theological Studies*. Vol. 59, No. 1, (March 1998): 51-60.

Myers, Ched. *The Biblical Vision of Sabbath Economics*. Washington D.C.: The Church of the Savior, 2001.

Neyrey, Jerome H. *Honor and Shame in the Gospel of Matthew*. Louisville: Westminster John Knox, 1998.

Niebuhr, Reinhold. *Man and Immoral Society*. New York: Harper Collins, 1932.

———. *The Nature and Destiny of Man*. 2 vols. New York: Scribner's, 1941–1943.

North, Gary. *Victim's Rights: The Biblical View of Civil Justice*. Tyler, Texas: Institute for Christian Economics, 1990.

Nozick, Robert. "Anarchy, State, and Utopia." In *What Is Justice?* Edited by Robert Solomon and Mark Murphy. Oxford: Oxford University Press, 1990.

———. "Retribution and Revenge." Philosophical Explanations. In *What Is Justice?* Edited by Robert Solomon and Mark Murphy. Oxford: Oxford University Press, 1990.

O'Collins, Gerald G. s. v. "Crucifixion." *The Anchor Bible Dictionary*, Logos Library System, 1998.

Orloff, Leslye. *Brief Facts: Battered Immigrant Women Protection Act of 1999*. Hearing. Washington, D.C.: GPO, 2000.

Osborn, Bud. *Hundred Block Rock*. Vancouver: Arsenal Pulp Press, 1990.

Parens, Henri. "Rage Toward Self and Others in Early Childhood." In *Rage, Power, and Aggression: The Role of Affect in Motivation, Development and Adaptation*. 2 vols. New Haven: Yale University Press, 1993.

Park, Andrew Sung. *Racial Conflict and Healing: An Asian-American Theological Perspective*. Maryknoll: Orbis, 1996.

Park, Andrew, and Susan Nelson, eds. *The Other Side of Sin*. New York: SUNY Press, 2001.

Patton, John. *Is Human Forgiveness Possible? A Pastoral Care Perspective*. Nashville: Abingdon, 1985.

Paulk, Dave. "Recognizing Child Abuse, Child Abusers, and Individuals Who Are Likely to Abuse." *Physician Assistant* 23 (May 1, 1999): 38-42.

Pearsall, Paul. *Super Joy: In Love with Living*. New York: Doubleday, 1988.

Peck, Scott. *Further Along the Road Less Traveled: Blame and Forgiveness*. Audio. New York: Simon & Schuster, 1992.

Peters, Ted. *Sin*. Grand Rapids: Eerdmans, 1994.

Peterson Karen S. "Victims of Betrayal Must Learn How to Forgive." *USA Today* (18 August 1998): n.p.

Piers, Gerhart, and Milton B. Singer. *Shame and Guilt: A Psychoanalytic and a Cultural Study*. New York: Norton, 1971.

Plato. "From the *Republic*." In *What Is Justice?* Edited by Robert C. Solomon and Mark C. Murphy. Oxford: Oxford University Press, 1990.

Pleasants, Julian R. "Religion That Restores Victims." *New Theological Review*. August 1996.

Rall, Harris. s.v. "Guilt." The International Standard Bible Encyclopedia, Geoffrey W. Bromiley, ed. Grand Rapids: Eerdmans, 1979–1988.

Rauschenbusch, Walter. *A Theology for the Social Gospel*. New York: 1917.

Rawls, John. "Justice as Fairness and a Theory of Justice." In *What Is Justice?* Oxford: Oxford University Press, 1990.

Research News. "Low Social Support and Anger Accelerate Hardening of Arteries." *Heart Disease Weekly* (10-17 December 2000): 4-6.

Restorative Justice Fact Sheet. Monsey, N.Y.: Criminal Justice Press, 1994.

Ringe, Sharon H. *Jesus, Liberation, and the Biblical Jubilee*. Philadelphia: Fortress, 1985.

Rubinstein, Richard. *The Cunning of History*. New York: Harper Colophon, 1978.

Saiving, Valerie. "The Human Situation." In *WomanSpirit Rising*. New York: Harper and Row, 1979.

Salter, Daniel. "Development of Sexually Abusive Behavior in Sexually Victimized Males: A Longitudinal Study." *Lancet* 9356 (8 February 2003): 471-77.

Sanders, E. P. s.v. "Sin: NT." *The Anchor Bible Dictionary*, Logos Library System, 1998.

Schneider, Carl. *Shame, Exposure, and Privacy*. Boston: Beacon, 1977.

Schweizer, Eduard. *The Good News According to Matthew*. Atlanta: John Knox, 1975.

Sheler, Jeffrey L. "The Era of Collective Repentance." *U.S. News and World Report* (3 July 1995): 10-12.

Shogren, Gary S. s.v. "Forgiveness." *The Anchor Bible Dictionary*, Logos Library System, 1998.

Shriver, Donald. *An Ethic for Enemies: Forgiveness in Politics*. New York: Oxford University Press, 1995.

The Six Version Parallel New Testament. Wheaton: Christian Life Publications, 1974.

Smedes, Lewis B. "Keys to Forgiving." *Christianity Today* 15 (3 December 2001): 73.

————. *Shame and Grace: Healing the Shame We Don't Deserve*. San Francisco: Harper, 1993.

Steinem, Gloria. *Revolution from Within: A Book of Self-esteem*. Boston: Little, Brown, 1992.

Stuart, Charles. s.v. "Shame." *The International Standard Bible Encyclopedia*. Geoffrey W. Bromiley, ed. Grand Rapids: Eerdmans, 1979–1988.

Suchocki, Marjorie. *The Fall to Violence: Original Sin in Relational Theology*. New York: Continuum, 1994.

Summary Report: The Assessment of Restitution in the Minnesota Probation Service. Governor's Commission on Crime Prevention and Control, January 31, 1976.

Tangney, J. P. "Moral Affect: The Good, the Bad, and the Ugly." *Journal of Personality and Social Psychology* 61 (1991): 598-608.

Tangney, J. P., P. Wagner, C. Fletcher and R. Gramzow. "Shamed Into Anger? The Relation of Shame and Guilt to Anger and Self-reported Aggression." *Journal of Personality and Social Psychology* 62 (1992): 669-75.

Thomas, Owen, and Ellen Wondra. *Introduction to Theology*, 3rd ed. Harrisburg: Morehouse, 2002.

Tillich, Paul. *The Protestant Era*. Translated and edited by James Luther Adams. London: Nisbet, 1951.

————. *Systematic Theology*. 3 vols. Chicago: University of Chicago Press, 1951–1963.

Umbreit, Mark and Howard Zehr. "Restorative Family Group Conferences: Differing Models and Guidelines for Practice." *Federal Probation* 60, no. 3 (September 1996): 24-30.

Underwood, Robert A. Congressional Record. Daily ed. 150 (2 November 2001): E1980.

Villa-Vicencio, Charles. "The Road to Reconciliation." *Sojourners* (May/June 1997): 36-37.

Volf, Miroslav. "Washing Away, Washing Up." *Christian Century* 23 (28 August 1999): 820.

Vorlander, H., s.v. "Forgiveness." *The New International Dictionary of New Testament Theology*, Colin Brown, ed. Grand Rapids: Zondervan, 1975–1978.

Waltz, Tom, and Heather Ritchie. "Gandhian Principles in Social Work Practice: Ethnics Revisited." *Social Work* 45, no. 3 (May 2000): 213-23.

Weatherhead, Leslie. *The Will of God*. Nashville: Abingdon, 1944.

Weil, Simone. "From Random Thoughts on the Love of God." In *The Soul Is Here for Its Own Joy: Sacred Poems from Many Cultures*. Hopewell, N.J.: Ecco, 1995.

Weinfeld, M. "The Sabbatical Year and Jubilee in the Pentateuchal Laws and Their Ancient Near Eastern Background." In Timo Veijola, ed., *The Laws in the Bible and Its Environment*. Göttingen: Vandenhoeck and Ruprecht, 1990.

Weitekamp, Elmar. *Restorative Justice: An Ancient Approach to Improve Today's World*. Boulder, Colo.: Westview, 1997.

Wells, Jo Bailey. *God's Holy People*. Sheffield, England: Sheffield Academic Press, 2000.

Wesley, John. "Christian Perfection." In *The Complete Works of John Wesley*. The Ages Digital Library, 1997.

———. "The Great Privilege of Those Who Were Born of God." In *The Complete Works of John Wesley*. The Ages Digital Library, 1997.

———. "Justification by Faith." In *The Complete Works of John Wesley*. The Ages Digital Library, 1997.

———. "A List of Poetic Works." In *The Complete Works of John Wesley*. The Ages Digital Library, 1997.

———. "Minutes of Several Conversations Between the Reverend and Mr. John Wesley and Others: From the Year 1744 to the Year 1789." In *The Complete Works of John Wesley*. The Ages Digital Library, 1997.

———. "On the Discoveries of Faith." In *The Complete Works of John Wesley*. The Ages Digital Library, 1997.

———. "A Plain Account on Christian Perfection: Brief Thoughts on Christian Perfection." In *The Complete Works of John Wesley*. The Ages Digital Library, 1997.

———. "The Scripture Way of Salvation." In *The Complete Works of John Wesley*. The Ages Digital Library, 1997.

———. "The Spiritual Christianity." In *The Complete Works of John Wesley*. The Ages Digital Library, 1997.

Wiesel, Elie. *Messengers of God*. New York: Random House, 1976.

Will, George F. "The Journey Up from Guilt." *Newsweek* (18 June 1990): 68.

Williams, Collin W. *John Wesley's Theology Today*. Nashville: Abingdon, 1960.

Willimon, William H. "Our Kind of Crowd." *Reflections on Forgiveness and Spiritual Growth*. Nashville: Abingdon, 2001.

Wink, Walter. "Counterresponse to Richard Horsley." In *The Love of Enemy and Nonretaliation in the New Testament*. Louisville: Westminster John Knox, 1992.

———. *Engaging the Powers: Discernment and Resistance in a World of Domination*. Minneapolis: Fortress, 1992.

Wisdom, Kathy Spatz. "Victims of Childhood Sexual Abuse—Later Criminal Consequences." *Contemporary Women's Issues Database* (1 March 1993): 1.

Wolff, Christian. s. v. "Thanksgiving." *The Anchor Bible Dictionary*. Logos Library System, 1998.

Wolterstorff, Nicholas. "The Contours of Justice: An Ancient Call for Shalom." In *God and the Victim: Theological Reflections on Evil, Victimization, Justice and Forgiveness*. Edited by Lisa Lampman and Michelle Shattuck. Grand Rapids: Eerdmans, 1999.

Wright, Christopher. s. v. "Year of Jubilee." *The Anchor Bible Dictionary*. Logos Library System, 1998.

Yoder, John Howard. *The Politics of Jesus*. Grand Rapids: Eerdmans, 1972.

Zehr, Howard. "Restoring Justice." In *God and the Victim: Theological Reflections on Evil, Victimization, Justice, and Forgiveness*. Edited by Lisa Lampman and Michelle Shattuck. Grand Rapids: Eerdmans, 1999.